ANDREW MARVELL

POET · PURITAN · PATRIOT

ANDREW MARVELL

POET · PURITAN · PATRIOT

PIERRE LEGOUIS

Professor of English Language and Literature
University of Lyons

SECOND EDITION

OXFORD
AT THE CLARENDON PRESS
1968

Oxford University Press, Ely House, London W. 1

GLASGOW NEW YORK TORONTO MELBOURNE WELLINGTON
CAPE TOWN SALISBURY IBADAN NAIROBI LUSAKA ADDIS ABABA
BOMBAY CALCUTTA MADRAS KARACHI LAHORE DACCA
KUALA LUMPUR HONG KONG TOKYO

FIRST EDITION 1965
SECOND EDITION 1968

© OXFORD UNIVERSITY PRESS 1968

PRINTED IN GREAT BRITAIN
AT THE UNIVERSITY PRESS, OXFORD
BY VIVIAN RIDLER
PRINTER TO THE UNIVERSITY

IN MEMORIAM

H. M. MARGOLIOUTH

PREFACE TO THE
SECOND EDITION

In this second edition only a few corrections have been made to the text, affecting single words or at most single sentences. But there have been added, at the end of the volume: (1) some new pieces of information on various points with the reference to the page concerned; (2) a critical bibliography of recent books and articles published, or come to my notice, too late for consideration in the first edition.

PREFACE TO THE
FIRST EDITION

THIS is an abridged version of a bulky French book published in 1928. Since it was presented as a thesis for the *Doctorat-ès-lettres* it had, above all, to be thorough and produce evidence supporting every statement: hence the 1,566 footnotes, fair game at the time for the English reviewers in the more literary of the daily papers. All those notes have now gone by the board, save a very few considered important enough to be incorporated in the text: whoever questions a statement in this volume should consult the original.[1] But even after jettisoning the notes too much matter remained for the space available. Explanations necessary for the (largely theoretical) French general reader of 1928 but unwanted by his English equivalent thirty-odd years later were easily sacrificed. This was still not enough and I had, reluctantly, to reduce illustrations in number and in length, especially numerous quotations of Marvell's verse. So the reader should have a good edition of the poems by his side: I would like him to read, or reread, the passages preceding or following the surviving

[1] Since only 500 copies were printed and the book has been out of print for over twenty years many libraries possess no copy; but it is now again obtainable, having been reprinted by Russell and Russell, New York, in 1965.

quotations, and also those merely summed up in vile prose or just alluded to. Lastly, many details of my text that contributed to the delineation of Marvell, man and writer, had to be omitted. I have deliberately made compression bear more on the biographical than on the critical part. (In the original work the two parts were about equal in length, but the critical was the one that mattered most, so that I rather resent seeing my thesis listed, in some bibliographies, as a mere biography.) Yet the sacrifice has been painful to me, since Marvell's life is chiefly made interesting by casual glimpses requiring a good deal of preliminary explanation. Reduced to an outline one biography of him cannot look very different from another.

Needless to say, errors of fact have been corrected. And facts discovered since 1928, if of any importance, have been mentioned, either in the text or in notes giving references. But on matters of opinion I have changed very little, which may be due to mental sclerosis. I have not thought it necessary, even had it been possible, to discuss in detail the views of more modern critics when they differed from mine; I either reject them silently or refer the reader to articles, or reviews, where I have tried to refute them.

In order to facilitate the checking of statements and the finding of references in the French original, the order, not only of the chapters and sub-chapters but also of the paragraphs, has been as far as possible preserved. For the same reason Chapter II has been allowed to stand, though reduced to a few pages: already the shortest in the original volume, it contained mostly generalities on 'La Poésie lyrique en Angleterre au xviie siècle'; it now retains only its more modest sub-title: 'Les Maîtres de Marvell.'

Translating oneself is writing in fetters. Had I used English from the first the number of gallicisms would have been smaller and the vocabulary less pedantic, the style less stilted. But the necessity of abridging made it impossible for anyone save the author to do the translation. As a compensation and a corrective I have had the benefit of revision in this respect by the staff of the Clarendon Press, with their usual kindness and courtesy. The present book was also read in typescript by my two Marvellian corre-

spondents at Birmingham, Mrs. E. E. Duncan-Jones and
Mr. Norman Wall, who, besides helping to normalize my
English style, offered many suggestions for the bringing
up to date of the matter. I have adopted almost all of them
that could fit into the old frame, but since I have remained
obdurate on some points they should bear no responsibility
for any errors that stand uncorrected. For their assistance
in this final revision I owe them many thanks; but in fact
my debt to both began long before: for several years they
have untiringly answered the queries of one who suffered
from the disadvantage of writing on things English far
from the great English libraries.

Most of those I thanked in the preface to the French
volume are, alas! gone. One, however, is still alive and on
the active list of Marvellians: Professor Caroline Robbins,
of Bryn Mawr College. She has always generously com-
municated to me across the Atlantic all her more recent
finds on the poet and patriot to whom we each devoted our
earliest work and to whom we both revert now.

Among the departed I shall only name him who should
have written this English monograph himself, had not his
deeply religious soul been rapt away in middle age by William Blake and Traherne. I mean H. M. Margoliouth. Thus
he left Marvell to me when this volume was planned in
1956. I then relied on his assistance to carry the undertaking
through. He died, alas, before I had been able to submit any
part of my draft to him. His only contribution, then, besides
the invaluable help given to me for my French book, was
the additional matter in the second edition of *The Poems and
Letters of Andrew Marvell* (1952) in the Oxford English Texts,
from which of course I have taken my quotations.

For the prose works one has still to make do with Grosart's
volumes III and IV, in The Fuller Worthies Library
(1873–5). But I have, as far as possible, had his text checked
from the original editions. A critical and fully annotated
edition of the pamphlets, especially of *The Rehearsal Transpros'd*, remains a desideratum.

PIERRE LEGOUIS

Lyons
31 March 1964

CONTENTS

I

EARLY LIFE

At the beginning of the sixteenth century one or more families by the name of Marvell (or Marwell or Merwell) lived in two neighbouring villages of Cambridgeshire, Shepreth and Meldreth.[1] From the legacies in the wills of some of them we see that their income came from the land and that they were neither wealthy nor poor; we also see that as late as 1543 they retained the naïve piety of medieval times.

Between these possible ancestors and the poet's grandfather there is a break in this respect since we see him choose the puritan Emmanuel College, lately founded, for his son's education. This son, Andrew Marvell senior, had been born about 1586 at Meldreth, probably in a house still called 'The Marvells' in the nineteenth century. But the first certainty we find in his career is that he commenced B.A. in 1605. He proceeded M.A. in 1608 and took orders. Not later than 1608/9 he was curate at Flamborough in Yorkshire. On 22 October 1612, at Cherry Burton, he married Anne Pease; the bride's surname was that of an already well-known Yorkshire family. In 1614 he was presented to the living of Winestead-in-Holderness, where his five children were born: first, three daughters, Anne, Mary, and Elizabeth; then, 'the last day of March' 1621, 'being Easter-Eve', Andrew, the poet, who was baptized on 5 April; last, John, who died when one year old and was buried at Winestead on 20 September 1624.

A few days after this bereavement the family left the country to settle in a town, or a suburb. For on 30 September the burgesses of Hull had chosen the Reverend Andrew Marvell as lecturer in Holy Trinity Church. This entailed a considerable change in his activity and probably agreed better with his temperament. An enemy of his son, many

[1] The name can be traced in this area back to the year 1279. See L. N. Wall, 'Andrew Marvell of Meldreth', in *N.Q.*, Sept. 1958, pp. 399–400.

years later, was to note that in the 'late Rebellion . . . none were more conspicuous for loyalty than the Dignified Clergy, and none greater Incendiaries than the Mercenary Preachers and Lecturers, who subsisted purely by the Benevolence and arbitrary Pensions of the People'. The language is abusive but the remark well founded. Andrew Marvell senior died before the outbreak of the Civil War, but we can surmise that he would have sided with the Long Parliament.[1] 'Facetious and yet calvinistic', Anthony à Wood was to say of him, with obvious surprise. And another more moderate Royalist, Thomas Fuller, granted him this post-humous praise:

. . . in Hull . . . he was well beloved. Most *facetious* in his discourse, yet *grave* in his *carriage*, a most excellent preacher, who like a good husband never *broached* what he had new brewed, but preached what he had pre-studied some time before. Insomuch that he was wont to say that he would crosse the common proverb, which called *Saturday* the working day and *Munday* the holy day of preachers.

This popularity did not exclude some local animosities, and records survive of three quarrels in which he took part.

In addition to the lecturership, he held, also by election of the burgesses, the Mastership of the Charterhouse, this being the popular name of an almshouse founded in 1384 by Michael de la Pole; there he proved a good administrator. By the terms of his appointment, he was to live in a house provided for him almost a quarter of a mile north of the city walls, and only fifty yards from the river Hull. Gardens surrounded it, so that leaving Winestead did not imply for his three-year-old son being completely cut off from rural scenery.

Indeed, the enemy of Andrew Marvell junior already mentioned was to tax him with a 'first unhappy education among Boat-Swains and Cabin-boys, whose Phrases . . . [he] learn't in his childhood'. There may be this much truth in the charge that young Andrew enjoyed playing on the

[1] This surmise has been much strengthened by L. N. Wall's discovery, loc. cit., that one 'Andrew Marvell, yeoman', almost certainly the poet's grand-father, who was buried at Hull on 13 April 1628, had left Cambridgeshire rather than pay his assessment of £2 when Charles I levied a forced loan (1626/7) without parliamentary authority. Resistance to oppression ran in the family.

wharf, where the heart of Hull beat noisily. But he could not have idled much, since Anthony à Wood admits that when at the age of twelve he left school, he was 'well-educated in grammar learning'. This was Hull Grammar School, John Alcock's foundation, close to Holy Trinity Church. From the poet himself we hear that Latin verse and the art of 'scanning' held an important place in the very traditional teaching of the single master, who was assisted by but one usher.

On 14 December 1633 Andrew matriculated at Cambridge as a sizar of Trinity College. This shows him to have been precocious, though not exceptionally so. Still, for most of the seven years he spent at Cambridge, he was too young, one would suppose, to take more than a limited interest in the major problems of the University. So we shall only recall that Laud, made Archbishop of Canterbury in that same year 1633, and all powerful at Oxford as benefactor and Chancellor of the University, met with more resistance at Cambridge to his reforms, if only *vis inertiae*. Yet even here Puritanism and Calvinism seem to have fought a rear-guard action; and with John Harvard, of whom young Marvell may have caught a glimpse, they had apparently emigrated to the new Cambridge beyond the Atlantic. But the citizens of the old Cambridge mostly stuck to the strongly Protestant tradition started under Elizabeth by Thomas Cartwright. They flocked every Sunday (and some of the more sober students joined them) to the lecture given in Trinity Church by a clergyman of their own choosing. From 1636 the lecturer was Benjamin Whichcote, who was to become vice-chancellor when the Presbyterians ruled. A liberal-minded man, he indeed turned the Puritan spirit into new channels; under his influence a movement was then started later to receive the epithets of Latitudinarian and Platonist. Its Platonism, however, was derived chiefly from a more scholarly person, John Sherman, who from 1635 to 1640 preached in the chapel of Trinity, his own and Marvell's college, short sermons called 'Commonplaces'; he later published them under the significant title of *A Greek in the Temple*, using for their general text Τοῦ γὰρ καὶ γένος ἐσμέν (Acts xvii. 28).

The Ritualist stronghold was Peterhouse, of which
Richard Crashaw, Marvell's senior by nine years and already
famous for his Latin verse, became a Fellow in 1635. He
'*led* his life in St. Maries Church' nearby, 'lodged under
Tertullian's roofe of Angels', and there 'penned these poems,
Steps for happy souls to climbe heaven by'.

Half-way, in matter of churchmanship, between Peterhouse and his father's old college of Emmanuel, stood
Trinity; under its master, Thomas Comber, it avoided controversy and devoted itself to erudition. The choice of this
college for his son seems to imply that the Reverend Andrew
Marvell wanted him to steer a middle course, but what did
the boy himself think at the time? From his verse satires or
from his prose pamphlets (where he speaks more cautiously)
we know that the man, thirty-odd years later, held Laud, with
his inordinate fondness for 'ceremonies and Arminianism',
responsible for the Civil War. He may even have gone to
the length of calling Charles I 'a fool' because the King had
fought and died 'For the Surplice, Lawn-Sleeves, the Cross
and the Mitre'. So that, in the absence of any contemporary
evidence, we should incline to date Marvell's Latitudinarian
and Platonist tendencies from his time at Cambridge and
ascribe them to Whichcote's and Sherman's preaching.

But almost the only fact that has survived of these university years flatly contradicts the inference of logic: this fact
is the boy's conversion by 'Jesuits' and consequent flight
from Cambridge, probably in 1639. Though the circumstances do not clearly appear, and in spite of some dis-
crepancies in the evidence, we can accept the family tradition that the Reverend Andrew Marvell discovered his
runaway son 'in a *Bookseller's* Shop in *London*, and prevailed
with him to return to the College'. This misadventure, closely
paralleled by another that befell the son of the Vicar of
Welton, a parish only ten miles west of Hull, a year or so
later, denotes a certain slackness of discipline and inadequate
supervision. Yet caning, up to eighteen years of age, when
the student became *adultus*, remained in force, and with its
help Alma Mater taught her foster-children 'better arts and
better manners', as Marvell himself admitted near the end
of his life.

Those arts were the legacy of the Middle Ages; and a student's ability revealed itself in scholastic exercises. Marvell was to make fun of them when describing an adversary's career at the University: 'he ... became a competent rhetorician, and no ill disputant. He had learnt how to erect a thesis, and to defend it *pro* and *con* with a serviceable distinction'; while the truth came in at one door and went out at another.

Of the few attempts at modernization that took place in the thirties, such as the teaching of Arabic and Anglo-Saxon (by the same man, Abraham Wheelock), Marvell must have heard, but nowhere shows that he profited by them. However, since mathematics had not yet established its dominion at Cambridge in that pre-Newtonian age, most inquisitive minds turned to the study of languages. Thomas Comber, under whose authority Marvell found himself, 'excelled in the Hebrew, Arabic, Coptic, Samaritan, Syriac, Chaldee, Persian, Greek, and Latin languages, and also in French, Spanish, and Italian, which he not only understood but spoke'. Richard Crashaw, in the intervals of his ecstatic devotions, had mastered 'five languages (besides his Mother tongue) *vid*. Hebrew, Greek, Latine, Italian, Spanish, the last two whereof hee had little helpe in, they were of his own acquisition'. This last remark shows how difficult it is to assess Marvell's debt to Cambridge. From his works and other evidence we perceive the scope of his learning, but we cannot apportion the credit between his tutors, travel, the conversation of the best minds, and various reading. One thing we know: at Cambridge Marvell already composed verse, if not poetry.

On 17 March 1636/7 the Queen gave birth to her fifth child, Princess Anne. Each of the two universities put forth the customary volume. The Cambridge one, entitled Συνῳδία, included contributions by Joseph Beaumont, Richard Crashaw, Abraham Cowley, and Andrew Marvell. The last named addressed the King in Greek and Latin. The Homeric epithet Δυσαριστοτόκος, queerly applied to the number of the royal children, proves that the boy of sixteen indulged in the worst sort of conceits. But the Latin poem, a *Parodia* of Horace's ode to Octavius after Actium (i. 2), does not lack rhythm, even when it departs from the original, e.g. by

substituting for the description of the presages announcing
Caesar's death that of the plague that had just devastated
Cambridge:

> Cùm scholae latis genus haesit agris,
> Nota quae sedes fuerat bubulcis;
> Cùm togâ abjectâ pavidus reliquit
> Oppida doctus.

Happily the woes of England draw to an end: Charles and
Mary repeople the country; let us wish to preserve this
excellent sovereign as long as possible. And here we need
change only one word in Horace's strophe:

> Serus in cœlum redeas, diúque
> Laetus intersis populo Britanno,
> Néve te nostris vitiis iniquum
> Ocyor aura
> Tollat . . .

The year, we repeat, is 1637, which historians now call
decisive: no human wisdom can any longer prevent the
Civil War.

While young Andrew's education went on, various family
events, happy and unhappy, took place at Hull. In 1633 his
eldest sister, Anne, married James Blaydes, and in 1636 his
second sister, Mary, became Mrs. Edmund Popple. By these
two alliances the Marvells struck roots in the town, where
the Blaydes and the Popples, wealthy and esteemed, took an
increasingly important share in municipal affairs. These advantageous unions show not so much the charm of the
daughters as the good opinion the Hull merchants entertained of the father. This regard even rose to admiration
for his conduct during the plague that raged at Hull, with
a few lulls, from 1635 to 1639. The Lecturer of Trinity
Church did not desert his congregation, and when the
mayor, William Ramsden, died in December 1637, he 'ven-
tured to give his corpse Christian burial, and preached a
most excellent sermon, which was afterwards printed' (it
has, it seems, disappeared).

The next year young Andrew's mother died; she was
buried on 28 April. With a haste not then uncommon among
the opponents of ecclesiastical celibacy, the Reverend Andrew

Marvell married, at Norton in Derbyshire, on 27 November, Lucy Alured, herself a widow for the second time, over fifty, and 'generosa' according to the parish register. We do not know how the boy of seventeen took this union (unless we ascribe to it his conversion to Rome), but it proved short-lived: 'It happened that Anno Dom. 1640 [o.s.] Jan. 23, crossing *Humber* in a *Barrow-boat*, the same was sand-warpt and [the Rev. Andrew Marvell] drowned therein, by the care-lessness (not to say drunkenness) of the boatman.' So says Thomas Fuller, and his narrative, the first in point of time, bears the mark of brutal reality; but popular imagination, struck by the sudden departure of a beloved minister, sur-rounded it with romantic and supernatural details, which biographers fond of the marvellous kept embellishing in the eighteenth and nineteenth centuries. Only one of these cir-cumstances appears to rest on some foundation, namely that Fuller himself gives it in a marginal note: Mr. Marvell was drowned 'with Mrs. Skinner (daughter to Sir Edward Coke) a very religious Gentlewoman'. Yet we know for certain that the great juris-consult's daughter was not drowned in 1640/1 or later. Some biographers, having realized the impossibility of this, tried to arrange matters by sacrificing to Neptune one of Mrs. Skinner's four daughters, instead of their mother; but here again inexorable scholarly research deprives us of these tearful delights by proving that Bridget, the only possible candidate for the honour of having been drowned with the poet's father, in fact died almost a centenarian, some eighty years after the Reverend Andrew Marvell. In another version, not found in print before 1760, the drowned girl's mother (not named) 'sent for our author, charged herself with the expense of his future education, and at her death left him her fortune'. Then a plausible contamination made of Mrs. Skinner the adoptive mother of the young orphan; here again research workers have clipped the wings of legend: this lady's will does not mention our poet. And yet the Marvell and Skinner families were already acquainted at the beginning of Charles I's reign, and they still kept in touch under the Restoration; so for this full-blown and age-long tradition there may have been a germ of fact, were it but a grain of mustard seed.

Thirty years later the poet's enemies tried to injure him by attacking the memory of his father, whom they called a rebel and a schismatic. Filial piety then expressed itself with dignified simplicity: 'he dyed before ever the War broke out, having lived with some measure of reputation, both for piety and learning, and he was moreover a Conformist to the established rites of the Church of England, though I confess none of the most over-running or eager in them.' And yet this lukewarm Conformist had clashed with some of the Antiritualists of Hull. His prudent advice had brought back on him the charge of doctrinal errors. A conference between him and the Anabaptists and other sectaries had not helped much. Thus, beyond the quarrel between Arminians and Calvinists, another one was breeding within the Puritan camp between Presbyterians and Independents.

About the time, and perhaps on account, of his father's death Marvell left Cambridge. In April 1638 he had been made a scholar of Trinity. In 1638/9 he had commenced Bachelor of Arts. In 1639 and 1640 he continued residence and drew his *stipendium*: no doubt he still aimed at the degree of Master of Arts. But he must have given up this plan since, under date of 24 September 1641, the Conclusion-book records that several scholars, one of them 'D^s Marvell', 'in regard yt some of them are reported to be married and yt others look not after yeir days nor Acts . . . shall be out of yeir [their] places unless yei [they] shew just cause to ye Coll for ye contrary in 3 months'. Marvell's worst enemy will say of him after his death: 'a patre abdicatus, ab academia pulsus'; the former taunt seems untrue, the latter inaccurate.[1] Yet an impression persists that the young Marvell was not, at any rate in his last years at Trinity, a model

[1] One of the Senior Fellows constituting the governing body of Trinity College at this time was the Rev. Herbert Thorndike, to whom Marvell makes unfavourable references in *The Rehearsal Transpros'd* (Part I). The editor of Thorndike's works (A. W. Haddan, 1844–6) says he must have had a share in expelling Marvell; Haddan also accuses Marvell, quoting one of Thorndike's pamphlets from memory, of making Thorndike say the opposite of what he in fact wrote. (Information received from Mrs. Duncan-Jones.) Marvell has no doubt distorted Thorndike's thought but the Anglican divine had invited a castigation, if not by his theology at least by his prose style, involved and crabbed almost to the point of unintelligibility.

student. In 1640 he did not contribute any piece of verse, Greek, Latin, or English, to *Voces Votivae* on the occasion of the birth of the future Duke of Gloucester; whereas Crashaw, Cowley, and Beaumont again seized the opportunity to vent loyal feelings, made more valuable by the pitiful issue of the First Bishops' War. The Second War proved even more disastrous for the King, and in October of the same year England elected the Long Parliament. Cromwell, already sent to the Short Parliament by the borough of Cambridge, retained his seat in spite of the efforts of Cleveland, then a Fellow of St. John's; this poet, whose disciple in satire Marvell was to become, cried out when the return for the election was made that 'that single vote had ruined both Church and Kingdom'.

How Marvell behaved during this general election we do not know, nor indeed do we know where he was. A local tradition says that 'he served his clerkship' at Hull without defining the date and length of this episode. A reasonable guess has been made that soon after his father's death he entered the trading-house of his brother-in-law Edmund Popple, a shipwright and merchant; this would account for the inside knowledge of commercial and maritime problems he was to evince as a Member of Parliament.

We find ourselves on firmer ground with one of Milton's letters written in 1652/3, which says of Marvell: 'he hath spent four years abroad in Holland, France, Italy, and Spain to very good purpose . . . and the gaining of these four languages'. Since he had returned to England by 1649 certainly, by 1646 possibly, Marvell may have left it as early as 1642, the year when the Civil War broke out. If so, did he deliberately shun the shedding of blood, including his own? Though Milton left 'the labour of the camps to any ordinary man', he had at least decided from the first (so he says) to share the dangers of his countrymen; and Marvell himself was to praise magnificently the *Defensio Secunda* from which that personal statement is extracted, though he may have had some difficulty in swallowing the epithet 'turpe' there applied to a conduct that had been his own. Thirty years after these events, in a pamphlet advocating religious tolerance, he wrote:

Whether it be a war of religion or of liberty, is not worth the labour to inquire. Whichsoever was at the top, the other was at the bottom; but upon considering all, I think the cause was too good to have been fought for. Men ought to have trusted God; they ought and might have trusted the King with that whole matter. 'The arms of the Church are prayers and tears'; the arms of the subjects are patience and petitions. The King himself, being of so accurate and piercing a judgment, would soon have felt where it stuck. For men may spare their pains where nature is at work, and the world will not go the faster for our driving. Even as his present Majestie's happy Restoration did it self, so all things happen in their best and proper time, without any need of our officiousness.

But even if he thus revealed his real mind of 1673, which we may well doubt, does it account for his abstention of 1642? His enemies, of course, were to tax him with cowardice for this refusal to join either camp; a charge that the courage he showed in his later life, not only moral but physical, seems to rebut. So that the enigma remains unsolved.

Anyhow, while Hull withstood two royalist sieges, which entailed the blowing up of part of the Charterhouse buildings; while at Cambridge Royalist and Anglican Masters, Fellows, and Scholars were deprived and expelled, and Manchester's and Cromwell's soldiers purged the college chapels from idolatry, Marvell went through the Grand Tour, that aristocratic complement of an insular education. With what money? His biographers answered that it was with Mrs. Skinner's legacy, until this explanation was exploded. But an ingenious conjecture makes him travel as tutor to the lady's eldest son.[1] Whether with this young gentleman or another one in his charge, Marvell, like Ben Jonson before him and many another English writer after him, most likely acted as bear-leader, since otherwise he could hardly have afforded to travel in so leisurely a manner. Besides, between the years 1650 and 1657 he certainly made a living almost continuously as a private tutor. It has therefore been argued that his life falls in three parts: childhood and education, 1621–42 (?); tutorships, 1642 (?)–57; political

[1] This conjecture, however, appears very fragile in the light of recent research: see L. N. Wall, 'Marvell and the Skinners', in *N.Q.*, June 1962, p. 219.

life, 1657–78. Yet it seems fitter here to consider Marvell's Grand Tour as part of his own education since he must have been then little older than his supposed pupil.

That he acquired the reputation of a travelled man, his epitaph witnesses, as also does the abuse of his enemies, eager to turn against him the prejudices of the true-born Englishman against continental, and particularly Italian manners.

Thus Marvell visited Holland, France, Italy, and Spain, presumably in the order in which Milton enumerates them. Of the first of these countries he was to compose some twelve years later, a portrait, or rather a caricature, prompted by national rivalry, yet bearing the mark of amused observation and a retentive visual memory. The description of Dutch women 'Reeking at *Church* over the *Chafing-Dish*' recalls the manner of the Van Ostade brothers.

Of his first visit to France nothing survives except three unsavoury lines inserted in an early satire by way of burlesque comparison. Geneva, though not mentioned by Milton, was visited by Marvell, who found it less Puritanical than he expected, rather to his surprise than to his disappointment. Possibly he followed the Rhône southward through Bellegarde, Lyons, and Avignon, but the only certainty about his whole tour is his presence in Rome in 1645, 1646, or 1647 at latest, since there he met a fellow-countryman of his, Richard Flecknoe, on whom he wrote his first English verse that we can date with something like precision.[1] Flecknoe, an English priest (not an Irish one as Dryden's *Mac Flecknoe*, misinterpreted, has caused critic after critic to repeat), survives only as a butt for satirists, save that Lamb paid him the compliment of using a stanza of his piece 'On Silence' as the epigraph of 'A Quakers' Meeting'. Marvell in his poem showed himself pitiless to his brother-poet, but never printed his satire. Flecknoe's famished condition, resulting in incredible leanness, provides Marvell with opportunities for conceits of which he

[1] With the exception of 'A Dialogue between Thyrsis and Dorinda', set to music by William Lawes (a Royalist, by the way) *c.* 1645, and probably written a little before. See John P. Cutts's letter in *T.L.S.*, 8 August 1952, p. 517.

makes full use. The event that gave occasion for the satire, Marvell's visit to Flecknoe in his tiny room at the Pelican inn; the 'Martyrdom' inflicted on the visitor by 'hideous verse' read in 'a dismal tone'; the arrival of a third party and the wit-combat that ensues at the door of the already packed 'Cell'; the dinner to which Marvell takes Flecknoe and the other visitor, and which ends in the traditional quarrel caused by poetic vainglory and touchiness; the host's escape and the mock *ex voto* to be hung by him in Saint Peter's— all these incidents create the impression of a rather conceited young man who complacently repeats his own *bons mots* and boasts of his heavier purse.

In Spain, among other arts, swordmanship flourished. Marvell, more and more of a fine gentleman, took lessons he was to recall a quarter of a century later when writing to a friend: 'My Fencing-master in *Spain*, after he had instructed me all he could, told me . . . there was yet one Secret, against which there was no Defence, and that was, to give the first Blow.' He seems to have attended at least one bullfight: in spite of the love for animals expressed in 'Upon Appleton House' he introduces into this poem a comparison—free from any censure of the bloody entertainment—of the smooth meadows, newly mown, to the 'Toril [meaning the arena] Ere the Bulls enter at Madril'. He may also remember Andalusia when in 'Bermudas' he describes, not only 'the Orange bright' hanging 'in shades . . . Like golden Lamps in a green Night', but 'the Pomegranates' enclosing 'Jewels more rich than *Ormus* show's'.

Here he is again in England, without any fear of the scholar's being detected under the gallant by his noble friends. For he mixes in London society, whose prestige survives its political influence and even its wealth. To this fashionable phase in his life belong two, possibly three, pieces of poetry. The doubtful one is an elegy on the death of Francis Villiers, the first Duke of Buckingham's younger son, killed on 7 July 1648 in a rash Royalist rising;[1] the author hopes to hear:

[1] E. E. Duncan-Jones, 'Notes on Marvell', in *N.Q.*, March 1953, p. 102, has identified 'the matchless Chlora' (l. 69) whom Francis loved, with high

How heavy *Cromwell* gnasht the earth and fell.
Or how slow Death farre from the sight of day
The long-deceived *Fairfax* bore away.

If Marvell's authorship were established it would only proclaim more loudly what the other two poems tell plainly
enough: his sympathy went to the Cavaliers; and among
them to the poet who in a few immortal stanzas has en-
shrined the best of the Cavalier spirit, Richard Lovelace.
Marvell's elder by eight years and an Oxonian, we do not
know how he became acquainted with the younger Cantab.[1]
In October 1646 Lovelace was still fighting in Flanders
under Condé, but he imprudently returned to England,
which led to his (second) imprisonment from June 1648 to
April 1649. *Lucasta* came out in 1649, but Marvell's com-
plimentary poem seems to have been written when the
granting of the licence hung in doubt, i.e. before 4 February
1647/8. It is one of fourteen but Marvell's ranks *facile prin-
ceps*. In another poetical collection that came out in the same
year, *Lachrymae Musarum*, to mourn the premature death of
Henry, Lord Hastings, only son of the Earl of Huntingdon,
competition for the palm was more severe since thirty-six
poets entered the lists, among them Herrick, Denham, and
Dryden; yet we do not consider it partiality to rank Marvell
first: Herrick was ageing and Dryden was young. This does
not mean that Marvell's elegy is a good one, only that it is
better than, or not so bad as, the others. But the literary
quality of this volume, like that of the pieces composed in
Lovelace's honour, matters less here than the social and
political atmosphere in which these pieces were steeped.
Now the Earl of Huntingdon seems to have been a royalist
at heart, though a far less consistent and devoted one than
Lovelace, and the friends of each held the same faith. No
one expressed his royalism more fervently than a certain

probability. She must be Mary Kirke, daughter of the Court poet Aurelian
Townshend. But this brings us no nearer to Marvell, unless she also is the
Chlora of 'Mourning' and the Clora of 'The Gallery'.

[1] After leaving Oxford Lovelace spent a short time at the sister University
during Marvell's stay there. C. H. Wilkinson assumes that it was at this time
(1637) that Lovelace made the acquaintance of Marvell and other Cambridge
men who wrote verses for *Lucasta*. (Information received from Mrs. Duncan-
Jones.)

Samuel Bold, who congratulated Hastings upon his having left Babylon for Sion: there is 'In Heaven both Monarch, and an House of Peers'; bishops, and 'an Academ, though here's none now'. But the other poets do not lag far behind. If a man is known by the company he keeps, then it may be said that Marvell curses the new-born Commonwealth and laments for the Royal Martyr. His own words do not invalidate this presumptive evidence: he attacks the 'barbed Censurers' of the Press and praises the Kentish Petition, which had first brought down the anger of the Commons on Lovelace. In the same spirit Hastings's early death is ascribed to the envy of 'the Democratick Stars', which 'all that Worth from hence did Ostracize'. Lastly, to the Cavalier scorn for the vulgar herd Marvell adds the Cavalier's gallant language, as when he shows us Lovelace's innumerable female admirers coming to his rescue, 'though yet undrest': one of them, mistaking Marvell for one of her favourite's enemies, 'invades' his eyes, because she knows what pain it would be for him to lose the sight of her.

In later days the champion of religious tolerance 'will confess', apropos of the persecuted Arians of old, that he found himself 'inclinable to favour the weaker party'; and perhaps his sympathy with the conquered Royalists came chiefly from that inclination. Therefore we need not be overmuch surprised at the very different tone Marvell adopts in June 1650 in his best-known poem, 'An Horatian Ode upon Cromwel's Return from Ireland'. The conqueror of Drogheda had not quite completed the pacification, in his own style, of the sister island, when the threat of a Scottish invasion of England under Charles II caused the Long Parliament to recall its best commander. The reader of the 'Ode' must see Cromwell at this moment of his career as he is seen by the poet, who yet allows himself free scope to recall the past and even to forecast the future. This examination of a man, the object then and since of such conflicting judgements, has the merit of complete independence, nay, of an almost inhuman aloofness. If the poet errs in his interpretations or previsions it is not because the hero dazzles him or the regicide horrifies him. For the only time in his life he speaks *sine irā et studio*, and for over two centuries he remains the only one to have thus spoken of those events. Cromwell's worshippers, *à la Carlyle*, may find the praise in the 'Ode' qualified by too many hinted reservations; they may feel indignant because the three most perfectly beautiful stanzas are devoted not to the Lord General but to the King, that weak and lying monarch who had so richly deserved the block. But those stanzas are only a digression that proves the impartiality of the poet: Cromwell fills all the others, a Cromwell who compels admiration less by his virtues or even his genius than by the mission with which he has been entrusted, a kind of Scourge of God, or rather, since there is nothing Christian in this ode, which borrows from Latin poetry not only its form but its fatalistic philosophy, Fate's executioner.[1] One may now think this view erroneous or at least inadequate, but one must acknowledge that it is the view of an historian and philosopher, wholly intellectual, without any alloy of sentimental sympathy or antipathy. Marvell, it seems, had nothing to gain by writing this ode, which in fact was not published until long after his death. It would probably have displeased both parties had they read it. Yet its effect, at least temporarily, would have been to strengthen the *de facto* government, to teach the conquered resignation, and so make them give up the thought of appealing from ordeal by battle:[2] the same lesson, in fact, that appeared in number after number of *Mercurius Politicus* from the mercenary pen of Marchamont Needham, a former Royalist, starting in June 1650, the very month in which the 'Horatian Ode' was written. Milton later contributed to the same official newspaper and may have harped on the same argument, 'the power of the Sword'; at any rate he had played a part in Needham's political conversion.[3] Milton's political opposite, Hobbes, in his *Leviathan*,

[1] Gallicè, 'l'exécuteur des hautes œuvres du Destin'.
[2] Gallicè, 'le jugement de Dieu'. George R. Hibbard, 'The Early Seventeenth Century and the Tragic View of Life', in *Renaissance and Modern Studies*, 1961, pp. 5–28, places the 'Horatian Ode' flatteringly at the beginning and end of a rather rambling paper, and makes interesting, though somewhat forced, remarks on the parallel political conversions of Horace and Marvell.
[3] Marvell's indebtedness to Needham's pamphlet, *Case of the Commonwealth of England stated*, 1650, is proved by verbal echoes. See E. E. Duncan-Jones, 'The Erect Sword in Marvell's *Horatian Ode*', in *Études anglaises*, 1962, p. 172.

published (in Paris) less than a year later, came by a different
road to a not very different conclusion: while he severely
condemned rebellion in its inception he seemed to admit
that the authority of a new régime is established by con-
quest when the former sovereign can no longer help his
loyal subjects, for 'the end of obedience is protection'.

Whatever echo the politics of the 'Ode' may now find in
England or elsewhere, it should not be read for first-hand
historical information on Cromwell and his actions. Marvell
is as yet a mere private person, lost in the crowd, from which
he distinguishes himself only by his vigorous intellect and
his poetic gift. The gravest of modern historians, for instance, does not give any credit to the rumour, accepted by
the poet, that Cromwell 'wove a Net' and thus 'chased'
Charles 'To Caresbrooks narrow case'. But where all Royalists and some Republicans denounced perfidiousness Marvell sees only 'wiser art' in accordance with Machiavelli's
patriotic maxims. Likewise, later events have sufficiently
shown that for Cromwell obedience to the civil power had
its limits, while religion directed his conduct to a degree
entirely unsuspected by the poet. Lastly, the Irish have
never ratified and doubtless never will ratify the 'praises'
Marvell so generously bestowed on Cromwell in their name.
But these errors leave the conclusion of the 'Ode' intact:
the Man of Destiny, the destroyer of decrepit institutions,
irresistible so long as he wields the sword, is doomed never
to lay it down. We know today that after the expulsion of
the Long Parliament the Protector aspired to nothing else
but a return to legal order: he was to discover by experience
the truth that one can more easily establish a dictatorship
than restore freedom. No doubt familiarity with Greek and
Roman history served Marvell well and partly accounts for
his perspicacity; but erudition alone could not serve since,
among many contemporaries of our poet as learned as he,
not one rises to the same intellectual height. Some cheer the
Republican general; the greater part see only an ambitious
hypocrite. A few days after his arrival in England Cromwell
found himself more than ever exposed to envy and calumny,
owing to the resignation of his one military superior, Fairfax, since 1645 commander-in-chief of the Parliamentary

armies. And, through a freak of Fortune, Marvell entered
into the service of the same late General, now again a private
person, just after having written his 'Ode' to the glory of
his successor.[1]

Thomas, third Baron Fairfax of Cameron in the peerage
of Scotland, belonged to an old Yorkshire family firmly
rooted in the soil and wise enough to have resisted the lure
of the Court, where they could not have made a figure without becoming impoverished. Much beloved in the district
limited by the Nidd, Wharfe, and Ouse, the Fairfaxes had
all taken the side of Parliament in the Civil War. Thomas
had there evinced such boldness that his censurers called
him a hothead and questioned his capacity as a general. At
any rate he was no braggart: his modesty equalled his
courage. Save on the battlefield he even lacked self-
confidence. From 1646 to 1650 his political action had

---

[1] I have translated my analysis of the 'Horatian Ode' from the French
text of 1928 as closely as possible, neither adding nor omitting. What I think
of later studies devoted to this poem, up to 1955, by Cleanth Brooks, Douglas
Bush, and L. D. Lerner, will be found by the curious reader in 'Marvell and
the New Critics', in *R.E.S.*, 1957, pp. 387–8. They left me much where I was.
There have since appeared more profitable contributions: Joseph E. Mazzeo,
'Marvell's Machiavellian Cromwell', in *Journal of the History of Ideas*, 1960,
pp. 1–17, develops a hint thrown out by me (*v. supra*) with far superior com-
petence and great argumentative power; indeed he proves too much and
deserves the correction administered by Hans Baron, ibid., pp. 450–1: Marvell probably understood *The Prince* and *The Discourses* (if he had read them)
as his most enlightened contemporaries did and no better. R. H. Syfret,
'Marvell's *Horatian Ode*', in *R.E.S.*, 1961, pp. 160–72, is so far the most
balanced study of the poem, especially as regards its Latin sources (Lucan's
Pharsalia and Horace's *Odes*). While it certainly reveals more complexities in
Marvell's view of Cromwell it does not seem to me that her conclusion contradicts mine; I only demur to her denial of 'admiration' as well as of 'moral
acceptance' on the poet's part: the latter is indeed unnecessary (in the
Machiavellian atmosphere of the poem) but the former is unquestionably
there, since we often bestow it without regard to the morality of its object.
John M. Wallace, 'Marvell's *Horatian Ode*' in *PMLA*, 1962, pp. 33–45, gives
a full—indeed overfull—commentary and adduces much contemporary
evidence to support an interpretation broadly similar to the one given by
me in 1928; but he damages his case by some inaccuracies and rash statements, e.g. when he makes Charles I abdicate on the scaffold, free his subjects from their oath of allegiance, and 'surrender . . . to Cromwell', all this
tacitly of course. E. E. Duncan-Jones, 'The Erect Sword in Marvell's
Horatian Ode', in *Études anglaises*, 1962, pp. 172–4, by providing for the first
time a satisfactory explanation of the image (derived from the Νέκυια) has
fully confirmed—against some intervening critics, perhaps pietistically inclined—the pagan character of the whole, as asserted above.

proved mostly ineffective. He could not prevent the King's execution, of which he strongly disapproved, and yet went on serving the Commonwealth after it for seventeen months. When he resigned, on 25 June 1650, he invoked a scruple: the war against the Scots, so briskly heralded by the 'Horatian Ode', Fairfax would not have an offensive one. The advice of Cromwell, whom legal subtleties did not embarrass, prevailed with the Rump, and the victory at Dunbar (3 September) showed that the Lord of Hosts was agreeable. It seems that the Lieutenant-General had honestly done his best to persuade the General to remain at the head of the Army, and there was no open breach between the two, but their paths henceforth diverged for ever.

Almost at once Fairfax left London for his Yorkshire estates. Although he was only thirty-eight his health was undermined by an ague, his wounds, and the gout. His portrait, painted by Walker about that time, gives him a sad and ailing countenance. He had already had to forgo hunting, the favourite pastime of his earlier years. Fortunately he had received a literary education worthy of his great-uncle, Edward Fairfax, the translator of the *Gerusalemme Liberata*. He had been at Cambridge for three years and was a good Latin scholar. Later he had spent a year in France and could write and speak French and Italian. He loved books and medals, which he collected. He himself wrote, though not for publication, on various subjects: horse-breeding and Church history; he translated from the French *Mercure Trismegiste*, with a commentary, and from the Latin Flavius Vegetius' *Epitoma Rei Militaris*. The picturesque medley calls up before us an age, a country, and a class. Lastly, the former General was a poet; mostly he composed religious poems, but also some secular ones, without ever flinging aside his dignity, even when he dissuades ladies from wearing patches. To make up for the lack of the poetic gift he has a genuine feeling for natural beauty that must have created a fellowship at once between him and Marvell. And in fact, when reading some poems, or at least lines, of his, one seems to hear a faint echo, or see a faint copy, of Marvell's rural poems: they lovingly describe the same landscapes.

By Fairfax's side his wife has a niche in history. She was the niece and daughter of the Vere brothers, the best English soldiers of the beginning of the century. She had spent her childhood and youth in the camps of the Low Countries, and had made her future husband's acquaintance at the siege of Bois-le-Duc. Without beauty or even grace, bluff but frank, she was to Fairfax a trusty and devoted helpmate. A determined Presbyterian, she detested Cromwell and the Independents; she displayed her hostility to them in a spectacular way by twice interrupting, from a gallery, the proceedings at Whitehall (20 and 27 January 1648/9). According to one report she shouted 'Oliver Cromwell is a traitor'. She had always encouraged her husband in the fight against arbitrary government but she would have had him use even violent means to save Charles I. In this she failed but when he resigned his command the Republicans ascribed this decision to her influence and suggested that the General was henpecked.

Who recommended Marvell to Fairfax as a tutor for his only child, then twelve years old? We cannot tell; possibly another Yorkshireman. We know this much from Milton's letter to Bradshaw of 21 February 1652/3: 'he [Marvell] now comes lately out of the house of the Lord Fairfax . . . where he was intrusted to give some instructions in the languages to the Lady, his daughter'. Marvell's pupil, by the way, had known much more of the dangers of the Civil War than he had: carried on horseback before her nurse, she had accompanied her father when in 1643 he sallied out of besieged Bradford and slipped through the enemy lines; she had crossed the Trent and been left exhausted at a farm; Fairfax, lucky beyond belief, had managed the next day to bring her safe to Hull. In spite of this romantic childhood Mary's characteristic trait seems to have been her placidity, and this she preserved even after she had married, in 1657, one of the worst rakes of the age, the second Duke of Buckingham, elder brother to the Francis Villiers whose death Marvell had perhaps lamented in verse. A portrait of Mary, aged twenty-four, shows a stoutish young woman, with a plain but kindly countenance. Hamilton was to call the Duchess of Buckingham 'une petite ragote'. Marvell praises

his pupil's precocious gravity, good sense, and sweet disposition, rather than her looks. In 'Upon Appleton House'
he stimulates her by delicate praise to study 'all the languages
as hers' but the true aim is *Wisdome* defined as *Heavens
Dialect* (ll. 707–12).

Marvell may have joined the family before they left London, as soon as the need for a tutor became obvious owing
to the former General's decision to withdraw to his native
county. Fairfax had a mansion at York, but he preferred his
seat at Denton and, even nearer his heart, his more modest
manor-houses at Billborow and Nun Appleton.[1] Thus these
two years or so of Marvell's tutorship of Mary Fairfax were
spent in the country, and so far as we know they were the
only years (save for the first three of his life) he ever did
spend there. Then his lyrical talent came to its full bloom.

[1] A new biography of *The Lord General*, by M. A. Gibb, appeared in 1938.
It is very readable but adds little matter for our present purpose.

II

MARVELL'S POETICAL MASTERS

IT is no longer necessary to describe for the English reader the condition of English poetry when Marvell joined the *chorus vatum*. The vogue of Donne during these fifty years, a vogue by which most of his followers have benefited, makes the first half of the seventeenth century one of the best-known periods in the whole history of English literature. It would be impossible here to name all, and invidious to name some, of those who have contributed in bringing about this enlightenment. But since those critics do not lay the same emphasis on the several characteristics of the age we shall briefly state our own views (by no means original) and ask the reader to accept them, temporarily, as postulates.

First we consider 1660 the most convenient date for dividing the Renaissance, giving the term its broadest extension, from the neo-Classic age. But to define the former by the supremacy of feeling and the latter by that of reason seems to us questionable, even as an acknowledged simplification. Rather let us say that the intellect holds the helm all through the seventeenth century. In this respect the change comes with Donne, even before 1600, whether we ascribe it to his exceptional temperament or see in him the mouthpiece of the new *Zeitgeist*. So is born the metaphysical school (we shall not discuss the fitness of the epithet, invoking only its prescriptive title and the failure of all attempts to provide a substitute).[1] There follows on this first assumption the

---

[1] The most interesting of these attempts has been made by George Williamson: 'Strong Lines', in *English Studies*, 1936, pp. 152–9 (reprinted in *Seventeenth Century Contexts*, 1960). Unfortunately it does not lend itself to the coining of a handy epithet. We give 'metaphysical' a purely historical meaning, as wide as possible. More critical, and even philosophical, definitions tend to be very restrictive, e.g. the most recent and deepest of all, given by Robert Ellrodt, in *L'Inspiration personnelle et l'esprit du temps chez les poètes métaphysiques anglais*, 1960. On the other hand, Rosemund Tuve tends to rub out distinctions between *Elizabethan and Metaphysical Imagery* (1947) in order

assertion that Spenser's influence had by the end of the sixteenth century lost most of its efficacy, though of course we recognize the existence of some Spenserians in the early seventeenth century. As regards Ben Jonson, often mentioned as the third member of a poetic triumvirate, though the 'Sons of Ben' were not such exclusively within the Apollo Room of the Mermaid Tavern, yet his example either confirmed that of Donne (a certain *brusquerie*, energy sought in concision) or else qualified, often felicitously, Donne's metrical and stylistic audacities, but without exorcizing his spirit. The results of a mixed discipleship may best be seen in Thomas Carew, whose shorter lyrics—very short indeed—recall, and even surpass, Jonson's in classical finish, but whose strongest pieces read Donne all over. Indeed, one of the two (the other being 'The Rapture') is the finest tribute in verse ever paid to the master, 'An Elegie upon the death of the Deane of Pauls, Dr. John Donne', and a rare example of critical perspicacity at close range.

Marvell himself stands in much the same relation as Carew to his English predecessors. Spenser is to him, like Chaucer, a great name of the past. Ben Jonson impresses him even more by his character than by his art. For Donne his admiration, manifested in almost every piece of his verse through verbal imitation, survived his youth as a living force. He has left a testimony of it in a pamphlet written only four years before his own death. Here he brings in Donne's 'Progress of the Soule' with the thinnest possible excuse. He is trying to persuade the Anglicans not to persecute the Puritans, and he quotes what is in fact a bitter attack on Queen Elizabeth, composed by a very imperfect convert from Roman Catholicism, apparently on the road to atheism, and unafraid to couple Luther with Mahomet as perturbers of religion. Marvell ignores the glaring im-

to oppose both poetic periods, considered as one, to the present poetic and critical age. While we approve her method and admire her learning, acuteness, and cogency in argument, we think that she has carried a useful reaction too far, e.g. pp. 325–6: Marvell's 'Definition of Love' and Spenser's *Amoretti*, XLVI, to us remain poles apart even as regards imagery. Here I side with Bonamy Dobrée, 'Milton and Dryden: A Comparison and Contrast in Poetic Ideas and Poetic Method', in *E.L.H.*, 1936, pp. 85–86, whom Rosemund Tuve is trying to refute.

propriety of this digression, indeed one of many in his pamphlet but certainly the most awkward, and he does so because Donne's poem, then over seventy years old, still appeals to him as a 'witty fable'.

The master's influence on Marvell was reinforced by that of earlier disciples, George Herbert and Crashaw. The latter he may well have known personally, since they were at Cambridge together. As regards Cowley, Marvell's senior by only three years but a far more precocious poet, their acquaintance hardly admits of doubt since from 1637 to 1641 they belonged to the same College. And when *The Mistress* came out in 1647 Marvell at once read it and turned it to his own use. His most passionate love poems derive their themes and some of their imagery from pieces written, as Cowley himself acknowledged in a notorious passage of the preface to the 1656 edition, with the sole motive of conforming to an immemorial poetic tradition.

Henry Vaughan and Marvell were born in the same year, but, so far as we know, their careers did not bring them together, and the few resemblances one can trace between their respective poems, probably accidental, weigh little against the essential dissimilarity of their genius and inspiration. To sum this up in two words, Vaughan attracts us by his mysticism and Marvell by his art.

Marvell's kinship with Carew, Suckling, Lovelace, and the Cavalier poets generally is more obvious but still superficial, and shows best in some pieces of impertinent gallantry. These poets treated women little less contemptuously than Donne, but their manner was decidedly more courtly. Marvell was at times content to adopt their tone.

Of Marvell's friendship with Milton we shall speak later; suffice it to say that already at Cambridge the younger poet could not well fail to hear of the older one and read 'Lycidas' when it came out in 1638. He may have just reread it in the 1645 edition of the *Poems of Mr. John Milton* since he parodies one noble line of it in his own 'Fleckno'. A few other imitations or echoes collected by modern scholars hardly amount, however, to a proof of influence.[1]

---

[1] Since 1928 many parallels with or echoes from English poems and romances have been discovered in Marvell's poetry. We only mention here

To the Italian and Spanish poets Marvell should have a debt, like several of his contemporaries, since he had certainly read some at least of their verse at a rather early and still impressionable age. But nobody has yet pointed out any borrowings, and he refers to none by name save Ariosto, Aretine, and Guarini: to the first for his mock-heroic exaggerations, to the second for his malignity and atheism, to the third for his effeminate and immoral amorousness, expressed in 'whining Italian'.

Rather unexpectedly, Marvell's indebtedness to French poetry may have been somewhat more substantial. His only acknowledgement of it is a translation into Latin of two couplets out of Brébeuf's *Pharsale*, on the invention of the alphabet. Since Corneille is said to have thought highly of those lines, over-ingenious and affectedly elegant as they seem to us, we should not tax Marvell's taste on account of his choice. But on another occasion he quoted, as by 'Bassompierre or Aubigné' (meaning no doubt the author of *Les Tragiques*), two lines, far more obscene than witty, and he managed to destroy the rhythm thoroughly by the insertion of extra syllables, thus proving that his ear was never attuned to French prosody. Nevertheless Théophile de Viau, still at the height of his fame and yet unquelled by Boileau, and Saint-Amant, the other major figure among the *poètes libertins*, may have appealed to Marvell, chiefly by their praise of solitude. Even if he had not read them himself in France he found at Nun Appleton a dilution of their poetry in Lord Fairfax's rather bloodless imitations. But the French

the more plausible ones: Bradbrook and Lloyd Thomas, *Andrew Marvell*, 1940, p. 25 (Mildmay Fane's *Otia Sacra*); Pierre Legouis, 'Marvell and Massinger', in *R.E.S.*, 1947, pp. 63–65; L. C. Martin, 'Marvell, Massinger, and Sidney', ibid., 1951, pp. 374–5; Douglas Bush, 'Marvell and Sidney', ibid., 1952, p. 375; Eleanor Withington, 'Marvell and Montague', ibid., 1953, pp. 261–3 (these four concern 'The Definition of Love'); F. Kermode, 'Two Notes on Marvell', in *N.Q.*, 1952, pp. 136–8, 218 (Thomas Randolph); E. E. Duncan-Jones, 'Notes on Marvell's Poems', ibid., 1953, pp. 430–1 (Suckling, King, and Shirley); L. N. Wall, 'Some Notes on Marvell's Sources', ibid., 1957, pp. 170–3 (Lovelace, Edmund Spenser); Dennis Davison, 'Notes on Marvell's Coy Mistress', ibid., 1958, p. 521 (John Bodenham, Habington, Lord Herbert of Cherbury, Herrick, Quarles, Lovelace, this last one misleading); Robin Skelton, 'Rowland Watkins and Andrew Marvell', ibid., 1958, pp. 531–2, does not convince me that 'The Nymph complaining . . .' borrows from *Flamma Sine Fumo . . .* (1662).

contemporary poet closest akin to Marvell (whether read
or unread by him) is Tristan L'Hermite, whose 'Promenoir
des deux amants', no less than 'The Garden', deserves to be
praised for 'witty delicacy'.[1]

For completeness' sake Dutch poetry should be mentioned: it was then in its Golden Age, and the conjecture that
Milton knew Vondel's work has had several upholders. But
with respect to Marvell not even a conjecture has so far
been advanced.

Donne apart, it may be doubted whether any modern
writer, or, to speak more accurately, any writer in a modern
language, influenced Marvell's style as much as the Latin
poets, both ancient and recent, did. Like every schoolboy
of his age he read Latin and Greek authors by compulsion
before he read English authors voluntarily. More than others
(especially Donne, whose studies had not gone so strictly
by rule or routine) he learnt much from Horace, the finished
if somewhat stilted Horace of the *Odes*. Yet he may be
imagined to have found more congenial spirits among the
poets of the Silver Age, especially the elegiac; the Latin
verse he composed to the end of his life aims at effect rather
than chastity; he takes far more liberties with classical idiom
than Milton. Even in his English verse many of the conceits had done service long before Donne, even before
Petrarch, with Ovid and his more decadent successors, if not
with the Alexandrines. And Marvell's hardly explored debt
to the modern Latin poets may well prove considerable.[2]

---

[1] English critics have been very generous in their estimate of French
poetic influence on Marvell, beginning with Geoffrey Woledge, 'St Amand
[*sic*], Fairfax, and Marvell', in *M.L.R.*, 1930, pp. 481–3; then came M. C.
Bradbrook, 'Marvell and the Poetry of Rural Solitude', in *R.E.S.*, 1941,
pp. 37–46, where far more is made than I durst make in 1928 of similarities
with Théophile and Saint-Amant; see also Ruth Wallerstein, *Studies in Seventeenth Century Poetics*, 1950, pp. 306–31. Miss Bradbrook suggests Mildmay
Fane, Earl of Westmorland and Fairfax's brother-in-law as the introducer
of Saint-Amant's poetry to Marvell, presumably *c.* 1650; but Marvell cannot
well have missed hearing in France, *c.* 1643, of Saint-Amant, then at the
height of his fame, and quite a character.

[2] In addition to the borrowings from Horace and Lucan in the 'Horatian
Ode' (see p. 17, n. 1 *supra*) many more or less convincing ones have been
pointed out in other poems since 1928. Here I shall only mention one from
Virgil noted by Kenneth Muir in *N.Q.*, 1951, p. 115, and one from Lucretius
(through Statius?) suggested by E. E. Duncan-Jones, 'The First Sunset', in
T.L.S., 3 April 1959, p. 193. It does not seem that anybody has yet pointed

In a sense Marvell's culture when he came back to England was broadly European; this was due to the common basis of classical learning, but also to the international fashions prevailing more or less in all the western countries. Yet Mary Fairfax's tutor in modern languages remained rather insular. He praises his pupil in verse for preserving 'English thoughts' even when she 'doth them fitly fit' with French or Italian words. Doing otherwise would, it is hinted, endanger a young woman's virtue. This principle, if adhered to in practice, must have made Marvell a poor teacher, but his refusal to bend his mind to the thought of other peoples may well have made him the better poet. We shall now see how he could be himself by being intensely English.

out in print that 'Damon the Mower' is a (characteristically free) imitation of Virgil's 'Alexis' (*Bucolics*, ii). But no reader who had had the advantage of a classical education could read 'Nor am I so deform'd to sight . . .' (l. 57) without remembering 'Nec sum adeo informis: . . .' (l. 25)—and, beyond Alexis, Theocritus' 'Cyclops' (*Idylls*, xi), to whom, as well as to the Cowherd (ibid., xx), I referred in *André Marvell*, chapter III, n. 101). The only modern Latin poet for whom such a claim has been made is the Pole Sarbiewski; see Maren-Sofie Røstvig, 'Benlowes, Marvell, and the Divine Casimire', in *Huntington Library Quarterly*, 1954, pp. 13–35. On Marvell himself as a modern Latin poet see Carl E. Bain, 'The Latin Poetry of Andrew Marvell', in *Philological Quarterly*, 1959, pp. 436–49.

III

THE LYRICAL POET

THE two great sources of inspiration for the meta-physicals are human love and divine love. Both are found in Marvell; but, almost alone among Donne's disciples, he adds a third, the love of nature. Leaving aside for the present his political poems, some of which take lyrical forms, a three-forked division according to the themes forces itself upon us. This question, however, remains open: did Marvell write his amorous, his religious, and his descriptive verse simultaneously or successively?

Those of the last sort are the most easily dateable, at least roughly. 'Upon the Hill and Grove at Bill-borow' and 'Upon Appleton House' are both addressed to Fairfax and describe his Yorkshire estates; they were written during Marvell's residence with the former General. The four Mower poems seem related to stanzas LIII–LV of 'Upon Appleton House'. 'On a Drop of Dew' and 'The Garden', with their Latin versions, have been conjectured to belong to the same years of rural retirement, and a certain similarity in the feeling invites us to accept this conjectural dating.[1]

Those pieces that have woman for their subject offer more variety of tone and may belong to a longer period. Some that breathe the air of fashionable society may well have been composed in London, when Marvell sought the company of the Cavaliers, between 1646 and 1650. 'The Gallery', in its original text, may have referred to the collection of pictures at Whitehall in the present tense, i.e. before its dispersion in 1648/9. If 'The Picture of little T.C. in a Prospect of Flowers' borrows from Benlowes's *Theophila*, it was written

---

[1] Yet L. N. Wall, 'Some Notes on Marvell's Sources', in *N.Q.*, 1957, p. 173, points out that the garden described in the poem by this title does not resemble Fairfax's at Nun Appleton. He asks whether 'The Garden' may not have been written at Eton (see Chapter IV, *infra*)—possibly with Windsor or Hampton Court in mind, if there was a floral sundial at either of these places.

not earlier than 1652.[1] Even more elusive is the connexion
of 'To his Coy Mistress' with Yorkshire since 'the Tide of
Humber', by which the poet would complain, observed by
him as a boy, certainly ran all his life long in his imagination.[2]

If Marvell wrote any erotic verse while under Fairfax's
roof he must have kept it very secret. Conversely he found
there an atmosphere entirely favourable to the composition
of his religious pieces. Essentially independent of time and
space (save 'Bermudas', which we shall examine later) they
at least contain nothing irreconcilable with their having
been composed in the same years as the poems descriptive
of nature. Two of them, 'Clorinda and Damon' and 'The
Coronet', would seem to refer to a conversion, a 'late
change', from 'Pastures, Caves, and Springs' and 'fragrant
Towers / That once adorn'd [his] Shepherdesses head' to
an austerely Puritan way of life. But Marvell did not pass
from his Cavalier laxity (which need not have been very lax)
straight to the austerity (such as it was) of his Cromwellian
period; so that any dramatic incident in his spiritual life
seems excluded.[3] He may have changed his mind from day
to day on the lawfulness of the love of nature as of the love
of music, denounced in 'A Dialogue between the Resolved
Soul, and Created Pleasure' as the Tempter's supreme snare
but praised in 'Musicks Empire' with the sole reservation
that she should pay her 'Homage' to a still 'gentler Conqueror', modest and pious, whom we identify with Fairfax
rather than with Cromwell, lover of music as the Protector was.

---

[1] See E. E. Duncan-Jones, letter to *T.L.S.*, 30 October 1953, p. 693, and
'Benlowes, Marvell, and the Divine Casimire', in *Huntington Library Quarterly*,
1957, pp. 183–4.

[2] Roger Sharrock thinks that 'the Conversion of the *Jews*' referred to in
this poem dates it *c.* 1653. More ingeniously E. E. Duncan-Jones argues for
1646 from the 'ten years before the Flood', which event took place in 1656
(*anno mundi*). See their letters to *T.L.S.*, 31 October and 5 December 1958,
and 16 January 1959.

[3] For 'A Dialogue between Thyrsis and Dorinda', see *supra*, p. 11, n. 1.
J. B. Leishman, 'Some Themes and Variations in the Poetry of Andrew
Marvell', in *Proceedings of the British Academy*, xlvii, 1961, attempts to distinguish between the less and the more mature of Marvell's lyrical poems, as
a preliminary to a sensitive study 'of the ways in which tradition and originality
are combined in our poet'. It is some comfort for Mr. Leishman's tragic
death that it has not prevented the publication of the book on Marvell's
poetry he had been working at for many years.

Let us tarry no longer in the walks of an uncertain chronology, but conclude: there are few non-political pieces that
may be certainly or even plausibly ascribed to years later
than 1652. Now then is the time to take a general view of
Marvell's lyrical work. It contains little more than 2,000
lines, but within this small compass it presents a variety rare
in any age, exceptional in the mid-seventeenth century. It
is thus as easy as it is fitting to take stock of all its wealth.

Towards woman Marvell adopts diverse poetic attitudes.
Respect for her does not appear in all. Donne had given the
lead in irony, sharply interrupting the Petrarchan tradition
of English lyrical poetry:

> Hope not for minde in women; at their best
> Sweetness and wit, they'are but *Mummy*, possesst.

Then Suckling had made female inconstancy (amply reci-
procated) the main theme of his poetry. In 'Mourning'
Marvell follows this Cavalier fashion very closely. Why, he
asks, these tears of late in Chlora's eyes? Does she really
mourn for her dead lover? After devoting several stanzas to
ever more mischievous conjectures, the poet concludes, with
affected magnanimity, that he 'keeps' his 'silent judgment':

> But sure as oft as Women weep,
> It is to be suppos'd they grieve.

Of its kind this piece is excellent: no feeling but no heavy
insistence either; the restraint essential to such badinage is
preserved in spite of two conceits, the one mythological and
the other learned. Even in France, where raillery of the fair
sex was then reaching perfection through politeness, did
ever poet surpass Marvell in the shooting of the final dart,
so delicately sharpened?

'Daphnis and Chloe', implicitly placed under the invoca-
tion of Sáint Longus, the patron of libertine naïvety, at first
seems more tender. The shepherd has lost all hope of persuading the cruel fair one. But she, coquettish of course yet
enamoured as deeply as woman can be, when told he must
depart 'would gladly yield to all / So it had his stay com-
priz'd'. He unfortunately does not 'see he might be blest'
until it is too late to cancel his departure; half amused, half

serious, the poet reports the lover's lamentations. The climax is reached when Daphnis tears himself away:

> At these words away he broke;
> As who long has praying ly'n,
> To his Heads-man makes the Sign,
> And receives the parting stroke.

Marvell seems to have laid by his rural pipe to blow the trumpet of the 'Horatian Ode'. Did the poem end here we should preserve an inconsistent impression of sentiment not free from sensuality, of tenderness seasoned with bantering, of a pastoral poem now sincere now burlesque, rising to a tragic note. Was it in order to make his intention perfectly clear that Marvell wrote, perhaps later, two cynical final stanzas? Daphnis has had enough of Chloe's coyness:

> Last night he with *Phlogis* slept;
> This night for *Dorinda* kept;
> And but rid to take the Air.

—with the poet's approbation. How are we to account for this catastrophe? Probably by nothing more than a mood of rebellion against courtly conventions.[1] Anyhow, Marvell, having once given full vent to his pertness, avoided the fault of too many of his immediate predecessors—and successors—and moved on from this negative presentation of love. 'The Gallery' already shows him capable of true sensibility, even when dealing with a coquette.

The poet invites Chlora to visit his mind 'Compos'd into one Gallery' where portraits of her in various garbs face one another: on the one side 'an Inhumane Murtheress' or an 'Enchantress' in the Canidian line; on the other Aurora or 'Venus in her pearly boat'. So far the poet's fancy has been at play, but the last stanza strikes a more moving note; he remembers 'the Look . . . with which [he] first was took', and wistfully recalls

> A tender Shepherdess, whose Hair
> Hangs loosely playing in the Air,
> Transplanting Flow'rs from the green Hill,
> To crown her Head, and Bosome fill.

---

[1] Dennis Davison's commentary on this poem strikes me as unduly tragic; see *Andrew Marvell Selected Poetry and Prose*, pp. 37–40.

That a lover's heart contains his mistress's picture had already been said, among others, by Donne and Carew; but Marvell renovates the hackneyed metaphor by enlarging it. His imagination reveals itself spacious without strain. At the same time the rural verdant freshness of the description and feeling, in which one already foresees the singer of the meadows and gardens, takes us far away from the urban crispness of the Court poets.

The same freshness gives value to a short piece where love appears only in the bud, but which the *odor di femina* permeates. 'The Picture of little T.C. in a Prospect of Flowers' is stamped with a certain witty melancholy. In today's child the poet sees tomorrow's maid, and professes fear of finding himself among the future victims of her beauty associated with scornful chastity. Yet the last two stanzas revert to the initial theme of harmony between the background and the figure, the flowers and the little girl, whom the poet would teach to respect Flora's 'infants'.

'Young Love' might have been written for the same T.C. a little later (if she lived long enough) but before she came to be 'ripe for man' even by the seventeenth-century dramatist's standard. Marvell does not quite avoid the unpleasantness that lurks in such a subject. He anticipates the French metaphor of the *fruit vert*, too eagerly sought by elderly gentlemen, with his statement that the girl's 'fair Blossoms are too green' (subject and predicate do not agree at all well) 'Yet for Lust, but not for Love'; the distinction hardly saves the situation. As for the next stanza it anticipates, by a century and a half, the very English and humorous phrase 'calf-love':

> Love as much the snowy Lamb
>   Or the wanton Kid does prize,
> As the lusty Bull or Ram,
>   For his morning Sacrifice.

Hardly have we smiled at this conceit when the poet turns into a dialectician in verse, clearly in imitation of Donne, rather pedantically at first but ending on a truly eloquent note.

This rather incoherent piece where badinage straining to be light unexpectedly gives way to the language of passion, may serve as a transition to the consistently passionate pieces. Yet in 'The unfortunate Lover' hyperbole rises to such a height that a man of today suspects intentional parody: this character, shipwrecked while in his mother's womb, 'called to play / At sharp' with Fortune in order to entertain 'angry Heaven' with 'a spectacle of Blood', this 'only *Banneret* / That ever Love created yet, . . . In a Field Sable a Lover *Gules*', does he not come fully armed from the French, or better, the Spanish, romances? Amadis de Gaule, here then is thy caricature? Nothing is less certain. Raillery, if it exists, is tinged with sympathy, and we even think that sympathy predominates. Cervantes himself could not have created Don Quixote had he never been in love with chivalry. Now Cervantes is a classic, while Marvell here anticipates all the grotesque verve of the Romantics, not only in his tumultuous metaphors but also in his conception of a cursed hero after the heart of Byron or Hugo, of a *roseau sentant* who scorns the universe eager for his downfall.[1]

No less fundamentally extravagant is 'The Match', but here extravagance hides under logical, we might even say scientific, expression. The idea may have been borrowed from Shakespeare's Sonnet LXVII where Nature is shown making the poet's friend a treasure in which she accumulates all the riches of the Creation. Marvell divides the idea and develops the two halves symmetrically. The precious articles hoarded up by Nature and used by her with the utmost thrift drew together on account of their likeness; out of their union 'one perfect Beauty grew / And that was *Celia*'. At the same time Love stored fuel against the cold of old age. But nitre, naphtha, and sulphur combine 'magnetically' and a flame arises, never equalled in heat and height, 'And *Celia* that am I'. So that the two lovers, by this time more Donnean than Shakespearian, 'alone the happy rest, / Whilst all the World is poor'.

The modern mind will call this piece a *jeu d'esprit*.

[1] The interpretation of this poem as a political allegory with Charles, Prince of Wales, as its hero (see Bradbrook and Lloyd Thomas, *Andrew Marvell*, p. 29) never recommended itself to me, and its originator, Miss R. H. Syfret, informs me that she has long given it up. The connexion with the emblems (ibid.) presents better credentials.

Undoubtedly it is one, but in the seventeenth century the *bel-esprit*, wit, did not exclude passion; nay, passion hardly had any other interpreter. And if 'The Match' leaves the reader in doubt of the earnestness Marvell can pour into hyperbole, 'The Definition of Love' will convince him. No piece of his reveals more clearly the influence of Donne; no one better deserves the epithet 'metaphysical' and more fully justifies this perilous manner. It has now found its place in every anthology; so we shall only say that, while the most romantic guesses may be made, vainly enough, at the object of the poet's hopeless love, and though the phrasing has been resolved into a cento of reminiscences, passion rings through those stanzas. *Pace* Molière-Alceste, Dryden, and *The Spectator*, the heart speaks here, though it borrows the language of the brain. Besides, we are very far from the courtly love of the *précieuses* and the *ruelles* with this pre-Christian *Fatum*, which leaves the lovers no other issue than pessimistic stoicism.[1]

The same absence of Christian feeling is noticeable in Marvell's most erotic poem, 'To his Coy Mistress'. But this time his paganism recalls, though not Epicurus himself, yet those ancients called since Horace's time Epicureans. The poet handles the theme, tritest of all, of 'Carpe diem'. In France Ronsard and Tristan had composed on it their most beautiful poetry. In England, and close to Marvell in time, Herrick and Carew hardly ever gave any other moral advice, and the Court, though not the King, followed it only too well. Though each poet deals with the theme in his own way there is a family likeness between the poems. In this concert the dominant note is an elegant melancholy, somewhat sceptical and languid. Against this background Marvell's impetuosity stands out. Catullus alone, in a few immortal pieces, had written with such headlong speed, but even his raptures retain some touch of the effeminate. The

[1] H. E. Toliver, 'Marvell's "Definition of Love" and Poetry of Self-Exploration', in *Bucknell Review*, May 1962, pp. 263–74, however, suffers from an excess of philosophy, mostly Platonic, and fails to convince me of the general applicability of the 'Definition'; it suits Marvell's love and few others, or none. This sensitive study made us expect with interest the forthcoming publication of Mr. Toliver's Ph.D. thesis, *Ironic Vision; A Reading of Andrew Marvell*, but see *infra*, Bibliographical Appendix.

English poet is fuller-blooded, prouder too; possessed with a sensual frenzy heightened by his mistress's coyness, he means to triumph over this female reluctance through the male vigour of his intellect. This poem, which most of our readers will know by heart, is the work of a man neither blasé nor consumptive but robust, already mature and yet still young. Somewhat *précieux* at the start, the language becomes daring in the description of the corpse. To the Victorian anthologists the concrete use of 'Honour' (sc. *mulieris pudenda*), reinforced by the Shakespearian meaning of 'embrace', was too much and they left out those central lines. For us they suffice to settle contemporary doubts cast on the poet's virility, and to prove that he was at least once in love—body and soul—with a real live mistress.

After such transports, 'The Fair Singer' will sound like mere pretty amorousness, though the second stanza could compare not unfavourably with Campion's, Carew's, Herrick's, and even Milton's lines on the same theme: the irresistibility of female beauty when reinforced by vocal charm. Like those older poets, Marvell also loved music for itself, and in emulation of them he wrote his 'Musicks Empire', a quaint myth that sums up in a few stanzas the genesis and progress of that art.

We shall, by and by, find the love of women in a subordinate position, combining with the love of God or the love of nature, or else in conflict with both. But we can already assert the variety of Marvell's inspiration in this field. No poet of his or of the preceding generation has at his command so wide a gamut of feeling. Carew, though not incapable of strength, and Herrick may surpass him by their more careful workmanship, their more delicate sense of perfection; but their amatory verse, in spite of its limited extent, does not avoid monotony. Suckling is remembered for one attitude, that of the inconstant Cavalier, and Lovelace for the opposite attitude, that of the adoring lover; Habington praises his wife Castara's virtue with ever renewed wonder; in Donne, perhaps because he still is himself first and foremost, Petrarchan compliment and cynical defiance present a family likeness. But Marvell, a less pronounced but more versatile personality, manages not to

strike the same note twice. His compass extends from im-
pertinence to passion through exaggeration, infused in
various degrees with sincerity and voluptuous melancholy.
Only the Platonic worship of woman is absent from his
verse. This absence deserves all the more notice since his
sacred poems, as we shall now see, praise purity above all
and a Platonist influence may be recognized as one of the
sources of his Protestant idealist's creed.

For Marvell's religious poetry, less abundant and also less
various than his love poetry, makes him (at the feet of
Milton the great lonely one) the representative of the Puritan
current, so powerful in so many souls, but commonly contemptuous of literary expression. Among the metaphysicals
our poet is almost the only Calvinist (with qualifications)
facing numerous Catholics or Laudians. The son of the
Lecturer of Hull, in spite of his travels, his youthful friend-
ships, his literary admirations, still bears the Genevan impress, though sometimes concealed by other impresses.
Indeed two periods might be made out in his sacred verse,
the earlier more imaginative and sentimental, the later more
austere and bare; but succession in time is unnecessary to
account for an opposition not nearly so marked as many of
the other contrasts that together make up Marvell's physiognomy.

'Eyes and Tears', not an explicitly religious piece, derives
from Crashaw's 'The Weeper'. To Mary Magdalen, the
favourite saint of the baroque Italians, Marvell devotes not
only four English octosyllabics but two Latin elegiac distichs. Cromwell's Saints, though they wept unashamedly
when the Spirit moved them to it, would have frowned on
the worship of a woman and the indulgence in tender
emotions.

However, they might have thought better of a piece that
bears a superficial likeness to 'Eyes and Tears', namely 'On
a Drop of Dew'. Here again, and in the longer Latin version
entitled 'Ros', Crashaw's influence is felt. But some similarities of expression should not disguise the essential difference
of the two inspirations. Though the drop of dew in the
blowing rose (which stands for worldly beauty) looks 'Like

its own Tear', yet there is no luxuriating in tears. Even the former half of the poem reveals Marvell's preoccupation with purity; and the latter half presents the soul, whose symbol was the drop of dew, 'in its pure and circling thoughts', wholly intent upon 'excluding round' the World, 'disdaining' it, 'girt and ready to ascend'. In the Latin text two distichs:

> Quam bene in aversae modulum contracta figurae
> Oppositum Mundo claudit ubique latus.
> Sed bibit in speculum radios ornata rotundum;
> Et circumfuso splendet aperta Die

vaguely remind us of Horace's sage, 'teres atque rotundus'; but the spirit of the piece, in both versions, is that of Saint Paul interpreted by Calvin: divine grace, both necessary and sufficient, is here the ray that must pierce through souls; and in order to make these diaphanous any carnal alloy must be eliminated. Both versions express a religious feeling at once bright with purity and gloomy with horror at fallen nature. The little symbolic globe 'Shines with a mournful Light . . . / Restless it roules and unsecure, / Trembling lest it grow impure'. In the last four lines of each version a new comparison is introduced, that of the soul with 'Manna's sacred Dew / White, and intire, though congeal'd and chill'. The austerity of this couplet is not fully compensated for by the ecstasy in the next, and last:

> Congeal'd on Earth: but does, dissolving, run
> Into the Glories of th' Almighty Sun.

So, apparent impassiveness covers love, and the presence here of a truly Christian element must be acknowledged. Yet remembering the fervent joy of Crashaw or Vaughan one is struck chiefly by the Judaic aspect of this poem. The law of Moses, mostly negative, aimed at preserving the Chosen People from pollution: now, in spite of their indignant protests against the ritualistic survivals or revivals they detected in the Anglican Church, the English Dissenters remained faithful to the spirit whence the cleansing ceremonies had sprung, and the nickname of Puritan expressed not only their will to clear worship and dogma from all corruptions, i.e. additions to the Bible, but also their ambition to purify the soul from all the emotions and inclinations that did not tend solely to God.

Such exclusiveness may well entail impoverishment, but in this poem it is corrected by the delicate beauty of the form, at the cost, perhaps, of a certain inconsistency. Besides, the scorn of the sensible world is justified not only by the terrifying dogma of original sin but by the harmonious speculations of ancient Greece. What is that nostalgia of the soul 'Remembring still its former height, ... | And, recollecting its own Light', if not an echo of the theory of eternal ideas and reminiscence? Has this diffuse Platonism passed to Marvell through Saint Augustine, or some of the early Reformers, or one of the Cambridge dons when he was a student there? Probably from each and all, and the poet could well go to the fountain-head.

In 'The Coronet' there appears the Puritan mistrust of profane ornaments, even when presented to the Creator. Let us not admit into the Temple flowers under which the Serpent might lurk. The metaphorical flowers of poetry are no less dangerous: one imagines oneself to be glorifying God while one is only thinking of one's literary fame. One could thus procure one's damnation by writing sacred poems. Therefore the only use to which the poet can put his gift is not dedication but immolation to the Redeemer; or rather, since such a sacrifice exceeds the strength of man, prayer that fire from Heaven may, if necessary, kill the temptation without sparing the beauty. Three ample periods make up this brief poem, and argue with a nobility worthy of the theme.

The Calvinism of 'The Coronet' shows more clearly when it is compared with those pieces in which Donne and Herbert treat the same theme and which Marvell may have taken for his starting-point: 'La Corona' and 'Easter'. Donne has no doubt that his offering will find acceptance. Herbert indeed expresses a disappointment not unlike Marvell's, but while for the Anglican the flowers are superfluous, for the Puritan they are defiled; Herbert observes that he can give the Creator nothing that He does not own already; Marvell accuses himself of having offered a fragment of a Creation wholly given up to the spirit of evil. What might be objected to this view of the problem is that it dooms the poet to silence: when he had written 'The Coronet', consistency should have compelled him to lay down his pen, never to resume it. The triumph of the Puritan over the poet is made all the more decisive by the literary praise Marvell, in a dignified way, grants to his own verse: he cannot help regretting, while condemning them, their 'curious' (i.e. elaborate, finished) design and the words he had 'set with Skill and chosen out with Care'.[1]

Still more characteristic of this renunciation is 'A Dialogue between the Resolved Soul, and Created Pleasure'. This opens with a martial exhortation, versified from Ephesians vi. 14–16: the Soul must arm against temptation. Indeed, when the military metaphor is taken up by the Chorus we recognize the form (but not the spirit) of the Stoic adage: 'Ecce spectaculum dignum ad quod respiciat . . . Deus . . . vir fortis cum malā fortunā compositus.'[2] It is nevertheless significant that the poet should take his stand among those, numerous in his age and country, who see life as lists for single combat and refuse to come to terms with Nature, a perfidious enemy. But we should not accuse our poet of sacrificing easily what he cannot appreciate. Many Puritans, past and present,

> Compound for Sins they are inclin'd to
> By damning those they have no mind to.

Not so Marvell: the temptations undergone by the Soul lose nothing in his verse of their power and seductive charm. The personal note makes itself heard most distinctly when Created Pleasure borrows the language of Marvell's poetry: in the temptation through 'the Souls of fruits and flowers', which 'stand prepared to heighten' the poet's soul (tersely summing up the climactic stanzas of 'Upon Appleton House')—through woman (described in terms that recall the *Celia* of 'The Match')—through music, the most exquisite, hence the most dangerous of sensuous enjoyments

---

[1] J. E. Hardy devotes chapter iii of *The Curious Flame*, 1962, to this poem of Marvell's; he puts many otiose questions and provides some wild answers. To him the 'Shepherdess' of l. 8 is a 'recherché bawd'.

[2] L. N. Wall, 'Marvell and Seneca', in *N.Q.*, 1961, pp. 185–6, lists other possible borrowings from the moralist and tragedian.

(the metaphor of the 'sweet Chordage' reminds us of 'The Fair Singer'). Then, if 'minted Gold' does not seem ever to have wielded much power over him, the Tempter's supreme offer ('Thou shalt know each hidden Cause;[1] / And see the future Time:') appealed to Marvell, whose intellectual curiosity we know to have been wide. Yet he resists the *libido sciendi* as well as the *libido sentiendi*. He sacrifices to his God not only beauty but science. There is no limit to his Puritan intolerance.

But, some will ask, is the epithet necessary? Do not all Christians hold, in theory at least, that the senses and their objects are so many obstacles to salvation? Corneille's *Polyeucte* (a play performed when Marvell may well have been in France) proclaims this Puritanical faith and its hero acts upon it. Yet, in the seventeenth century the English Protestant Puritans as a body went furthest in this direction, and the author of that 'Dialogue between the Resolved Soul, and Created Pleasure' placed himself among them by renouncing all his worldly loves.

'A Dialogue between the Soul and Body', like the preceding one, is in the allegorical vein of the Middle Ages. It differs from the other in the absence of any conclusion; its effect is quite opposite, lacking the dogmatic assurance that baffled the strivings of Created Pleasure. In this *estrif* or *disputoison*, scholastic in its subtlety, where Soul and Body both seem to be in the right when railing at each other, Marvell seeks rather to parade his ingenuity than to persuade or move; if he at all gives the impression of sincerity he owes it to the confession of his perplexity when confronted with one of the most abstruse problems of divinity and philosophy. Besides, he but puts here in dialogue form the arguments pro and con scattered over the poetical works of John Donne, whose restless mind, in the 'Second Anniversary' and, even later, in a verse-letter to the Countess of Bedford ('T'have written then, . . .') raised difficulties rather than provided solutions. Marvell indeed does not go so deep as his master had done into the mystery of man's double nature. The Soul in his poem is a Platonist, as might

[1] This, of course, derives from Virgil: 'Felix qui potuit rerum cognoscere causas . . .' (*Georgics*, ii. 490).

be expected. But the Body, having read Saint Augustine, rejects and rebuts the charge of having corrupted its mate. As regards the poet, he remains in a wholly Pyrrhonic suspense.

The other two dialogues forming part of Marvell's religious poetry are set in a pastoral frame. They have this in common that the shepherd converts, easily enough, the shepherdess to his neophyte's faith. The former of the two pieces, 'Clorinda and Damon', need not detain us, for it contrasts in the crudest manner pagan sensuality and Christian, or Protestant, purity. Shameless Clorinda tries to draw Damon to an 'unfrequented Cave', raised by her to the dignity of 'Loves Shrine'.[1] To Damon such a prospect 'once had been enticing', but he has lately met Christ, called 'great *Pan*' in agreement with the pastoral tradition, and now '*Clorinda*, Pastures, Caves, and Springs' have lost all their power over him. Pan's name alone 'swells [his] slender Oate'. Nothing more trite as regards matter, or more insignificant as regards form, could well be found than this idyll.

On the contrary 'A Dialogue between Thyrsis and Dorinda', if carelessly worked out by a yet immature artist, reveals, in an unexpected light, a mystical Marvell with heterodox yearnings. Not that the description of life everlasting made by the shepherd to his wife contains anything original; in Paradise, called 'Elizium' in the approved Renaissance manner, 'sheep are full / Of sweetest grass, and softest wooll'; and the rest agrees. Yet Thyrsis' lines, insipid as they are, plunge Dorinda into an almost hysterical

---

[1] In the first of the 'Two Songs at the Marriage of the Lord Fauconberg and the Lady Mary Cromwell', l. 49, this 'Cave' will reappear, rather unexpectedly, and Cynthia's objection to its darkness will be easily overcome by Endymion's 'Then none can spy'. Thus is Cromwell's younger daughter wooed and won.—For a more favourable view of 'Clorinda and Damon' see John D. Rosenberg, 'Marvell and the Christian Idiom', in *B.U.S.E.*, Autumn 1960, pp. 152–61: not the least beauty of the poem is an 'ambiguity' in the word 'Temples', which besides its face meaning is said to refer to 'religious buildings'. This may well be the limit in misused ingenuity. Also partial to 'Clorinda and Damon' but of more interest is H. E. Toliver's 'Pastoral Form and Idea in Some Poems of Marvell', in *The University of Texas Studies in Literature and Language*, 1963, pp. 83–97; yet the critic's propensity to abstraction in vocabulary and thought overweights this and the other pieces considered.

fit of crying. She who at the start knew no 'Elizium' but
'home' now feels ready to swoon and 'fain would dye' at
once. In the language of *L'Astrée* he answers:

> I cannot live without thee, I
> Will for thee, much more with thee, dye.

Up to this point the reader might take it that by death, only
dying to the world is meant, a metaphor familiar to monastic piety but also in frequent use among the Puritans. Yet
the conclusion, sung by the couple as 'Chorus', must, it
seems, be taken literally:

> Then let us give *Carillo* charge o' the Sheep
> And thou and I'le pick poppies and them steep
> In wine, and drink on't even till we weep,
> So shall we smoothly pass away in sleep.

We cannot discover any orthodox meaning for these poppies.
And anyhow we find ourselves right at the centre of incoherence: the sheep that were to enjoy such happiness in
'Elizium' remain limited to terrestrial fodder;[1] the poem,
begun with the assertion that the way to Heaven is a 'rugged
way', ends on an invitation to painless suicide. Hamlet
shirked freedom obtained 'with a bare bodkin' because of
the dreams that might disturb the sleep of the dead. Thyrsis
experiences no such doubt: he knows he is God's elect, and
he draws from the Calvinistic version of predestination the
inference that he can hasten the hour of bliss. Such heresy
would fill, not only Roman Catholics or Anglicans, but also
Presbyterians and Baptists with horror. In this England of
the Civil War, where sects swarmed, was there one that
feasted its communicants with the heady and muddy wine
offered by Thyrsis to Dorinda? We see no trace of such an
aberration, even among the most visionary Antinomians or
Quakers. The spiritual evaporations of young Andrew seem
to have no contemporary analogue in professedly religious
literature. We must go back to antiquity with Montaigne, in
his 'Apologie of Raymond Sebond', thus translated by
Florio: 'The forcible power of Platoes discourse of the
immortality of the soule provoked divers of his Schollers

---

[1] Gallicè 'les nourritures terrestres'.

unto death, that so they might more speedily enjoy the hopes he told them of'.[1]

Indeed, if the poet ever bent over the gulf he quickly controlled his fit of dizziness. Health, sanity, and balance of mind are among his most pronounced characteristics when we consider his work as a whole. But intellectual curiosity, a certain freedom in his manners, which in a spirit less strongly tempered by Puritan breeding might have turned to libertinism, a grain of mysticism that might have made of a less steady head an illuminato, give Marvell's individuality a somewhat elusive diversity of aspects that attract us to it all the more. This impression, already resulting from the study of his sacred poems, will be confirmed when we come to examine the religious feeling to which his love of nature rises.

For many who do not know him otherwise Marvell is the poet of gardens, and he fully deserves the title, especially when compared to his master Donne and the master's other disciples. Their poetry keeps to the town; it will haunt the *ruelles* or the Court; when they compose their verse in the

[1] Mrs. Duncan-Jones has pointed out to me that one of those disciples of Plato's was known by name to Marvell's contemporaries (who derived their information from Cicero, *Tuscul. Disput.* i. 34, and Ovid, *Ibis*, ll. 495–6, possibly through Montaigne, *Essays*, II. iii): Burton refers to Cleombrotus three times (*Anatomy of Melancholy*, Pt. I, Sect. II, Mem. III, Subs. X; Pt. I, Sect. IV, Mem. I; Pt. III, Sect. IV, Mem. I, Subs. III) and Milton places him in 'the Paradise of Fools' (iii. 471–3). Both these writers use the story of his suicide to illustrate the harm done by 'superstition, and blind zeal'. Jeremy Taylor, however, uses it (*Holy Living and Dying*, ed. Bohn, p. 391) merely to illustrate the possible strength of desire for a better world and abstains from reproving the means taken to reach it. While such leniency might well surprise us in any other Anglican divine it falls far short, to my mind, of Marvell's invitation (written at least six years before the publication, in 1651, of *Holy Dying*) to use 'poppies'.

Another anecdote familiar to the men of the Renaissance was that of the expulsion from Egypt by Ptolemy of the orator Hegesias, nicknamed Peisithanatos, because he 'so highly commended death the dispatcher of all evils, as a great number of his hearers destroyed themselves'; see Puttenham, *The Arte of English Poesie*, III. ii, and Donne, *Essays in Divinity* (published only in 1651/2), ed. E. Simpson, p. 65, who gives Valerius Maximus, viii. 9, as a reference. Here the incitement to suicide is the (Cyrenaican) desire to avoid suffering, not the appetite of bliss. But both stories have this in common, that they take place in the pagan world before the coming of Christ; and they form part of the humanist's stock-in-trade. Marvell's 'Thyrsis and Dorinda' belongs to the present, to the Christian England of the sixteen-forties.

country, as Herbert and Vaughan largely do, their engrossing preoccupation with the Creator prevents them from dwelling on description of the Creation. Apart from the neo-Classical school, which it heralds in this respect, no English literary movement ever breathed so little in the open air. Marvell is an exception: less exclusive and more versatile, he does not, save in an occasional mood, think it necessary to shut his eyes to the outside world in order to develop his inner life. Therefore, if in an anthology each poet were to be represented by one piece, more powerful erotic or more compact religious pieces would have to yield to 'The Garden', which treats, on a very personal note, the antique theme of the old man of Tarentum.

Yet even in the group of Marvell's nature poems 'The Garden' is not fully representative. To avoid misleading the reader, another piece, less beautiful and less famous indeed but even more original and unexpected in that age, should be added as a corrective. In 'The Mower against Gardens' Marvell follows no tradition. While in 'The Garden' he attacked the artificial life of courts and towns, their vain activity stirred by the love of glory, he now rails at Man when, living amidst Nature, he sets his mark on it, and at Nature so humanized. Marvell's religion may partly account for this uncompromising attitude: 'Nature . . . most plain and pure' must have had a Puritan's preference if he stopped just short of banishing all worldly affections. Here a conceit identifies the physical result of cultivation with moral degeneracy: 'The Pink grew then as double as [Man's] mind.' And the most heinous charge, that of having 'dealt between the Bark and Tree / Forbidden mixtures there to see' and thus produced 'uncertain and adulterate fruit', derives from the Mosaic law (Leviticus xix. 19; Deuteronomy xxii. 9).

In spite of this biblical reminiscence, the tone of the piece is only half serious. Besides, the poet's indignation is roused less by the gardener's art than by the desertion of 'the sweet Fields / Where willing Nature does to all dispence / A wild and fragrant Innocence'. True, 'Fawns and Faryes do the Meadows till,' and this mythological nature smacks to us of the seventeenth century; but to appreciate its originality we must think of the taste that prevailed when these lines were written. The Italians still held the lead in gardening; Versailles was still a mere hunting-lodge and Le Nôtre had not yet achieved fame; now Versailles, deliberate as its art appears to us, marks a step towards simplicity and a reaction against baroque excess. Our poet was ahead of his age when he exclaimed: 'Tis all enforc'd; the Fountain and the Grot', and obliquely censured the presence of so many statues. Yet he did not come first, even in his own country. Francis Bacon's essay 'Of Gardens' (1625) condemned some ornamental devices as worthy of a confectioner; it, however, recommended hiding, inside each leafy 'turret' raised above a hedge, a cage of birds, and between the turrets 'broad plates of round coloured glass gilt, for the sun to play upon'. Milton was to be hardly more thorough in his condemnation of artifice: *Paradise Lost* indeed places 'Nature boon / Powrd forth profuse on Hill and Dale and Plaine' above 'nice . . . Beds and curious Knots', but it soon qualifies this revolutionary preference by setting Adam 'to reform . . . flourie Arbors' and rid paths of 'dropping Gumms,—That lie bestrowne unsightly and unsmooth'. The old Puritan does not confuse liberty with licence. When he speaks of the 'wanton growth' of trees, the epithet, which on other lips might be if not laudatory at least indulgent and amused, expresses shocked reprobation of irregularity.

At times Marvell seems to go further than Bacon or Milton. Then one may see in him, without undue exaggeration, a forerunner of Kent, a prophet of the English parks that will be the glory of the eighteenth century. But one should not credit Marvell with a system or turn into a rigid attitude what was perhaps merely a mood, a fit of temper against contemporary artificiality. Our poet could play with a paradox without becoming its dupe or its captive, wiser in this than Jean-Jacques Rousseau; to the academic question: 'Whether the progress of gardening has contributed to the corruption or embellishment of nature', Marvell once answered: 'to its corruption', as much in the way of badinage as in order to express a fragmentary truth; but he did not feel bound to give the same answer always, nor to ban all polite inventions forever. He provides his own refutation in 'The Garden' where he presents himself lying 'at the Fountains sliding foot', the same Fountain he had lately censured as 'enforc'd'. He enjoys as a gourmet, but also as a poet, the company of apples, 'the luxurious Clusters of the Vine', nectarines, peaches, and melons. Leaving aside the grapes, a memory perhaps of the sunny days in France, Italy, and Spain, or a classical reminiscence, none of these fruits, not even the apple, would grow in England without man's enterprising spirit. The epithet 'curious', applied by the poet to the peach, has special relevance for our argument, since it then preserved its etymological meaning: what requires care; and it is far from pejorative here as it was for Milton in the above-quoted passage, or for Marvell himself in his more austere moments. But now comes a still more refined horticultural artifice, the poet's praise of which assumes its full value since it fills the last stanza of the poem: 'the skilful Gardner' has disposed flowers that open and close successively, each at its proper time of day, so as to form a sundial. And in the Latin version of the same poem, 'Hortus',[1] the poet's admiration is expressed at even greater length and with all the majesty of hexameters.

No less artificial, though in another way, is Fairfax's garden at Nun Appleton, described by Marvell with smiling love. When one of the 'Fairfacian' line, after campaigning in 'France and Poland' had 'retired here to Peace', he had laid it out 'In the just Figure of a Fort', with 'five Bastions'. An old soldier's fad, as inoffensive as Uncle Toby's. But Marvell fondly draws out this travesty of nature through four stanzas by his use of military metaphors. Here is one of them, addressed to the garrison artillery of flowers that have saluted their 'Governour' and 'Governess':

[1] Contrary to what I, after Grierson, thought in 1928, Carl E. Bain, 'The Latin Poetry of Andrew Marvell', in *Philological Quarterly*, 1959, pp. 438–43, argues that the English versions of 'Hortus', 'Ros', and the two distichs on Magdalen's tears came first, since the Latin versions show expansion. The question remains open. It is left so by George Williamson, 'The Context of Marvell's "Hortus" and "Garden" ', in *M.L.N.*, 1961, pp. 590–8, who yet stresses the difference in temper and moral of the two versions. He relates both of them to Cowley's 'The Wish', not mentioned by Margoliouth in his list of Marvell's borrowings from *The Mistress* (1647).

> Well shot ye Firemen! Oh how sweet
> And round your equal Fires do meet;
> Whose shrill report no Ear can tell,
> But Ecchoes to the, Eye and Smell.

'Shrill report' looks like an imaginative anticipation of the theory of ultra sound-waves. But the mere literary critic will rather think of Shelley's hyacinth,

> Which flung from its bells a sweet peal anew
> Of music so delicate, soft, and intense,
> It was felt like an odour within the sense.

Both poets present the metaphorical term as the direct expression of a fact, then give to the direct enunciation of the fact the appearance of an interpretation. The circuitous device is as artful in the seventeenth-century poet as in the nineteenth-century one, but there the resemblance ends. Marvell, using a less ample and rhythmical metre, is more concise, even epigrammatic. Above all, if each passage is replaced in its context, the same difference is found between them as between fancy and imagination according to Coleridge and Wordsworth.

The 'Fairfacian' infantry of flowers equals the artillery in discipline: 'Each *Regiment* in order grows.' Now Marvell at the beginning of the poem had introduced Nun Appleton thus:

> . . . Nature here hath been so free
> As if she said leave this to me.
> Art would more neatly have defac'd
> What she hath laid so sweetly wast;

This hardly agrees with Fairfax's horticultural amusements. But from what follows it appears that the opposition, in modern English, is not between Art and Nature but between buildings and grounds (the former were small at Nun Appleton when compared to the owner's other residences). For the seventeenth century all that is not made of hewn stone or carved marble is 'Nature'; in France, when you leave Paris you go 'aux champs', or even 'au désert', words that should not be taken at their face value. In the same manner one should tone down the epithets 'waste' and 'wild', used several times by our poet, and grown since

so romantically intense. In 'The Mower, against Gardens',
Nature dispenses to all 'A wild and fragrant Innocence'.
And 'The Nymph complaining for the death of her Faun'
describes her garden as 'a little wilderness'. In neither poem
is there an evocation of the virgin forests and savannahs,
reserved for Chateaubriand to bring into fashion, nor of the
Alpine ranges, which were to enrapture Shelley, nor even
of the Jura hills where Rousseau was to find a refuge, or the
Westmorland peaks on which Wordsworth was to complete
his spiritual recovery. On closer inspection Marvell's daring
then is more apparent than real. And even so it alternates
with recantations: he makes amends before the altar of the
goddess Rule; thus 'loose Nature', shamed by Mary Fairfax's precocious wisdom, 'it self doth recollect'; as in the
greater world 'Gulfes, Deserts, Precipices, Stone' are contained, so they are in the girl's 'lesser World' (i.e. Nun
Appleton), 'But in more decent Order tame'. While 'loose'
implies moral condemnation 'tame' here is a term of praise:
since 1800 it has settled into the most cruel of sarcasms.

It would serve no useful purpose, however, to convict
a poet of contradictions, or to break a Parnassian butterfly
on the wheel of logic. We only wish to prevent or correct
anachronisms: Marvell belongs to his age. He also belongs
to his country: the scenery in the foreign lands he visited
provided no inspiration for him; he described the Bermudas
and the Canary Islands without having seen them, Sweden
before he saw it, Holland as he could have done even if he
had not seen it. Everything in his descriptive poetry that
bears the mark of loving observation concerns Britain.
Even within his native island he ignores much. He may
have had no chance of visiting either Scotland or Wales,
but what of the Yorkshire moors? He probably knew
Denton, the wildest of Fairfax's estates as regards location,
up in the valley of the Wharfe; but he wrote no poem on it;
he only mentions it twice, and then briefly and without
affection. This lack of interest is significant: the lower valley
of the Wharfe partakes of the general characteristics of the
English landscape, which (as Vigny will say) 'a ceci de bon
qu'on y sent partout la main de l'homme'; moderate un-
dulations slowly recede from sight; through fat meadows

lazy rivulets flow brim-full. If by chance a crag rises in its midst, like Almscliff some fifteen miles from Nun Appleton, our poet's Latin elegiacs, without denying it praise, prefer to it the softly-rounded eminence of Bilbrough:

> Erectus, praeceps, salebrosus et arduus ille:
> Acclivis, placidus, mollis, amœnus hic est.

Reading these lines one can foresee that the Alps will long continue to carry 'the permission mountains have of being frightful rather too far'. Seventeenth-century taste, even in such independent characters as Marvell and La Fontaine, seldom reaches further than a 'softly undulated, placid, agreeable' countryside. In nature as well as in female attire Herrick seeks 'a wild civility'; in the same spirit Marvell uses the epithet 'courteous' of hills as well as of briars or glow-worms. Politeness, now at a discount, was then at a premium.

Thus circumscribing Marvell's rural poetry we run the risk of disappointing those who, on the evidence of a few extracts, saw in him a harbinger of the romantics. But regret would be as vain as blame. Rather than deplore his timidity in the choice of his landscapes we had better pay him a just tribute for the fidelity with which he has noted certain aspects of nature.

Woods (not forests) bewitch the poet. Among those that surrounded Fairfax's several manor-houses he has chosen two 'groves' in order to sing of them: the one at the top of Bilbrough Hill, the other overlooking the meadows of Nun Appleton. In this he feels so happy that he asks the 'briars' to 'nail [him] through' in the morning. But when evening comes he wants to be 'staked down' in the meadows. More than of flowers or trees, Marvell is the poet of grass.

With an amused mind and a gently affected heart he has watched the course of the seasons in the meadows of Nun Appleton: June and its 'Abbyss' of 'unfathomable grass', through which men are seen to 'Dive'; July and haymaking, when 'the Grassy Deeps divide' before the mowers as the Red Sea before the Israelites; August and the mown meadows where 'the Villagers in common chase / Their Cattle, which it closer rase'; Autumn and Winter, which

turn the metaphorical sea into a real one; lastly Spring,
which dries up 'the Meadows fresher dy'd / Whose Grass,
with moister colour dasht, / Seems as green Silks but newly
washt'. The Wharfe is the 'little *Nile*' that fertilizes this
Egypt, yet it leaves behind it 'no *Serpent* new nor *Crocodile*'.
When, near the end of this long poem of subtle analytical
description, Marvell re-composes the landscape, four nouns
(or their respective synonyms) recur again and again like
a burden: gardens (or flowers), woods (or bushes), rivers
(floods, brooks, springs, or streams), meads (meadows or
fields). Of these elements of the cosmos whose demiurge
is Mary Fairfax—by the virtue of her beauty or rather by
the beauty of her virtue—the poet has chosen the last as his
favourite theme.

Now the meadow, of all natural features, has received in
all ages least poetic attention. That statement may seem
a paradox if we remember the vogue of the pastoral in
Sicily, in Rome, and all over civilized Europe in the sixteenth and seventeenth centuries. But neither Theocritus
nor Virgil, nor Mantuan, nor Spenser, nor their more or
less servile imitators tarry to describe the grass by which
their herds or flocks live; when they have called it 'flower-
enamelled' they think they have done it full justice. Their
eclogues and bucolics bring us back to the Golden Age
when men did not suffer under the necessity of garnering
hay in Summer against Winter. Of all poets Marvell first
sang haymaking and set up the figure of the mower: this is
his discovery.[1]

Yet he did not wholly escape convention, so tyrannical
is the pastoral genre. Let us recall the three dialogues—
between Daphnis and Chloe, Clorinda and Damon, Thyrsis
and Dorinda; characters that, with their frames and pro-
perties, conform to innumerable precedents. To them may
be added 'Unconstant Sylvio' who once gave a fawn to a

---

[1] Here I pointed out, in 1928, that Theocritus (Idyl X) would have
anticipated Marvell had not his Battos mown corn, not hay; thereupon a critic,
presumably town-bred, protested he saw no difference.—Barbara Everett,
'Marvell's "The Mower's Song" ', in *The Critical Quarterly*, Autumn 1962,
pp. 219–24, deals with this character in a very subtle manner. She does his
'Song' the honour of comparison with some of the most dramatic lines in
Phèdre, intending, however, contrast rather than assimilation. See p. 90.

'Nymph', i.e. not to a rural deity but to a very much refined country girl. The 'Two Songs at the Marriage of the Lord Fauconberg and the Lady Mary Cromwell', in 1657, will array the lovers and the bride's father in pastoral garb. The first 'Song' once more calls up Endymion (but courting Cynthia with Jove's approval instead of being courted by her), and Anchises, formerly 'a *Shepheard* too', who stands for the bride's brother-in-law; the second 'Song', less mythological and more fresh, does not yet rise above hackneyed prettiness: Marvell's Hobbinol and Tomalin do not succeed any better than Spenser's in convincing us of their Englishness.

All this small change of Arcadian currency is worth less for us than a single one of the pieces stamped by our poet in the Mower's effigy. Marvell grants to this serf, *addictus glebae*, citizenship in Poetry; he makes him the equal of numerous shepherds, goatherds, cowherds, and even swineherds, who have preceded him. He shows him in love like them and complaining in verse, which means that we cannot expect a transcript of real life and that the mower Damon will chiefly be Marvell's mouthpiece, just as Colin Clout had been Spenser's. At least the Mower is distinguished, though not by his feelings, yet by his labour, gestures, and metaphors. While Marvell's art in no wise anticipates Crabbe's, neither does it betray the haughty ignorance of Samuel Johnson, describing rural life from a London garret with the help of Horatian reminiscences. Enough observation of reality seasons this poetry, which we beg leave to call 'fenisectoral', an ugly and pretentious word, no doubt, but the only one to fit the group of poems that includes (along with part of 'Upon Appleton House') 'The Mower against Gardens', 'Damon the Mower', 'The Mower to the Glo-worms', 'The Mower's Song', and 'Ametas and Thestylis making Hay-Ropes'.

Herdsmen of all varieties lived in delicious idleness; the coolness of the Vale of Tempe followed them everywhere; reclining in the shade of the wide-spreading beech Tityrus knew no harder work than studying his woodland notes on the thin pipe; his complexion could well remain milk-white and clear. Marvell's mowers are 'tawny', for they toil under

the July sun; sweat runs down their bodies; true, whether
as a relic of Renaissance pedantry or a concession to the
growing taste for dignity in verse, 'every Mowers whole-
some Heat / Smells like an *Alexanders sweat*' according to
Plutarch. But mowing is not only hard work, it is also
dangerous work. So Damon found when 'The edged Stele
by careless chance / Did into his own Ankle glance'. As
regards the women the difference appears no less clearly:
the shepherdesses awaited declarations of love in a voluptuous languor, a be-ribboned hook in their hands; the
mowers' mates have their own tasks, less strenuous than
the men's yet animated enough. Having compared to a
battle-field the mown meadow at Nun Appleton where the
grass still remains lying, Marvell goes on:

> The Women that with forks it fling,
> Do represent the Pillaging.

No very flattering comparison, worlds apart from Madame
de Sévigné's somewhat *précieuse* letter where 'faner' is as-
similated to 'batifoler'. Marvell preserves in his verse the
rather brutal energy of country toil. He can also represent
its moments of merry-making, such as the dances during
which the haymakers 'in *Fairy Circles* tread' the mead, each
ending with a kiss.

Yet it is not one of those clever handlers of rake and fork
but the 'fair Shepheardess' Juliana, indistinguishable from
so many disguised princesses, idle and cruel, who is Damon
the Mower's love. Did Marvell unconsciously yield to the
tradition? Or did he seek a contrast? Possibly, since the
poet, with Damon as his mouthpiece, sets shepherd and
mower the one against the other and proclaims the superiority
of the latter over the former. Unfortunately Juliana does
not yield to the poet's ingenious arguments; so that
Damon's love expresses itself in one long moan. From the
author of the impassioned address 'To his Coy Mistress',
the ironical 'Mourning', and the libertine 'Daphnis and
Chloe', a more virile note might have been expected. Damon
makes up for those *fadeurs*, to which the pastoral convention
condemned lovers less bold than constant, by using fresh
comparisons borrowed from his handiwork; for instance,

he had been happy till 'Love here his Thistles sow'd'. He
even uses his scythe as a looking-glass; and here one might
charge Marvell with excess of ingenuity and with inaccuracy,
since the blade of a scythe will at best prove a distorting
mirror. Artificial, and maybe absurd, this conceit at least is
not stale.

In one poem by substituting for Damon and Juliana the
astute Ametas and the not too coy Thestylis, Marvell even
managed to combine subtlety of thought with freshness of
phrasing. Not indeed for the first time is love compared to
a bond, but here the metaphor becomes at once more precise and more poetic, for the two characters talk while they
are 'making Hay-Ropes'. Ametas warns his mistress that he
will not love on indefinitely if she still answers him nay:
'Love binds love as Hay binds Hay' he argues. But Thestylis
quickly turns the tables on him:

> Think'st thou that this Rope would twine
> If we both should turn one way?
> Where both parties so combine,
> Neither Love will twist nor Hay.

Ametas retorts less brilliantly, but eventually accepts
Thestylis' offer of love without guaranteed constancy, and
concludes:

> Then let's both lay by our Rope,
> And go kiss within the Hay.

In spite of the elegant manner, which makes us think of a
(condensed) dialogue out of one of Marivaux's plays, this
piece produces an impression of truth to rustic life. We think
of Burns, the peasant poet *par excellence*, singing of his
Annie:

> I kiss'd her owre and owre again,
> Amang the rigs o' barley.

and of Angellier's comment: 'Avec Burns, la réalité ne
perd jamais ses droits. . . . Dans Burns, il y a toujours un
endroit où les blés sont couchés.' Therefore, Marvell deserves credit for having added to the effete pastoral genus
a more lusty species. Instead of an artificial and almost
evaporated perfume Marvell's poetry of the countryside
breathes the healthy scent of hay.

Yet in his verse the passages that appeal most to the reader of today present him alone with Nature, for instance in the wood at Nun Appleton where he feels secure from Cupid's darts. True, this emancipation will not last long; but, exceptional as they are in the poet's life, these instants have the same unique significance as their ecstasies have in the lives of saints. In fact they *are* ecstasies, or at least they end in a sort of ecstasy. Marvell, not much of a mystic when contemplating the Creator, becomes one in the midst of woods or gardens. He yearns to cross the boundaries of the self, in order to unite with vegetable and animal life, a life scorned by the ordinary man, whom Reason in her pride misleads. The leaves of trees are '*Sybils* Leaves' to the poet and:

> What *Rome, Greece, Palestine*, ere said
> I in this light *Mosaick* read.
> Thrice happy he who, not mistook,
> Hath read in *Natures mystick Book*.

This is a bold assertion if one remembers the absolute authority the Bible enjoyed among the English Puritans (the Quakers alone standing apart) in the years about 1650. The conceit, or rather pun, on '*Mosaick*', which alludes to the law given on Sinai, strengthens the impression that the written Revelation—'What . . . *Palestine* ere said'—might be dispensed with and that the poet receives a direct revelation from the God of Nature. The tone of the next lines changes to picturesque badinage, with images that the poet's 'Phancy weaves'. But now appears the physical exaltation that heralds ecstasy: we see him 'toss / On Pallets swoln of Velvet Moss'. Of course he leaves it to those who have known such moments to imagine the ensuing 'Rest', or rapture. While we should not blame him for failing to put the ineffable into words we may regret his ending brusquely on a frivolous conceit: the '*cool Zephyr's* . . . shed' his thoughts as well as his hair and 'Winnow from the Chaff [his] Head'.

The appeal of such transports to the post-Romantic reader's mind can easily be understood but we should resist the temptation to superimpose a pantheistic philosophy of which Marvell never thought: we must not see him through

Wordsworth. The passage just analysed and another one, in 'The Garden', somewhat more explicit and too well known for quotation, if they prove that Marvell knew mystic raptures,[1] would not justify our making these the chief source of inspiration in his poems devoted to Nature.

Neither shall we find this distinctive note in the minute observation of animals and vegetables. In the nineteenth century he was praised to excess for some details, as yet unused in verse, which indeed contrast with the generality and banality of neo-Classical descriptive poetry. The stock example is the couplet in which he

> [Does] through the Hazles thick espy
> The hatching *Thrastles* shining Eye,

and it fully deserves its fame, but one would be hard put to it to find others of the same sort. Making an inventory of Marvell's flora would not take long either, nor would the result justify the title of 'botanist' once granted to him. All his verse would not provide a longer list of flowers than one scene of *A Winter's Tale*, or so long a one as Shelley's 'Sensitive Plant'. Of fruit he has not named ten kinds, but since the enumeration of them, almost complete, is found in one famous stanza of 'The Garden', and the 'Horatian Ode' contains the fairly technical term 'Bergamot', hasty admirers have made of him, at little cost, an expert in pomology. The study of his fauna would lead us to an estimate just as modest.

True, the number of animals or vegetables named matters less than the precision and originality of the descriptions. But here again Marvell stands very far from a Tennyson, bent on discovering the new epithet, the concrete and almost imitative notation of sounds and hues. Our poet is readily content with traditional adjectives, moral rather than physical. Not seldom does his interest in plants go to their magic or their medicinal power or their use as civic rewards. Nor

---

[1] With Plotinus' *Enneads* as his Bible, says Milton Klonsky, 'A Guide through *The Garden*', in *Sewanee Review*, 1950, pp. 16–35—or without it. Ruth Wallerstein, *Studies in Seventeenth Century Poetics*, 1950, pp. 318–35, also draws on Plotinus but even more on twelfth- and thirteenth-century mystics, Hugh and Richard of St. Victor and Bonaventura. Unfortunately there is no evidence of Marvell's ever reading them. See p. 90.

does he limit himself to personal observation as regards the habits of animals. He even includes 'unnatural natural history' worthy of *Euphues*, as when (just after the 'hatching *Thrastle*' with its 'shining eye') 'The Heron from the Ashes top, / The eldest of its young lets drop' as a '*Tribute* to *its Lord*', viz. Fairfax. The praise of the '*Hewel*', or woodpecker, begins more in accordance with reality, but it soon turns to the sort of moralization found in the emblem-books. The ratio of ingenious ratiocination to observation appears even higher when Marvell deals with insects, the bee, the grasshopper, and the glow-worm.

No, neither his flora nor his fauna owe their worth to their copiousness or accuracy. He cannot be said either to have shown in the choice of his favourites among them the same originality as in his predilection for meadows among the elements of the landscape at Nun Appleton. With him the oak, the rose, the nightingale, the bee remain secure in their lordship of trees, flowers, birds, and insects. Yet once, at the cost of a contradiction—one more of them—he grew emancipated enough to prefer to Philomel's song 'A Sadder, yet more pleasing Sound: / The *Stock-doves*'. In this he had the good fortune of agreeing in advance with Wordsworth. But his description of the bird soon turns to a Puritan madrigal, such as could be appreciated in Fairfax's virtuous household.

Lastly, it often happens that the poet abstains from any attempt to introduce those concrete touches that since the Romantic age have been considered the salt of poetry. Marvell at these times speaks like Malherbe himself; from his pen flow 'les termes les plus abstraits et les plus généraux', to quote Buffon's famous precept, copied by Dr. Johnson: trees, flowers, plants, birds, fish, nay things. Even the neo-Classical periphrasis, which aims not at depicting but at disguising the object, is not quite unknown to him. He speaks of birds as 'winged Quires', of their love songs as 'their tuned Fires'. And it must be acknowledged that the charm of his descriptive poetry does not reside essentially in its precision, since those passages where he does not particularize are not the least delightful.

All these reservations made, it must still be granted that

Marvell possesses the power of giving life not only to one plant or one animal but even to an ensemble. The second stanza of 'Damon the Mower' makes us feel the oppressive heat in the 'Sun-burn'd Meadows' during the dog-days—not a mean feat with octosyllabics. This measure suits better the twilight on the Wharfe, centering on the flight of the 'Halcyon', or kingfisher. But those two pictures have this in common: what strikes us is not so much this or that picturesque touch (though some are bold enough) as that sympathy with universal life already noted in Marvell's ecstasies in wood or garden. He shares now the joys and now the sufferings of creatures—animals, plants, and even those beings that our limited science calls inanimate. The most moving instance of this sympathy is found in 'The Nymph complaining for the death of her Faun', where it assumes the form of sorrowing tenderness. Even if we find in the description of the fawn more grace than precision, we cannot resist this call of a compassionate soul.

Melancholy Jaques had already[1] lamented the fate of the hunted deer and railed at its persecutors. But Jaques was an eccentric character; his was a diseased mind; and Shakespeare, like the Duke, laughed at him. Here the rights of the animal are seriously set against the caprice of man. Later poets, each with his own note, echoed Marvell's protest, though often unconsciously. Thomson, pompous and awkward, condemned deer-hunting and hare-coursing, allowing, in England, fox-hunting only, always provided the fair sex should not join in it. Cowper improved upon that solicitude, with a queer mixture of eighteenth-century *sensiblerie* and Calvinistic gloom. Burns expressed emotion as deep but more manly 'On seeing a wounded hare'; he combined tenderness with the common sense of a countryman: he is chiefly indignant at the shooting's taking place in a season when all the does mother their young; he protests against the abuse rather than the use of the sportsman's gun. On the contrary the cockney Blake sees in 'Each outcry of

---

[1] Perhaps I should have looked for earlier instances of pity to animals; E. K. Chambers, *English Literature at the Close of the Middle Ages*, 1945, p. 126, provides one, 'The Mourning of the Hare', a fifteenth-century 'lament rather than a narrative'.

the hunted Hare' the tearing of 'A fibre from the Brain';
a quasi-Buddhist philosophy forbids any blood-shedding
and condemns the butcher along with the huntsman. This
anathema, in spite of all its poetry, sounds rather declamatory
when compared to the no less pathetic but gentler reproaches
of the Nymph. Likewise, Wordsworth's lines in 'Hart-
Leap Well' seem somewhat morose for all their nobility;
and yet their moral comes closest to that of Marvell's poem:

> Never to blend our pleasure or our pride
> With sorrow of the meanest thing that feels.

In 1800 Wordsworth had not yet returned to Christianity,
and the absence of forgiveness (granted by the Nymph to the
murderers of her fawn) along with the austerer style and
more majestic metre mark the difference between the
Romantic poet and his seventeenth-century forerunner.

Marvell would suffer as a man and a poet if identified
with his Nymph, who at the end of the poem will turn to
a weeping statue and thus retain the same attitude for ever.
This heart-melting, at times coming perilously near the
ridiculous in its phrasing, would cease to move us if it
lasted. With a sound sense of dramatic effect Marvell places
those lines in the mouth of a young female. When he speaks
in his own name he does not always show the same sensibility; he even confesses having 'seen with some pleasure
the hawking at the magpy' and describes this rural sport
with great gusto. It might be answered that he is then writing as a middle-aged controversialist, coarsened by politics.
But the 'Horatian Ode' contains a laudatory comparison of
Cromwell with a well-trained falcon. And in 'Upon Appleton House' Marvell presents himself as an angler, thus
neither better nor worse than Isaac Walton, to be denounced
by Byron as 'That quaint old cruel coxcomb'. Certainly
Marvell, once his emotion had evaporated, could speak
without tremor of the violent death not only of animals but
of men. The horror of bloodshed expressed in 'The Nymph
complaining for the death of her Faun' does not prevent
military metaphors from cropping up thick and fast in other
works of the writer, who yet had not seized any one of the
opportunities offered to him of going to the wars.

Whatever the shares of observation and feeling in Marvell's descriptions those two elements yield in importance to a third, namely wit. Nature in his poetry is a metaphysical Nature sprung from the brain rather than the senses. To speak more precisely, as soon as the senses have made their harvest, now plentiful now scanty, the brain begins its task: out of its object it abstracts the essential quality, which it substitutes for the object and on which it works, making it live and shine anew by dint of unexpected metaphors and of comparisons that suddenly bring to light unsuspected analogies. Here again Marvell follows Donne's lead; though the master devoted little space in his works to Nature, yet two of his verse-letters are seascapes where the disciples could find a method capable of use for the interpretation of landscapes. 'The Storme' describes less the historical storm that Donne endured with Essex's fleet on its way to the Azores than the idea of a storm, stormy perfection:

> All things are one, and that one none can be,
> Since all formes, uniforme deformity
> Doth cover, . . .

In plain English the passage means that confusion in darkness is the master-quality of the storm. To this 'The Calme' opposes perfect immobility:

> in one place lay
> Feathers and dust, to day and yesterday.

With less jerky strength Marvell puts as much intellection into his descriptions. He too stylizes his landscapes, e.g. 'the Hill at Bill-Borow':

> See how the arched Earth does here
> Rise in a perfect Hemisphere!
> The stiffest Compass could not strike
> A Line more circular and like;
> Nor softest Pensel draw a Brow
> So equal as this Hill does bow.

One thinks of the legend according to which Giotto's supreme ambition was the tracing of a perfect circle freehand; also of the actual work of the same old master who 'limns, not what he sees but what he conceives; accuracy, observation, are not his dominating characteristics; this art pertains less to the world of the senses than to the world of thought; its power wholly lies in its intellectual might, and only with Giotto's disciples will reason become less imperious and the artist more docile to his sensations'.[1] Even among these disciples and until the coming of Raphael many are the faces of the Virgin where the red spots on the cheekbones seem circumscribed with the help of a compass, like Billbrough Hill in Marvell's poem. For if the reader goes there on a Marvellian pilgrimage he will be surprised, and perhaps disappointed, to find a hillock whose shape does not come at all near perfect rotundity. Neither does the sight of the meadows at Nun Appleton, so well beloved of the poet, produce the impression of flat immensity that his verse tries to create. It is more difficult to convict Marvell of having transfigured the wood at Nun Appleton, for here the woodman's axe has since worked changes unknown to hill or meadow. Yet, whatever respect Fairfax may have shown to 'this Forrest', an operation of the mind must have been necessary to give it the perfection it possesses in the poem: the trees growing side by side for so many centuries have lost their individuality to become one solid substance, '*Wood*' (in other words: one cannot see the trees for the wood); only 'one great Trunk' results, 'as meant / To thrust up a *Fifth Element*'. Does the painter or the metaphysician come uppermost here?

In the description of the house itself the generating idea is the smallness of the building, apparently too 'strait' for the greatness of its owner but made adequate by Fairfax's modesty. Eighty lines are not, to Marvell's mind, too many for the development of this conception. The terms of comparison used by the poet, from the shell of the tortoise to '*Romulus* his Bee-like Cell' on Mount Palatine, picturesque as they are, appeal mainly to the intellect for they have no sensible feature in common with Appleton House. But now we plunge even deeper into the abstract:

> *Humility* alone designs
> Those short but admirable Lines,

[1] This quotation from Louis Hourticq, *La Peinture des origines au XVIe siècle*, 1908, p. 100, was aimed at the reader of 1928. The reader of 1964 may find analogies for himself in contemporary abstract art.

By which, ungirt and unconstrain'd,
Things greater are in less contain'd.
Let others vainly strive t'immure
The *Circle* in the *Quadrature*!
These *holy Mathematicks* can
In ev'ry Figure equal Man.

And now who can tell what the house looked like? The
only concrete touch hides in an enigma: 'where [Fairfax]
comes the swelling Hall / Stirs, and the *Square* grows Spheri-
call'. Perhaps the critic had better explain that a cupola sur-
mounted the central part of the house. This heroic effort to
give an intellectual meaning to appearances soon drops to
moralizing commonplaces. Be it not answered that Marvell
drew all this out of his head because the subject provided
him with no esthetic material: when, twenty years later, he
wrote Latin elegiac distichs in praise of the Louvre he still
stuck to abstraction; the same conceit, or very nearly, served
to magnify the Parliamentary General and the French King:

Atria miraris, summotumque Æthera tecto;
Nec tamen in toto est arctior Orbe Casa.

This device can be applied not only to a landscape or an
edifice but even to a whole country. From the notion that
Holland is a land created by the whim of the sea and the
labour of man, Marvell infers its physical appearance, its
history, and the manners of its inhabitants: thus will
Montesquieu deduce all the English Constitution from the
insularity of England. When it becomes the poet's task to
paint that earthly paradise the Canary Islands, he will use
only one trait, turned over and over in twelve lines: it never
rains there. As to Sweden, what is it but an icy desert where
'the terrible North Pole oppresses everything with the dint
of its fall'? Marvell, who has not yet visited this country,
asks an English friend there:

Quae Gentes Hominum, quae sit Natura Locorum,
Sint Homines, potius dic ibi sintne Loca?

Of course he is jesting, but when most in earnest he does
not proceed otherwise. We apprehend here how abstraction
leads to hyperbole: Sweden is a Northern country; it will
become a polar land, nay it will be the Pole itself, the only
place that comes up to boreal perfection.

The very animals or plants are described, or rather defined,
in the same conceptual way.[1] The fawn is lightness and
softness, but above all whiteness:

> Among the beds of Lillyes, I
> Have sought it oft, where it should lye;
> Yet could not, till it self would rise,
> Find it, although before Mine Eyes.

And the description ends:

> Had it liv'd long, it would have been
> Lillies without, Roses within.

How graceful! And how far apparently from the laboured
conundrums previously quoted! Yet colour separate from
any other quality, taken neat, is less of an impression than
an abstraction.

Therefore, when critics note Marvell's predilection for
green, they should add that this feeling regards the colour
itself, independently of the thing described at the time.
Naturally the woods he loves and his favourite meadows do
present to the poet many varieties of greenery; and his must
have been a trained eye to discover green in the shade of the
trees a century before Bernardin de Saint-Pierre discovered
it in the sky; and so determined an Englishman could not
prefer the warmer tints of Mediterranean countries to the
characteristic hue of his homeland; yet neither habit nor
observation suffice to account for the place held by this
colour in his poetry. A mystic concern should be added:
the quest for absolute unity through the elimination of all
adventitious or subsidiary elements. A century earlier Saint
John of the Cross had exclaimed: 'O prado de verduraz!'

[1] Conceptual but not allegorical, as divers critics have tried to prove in
diverse interpretations, beginning modestly enough with Bradbrook and
Lloyd Thomas, *Andrew Marvell*, pp. 47–50, and rising to a climax with E. H.
Emerson, 'Andrew Marvell's "The Nymph . . ." ', in *Études Anglaises*, 1955,
pp. 107–10, where it is followed by my answer, pp. 111–12. Ruel E. Foster,
'A Tonal Study: Marvell', in *University of Kansas City Review*, 1955, xxii,
pp. 73–78, gives a careful and moderate but rather wordy commentary on
this single piece. An attempt has since been made to turn 'The Nymph . . .'
into a mere love-poem: see Leo Spitzer, 'Marvell's "Nymph . . .": Sources
Versus Meaning', in *Modern Language Quarterly*, 1958, pp. 231–43; and my
answer, ibid., 1960, pp. 30–32. D. C. Allen, 'Marvell's "Nymph" ', in *E.L.H.*,
1956, pp. 93–111, collects much information on the deer in literature and
tries to reconcile the literal and the figurative (?) meanings.

Marvell, whether he had read him or not, follows him in the famous lines of 'The Garden' where he shows the Soul

> Annihilating all that's made
> To a green Thought in a green Shade.

Rather than 'in comparison to' we take this to mean 're-ducing to': this is more of a climax to the stanza; and it might be the climax of the poem, did not the next stanza startle us even more: in it abstraction itself vanishes, and from the intellectual we rise to the ecstatic. But we do so once, and briefly. The intellectual sphere remains Marvell's normal abode.[1]

So far we have considered Marvell's lyrical poetry in its diversity. We shall now consider the features common to all, or nearly all, the pieces of this modest collection. Com-position, style, and versification do not change materially according to the nature of the subject. The same ornaments that grace an amorous poem do not mar a religious effusion. The classical doctrine of the separation of genres and sous-genres, each with its proper tone, was only beginning to take shape in England about 1650, and here Marvell does not side with the innovators.[2]

As regards composition it must be acknowledged that he is short-winded, resembling in this respect most of his con-temporaries and his master Donne. 'Upon Appleton House' stands alone with its 776 octosyllabics. But in order to reach

---

[1] I must refer the reader to my article in *R.E.S.*, 1957, pp. 382–9, 'Marvell and the New Critics', for a discussion of various and conflicting interpreta-tions advanced for the poem, and especially this stanza (the sixth), beginning with William Empson's article in *Scrutiny* (1932). The only helpful comment has been provided, unexpectedly, by a quotation from the twelfth-century *Ancrene Riwle*, where the 'anchoresses' are said to be 'birds of heaven that . . . sit singing merrily in the green boughs; that is they meditate upwards, and upon the bliss of heaven that . . . is evergreen . . .'; see Katharine Garvin, 'Andrew Marvell the Anchorite', in *T.L.S.*, 11 August 1950, p. 508. Anthony Hecht, 'Shades of Keats and Marvell', in *Hudson Review*, Spring 1962, xv, pp. 50–71, praises 'The Garden' above the 'Ode to a Nightingale', but reads Keats's death-wish into Marvell's poem, whereas in 'The Garden' the only reference to death (and the next world) is brief (l. 55) and perfunctory.

[2] Of course he respected the Renaissance rule of decorum no less than Milton did; see Rosemund Tuve, *Images and Themes in Five Poems of Milton*, 1957. Yet that was freedom when compared with the cut-and-dried classifica-tion soon to come in force.

this exceptional length Marvell has to tack on to the descriptions and the few lyrical passages (taking the epithet here to imply the direct expression of personal feelings) a digression, narrative or, more exactly, mock-heroic, on the history of the manor, which occupies over one-fourth of the whole. If Marvell, as it seems, has here taken for his model, beside Jonson's 'Penshurst', Denham's *Cooper's Hill*, at that time in all its novelty, this poem may have suggested the backward glance at the past. But while Denham, proceeding allusively, sums up in fifty lines the widely known story of the Reformation in England, it takes Marvell 200 lines to tell a local incident pitting against each other a lay landowner and the prioress of a nunnery for the possession of an heiress and her inheritance; he even introduces a marked dramatic element by the use of the direct style for the speeches of his characters. It follows that Marvell's poem, composite rather than composed, misses unity of impression but avoids monotony. The order in which the themes succeed one another cannot be called inevitable, even if not faulty. But Marvell sins less against order than against sobriety. He babbles pleasantly, adds still more images, more sentiments, more descriptions, until he suddenly stops. He does not husband his inspiration; he exhausts it and only then does he end. This exuberance becomes patent when 'Upon Appleton House' is compared with the admirably concise 'L'Allegro' and 'Il Penseroso'.[1]

Therefore Marvell was right to limit his ambition in other poems. Only two other lyrical pieces exceed 100 lines, and

---

[1] Kenneth Muir, 'Andrew Marvell', in *University of Leeds Review*, 1952, 128–35, boldly called 'Upon Appleton House' a 'well-articulated whole'. Two recent, very detailed studies try to substantiate this praise: D. C. Allen, *Image and Meaning*, 1960, pp. 115–53, reviewed by me in *R.E.S.*, 1962, pp. 75–78, makes the poem rather sombre and reads much allegory, mostly political, into it. M.-S. Røstvig, ' "Upon Appleton House" and the Universal History of Man', in *English Studies*, Dec. 1961, pp. 337–51, while accepting Allen's interpretation almost unreservedly, superimposes on it an hermetic one. She may well be right as regards individual sentences or phrases but she entirely fails to persuade me of the intellectual and spiritual unity, at an exalted level, of this rather chatty poem. Joseph H. Summers devotes most of his introduction to a recent selection of Marvell's poetry (in 'The Laurel Poetry Series') to 'Upon Appleton House'; he too vindicates it from the charge of being 'poorly constructed' and 'afflicted with giantism', but remains more temperate in the ascription of allegorical meanings.

their author's optimum compass: neither the piquancy of
'Daphnis and Chloe' nor the tenderness of 'The Nymph
complaining for the death of her Fawn' combine with
strength so as to give the impression of an irreducible unit;
'The Garden' itself, though it contains only nine eight-line
stanzas, does not succeed (but does it even attempt to do
so?) in creating that impression. The two texts, Latin and
English, reveal by their differences the poet's uncertainty as
to what he should include and what exclude. The former
version confesses a lacuna: 'Desunt multa.' In the latter the
last stanza is a sort of postscript; retrenching it, we end on
a misogynous sally, good of its kind but a distinct anti-
climax after the raptures of stanzas vi and vii. Marvell's
nonchalance prevented him from giving 'The Garden' a real
conclusion. Not that he was unable to frame a poem strongly;
but he shows his mastery only in still shorter pieces: 'To
his Coy Mistress' (46 lines), 'On a Drop of Dew' and 'The
Match' (40 lines each), 'The Definition of Love' (32 lines),
'The Coronet' (26 lines), and a few others. Within those
narrow limits Marvell can knit together the parts of a whole
as tightly as Donne himself. They both applied to poetry the
scholastic training they had received at the University; it
appears in the frequent use of the argumentative conjunctions: for, yet, but, then, therefore. The poet's appeal 'To
his Coy Mistress' has the strictness of a syllogism. The major
is hypothetical affirmative: 'if time belonged to us I could
court you at leisure'; the minor is categorical negative: 'our
life lasts not long enough'; to make a perfect *baroco* the
conclusion should read: 'therefore we should not tarry in
the preliminary manœuvres of courtship'. But Marvell substitutes for this negation a vehement affirmation, equivalent
as regards meaning yet much better fitted to the logic of
passion: 'therefore we must grasp the fleeting instant for
love'. To the three divisions of the argument there corre-
spond three contrasted paragraphs: the first ample, majestic,
and yet subtle; the second anguished, almost brutal in its
vision of death; the third defiant, headlong, and so to speak
ravenous. 'The Coronet' is built almost in the same way,
save that the conclusion is, like its Serpent's tongue, bifid
('either . . . or . . .'). In those two pieces art underscores the

articulations of the thought. Contrariwise, in 'Eyes and Tears' the multiple and equal twinkling of the conceits at first hides the logical framework. Nevertheless one soon discerns, in the somewhat jerky succession of the quatrains each containing an image, the three movements of a demonstration or of a reasoned decision: (a) 'With the same Eyes [we] weep and see', thus the vain sight of the world calls forth tears; (b) yet happy they that weep! Nothing is fairer, more salutary than tears; (c) 'Ope then mine Eyes your double Sluice.' The poet establishes a fact, sees a hope, takes a resolve: such is the progress of those stanzas, apparently ornamental. It was for the sake of his demonstration, which he would complete, that Marvell did not end on the radiant image (the gem of the piece) of the stars as 'the Tears of Light'. More obviously 'The Definition of Love' illustrates that deductive method, since it assumes the form of a theorem, astronomical or astrological: 'Two perfect loves' cannot meet any more than the two poles of heaven; such is the truth demonstrated by those stanzas, sombre yet glowing with passion. In a slightly different way the internal symmetry of 'The Match', 'The Gallery', 'On a Drop of Dew', even 'A Dialogue between the Soul and Body' (though in this piece the conclusion is missing, or only implicit) bear the mark of a deliberate will to compose.

To sum up, Marvell has two manners: either he gives free rein to his fancy, or he concentrates, tightens, orders, aiming at a single effect. A graceful prattler when he relaxes, he can be when he pleases a logician in verse, but an impassioned logician. At such times we shall call him a classic in the highest sense, unless we allow ourselves to be deterred by what is bizarre in his style.

For Marvell's style is not that of a classic.[1] Yet here again a distinction should be made: if the expression of his lyrical poems presents difficulties, their language proper is as simple as it is pure. They contain a very small number of words not in the current vocabulary, a fact all the more remarkable

---

[1] I realize how odd my Gallic prejudice in favour of intelligibility must sound in its English garb, but I cannot root it out without pulling down the structure of the sub-chapter.

as in his satires and his prose-works Marvell was to reveal
his command of words bookish or vulgar, sometimes scurri-
lous, always bold and picturesque. Here he writes as a contemporary gentleman talked: no Spenserian archaisms, not
many Latinisms *à la Jonson*, very few of those special terms
the Renaissance had borrowed so widely from the technical
vocabularies. In this respect an English Malherbe would
have found little to cross out in Marvell's poems. Nor does
our poet often fall into the opposite error, the abuse of the
periphrasis with the aim of avoiding words rated as low by
the conventional standard of dignity; he thus remains almost
entirely free from the worst fault of the pseudo-classics and
true to the spirit of the genuine classics.

Marvell's syntax is no less normal than his vocabulary.
Negligence rather than affectation accounts for the few
deviations one could list: some harsh inversions or ellipses,
a few anacolutha and amphibologies. Seldom does he pack
those peculiarities so close as he does in stanza LV of 'Upon
Appleton House', and even there, though the grammarian
cavils, who runs may read. To one familiar with the English
of Dryden's verse Marvell's requires little introduction.

Nor does the difficulty of his style lie in the excess of
mythological allusion, the darling sin of the Renaissance.
Here he stands nearer to pseudo-classic triviality than to
Elizabethan pedantry, and he does not try modern ignorance
too severely. True, not all readers of today remember at
once that Phaeton's death made the Heliades 'brotherless'.
But as a rule Marvell keeps his most erudite learning for
his Latin poems, or, more unexpectedly, for his satires.
The vogue of Scarron's *Virgile Travesti*, the first part of
which came out in 1648, marks in a sense a loss of prestige
for the ancient gods. But already Donne had banished them
from serious poetry, and Marvell may just follow him here
as elsewhere.

The poet who rejects traditional mythology is induced to
create one for himself; the names given to deified natural
powers change with belief or fashion, but the instinct is
eternal that drives man to lend inanimate objects (and also
abstractions) feelings similar to his own, though stamped
with greater majesty. Marvell would probably not have

escaped the common fate of poets, even if he had not, like all his contemporaries, undergone the still living influence of the *Arcadia*. Something of the freshness that redeems in Sidney the over-indulgence in what we now call the pathetic fallacy is occasionally found in Marvell's poems; but too often spontaneity yields to the sort of artifice that Wordsworth was to condemn in eighteenth-century poetry. 'Courteousness' is ascribed to a hill, to briars, to glow-worms. The wood at Nun Appleton 'draws a Skreen' about Mary Fairfax to hide her beauty. The Sun (and here oddity comes near to indecency, especially if we remember that this compliment is paid to a girl in her early teens), when the same paragon of virtue appears, 'lest she see him go to Bed, / In blushing Clouds conceals his Head'. Before the Reformation '*Virgin Buildings* oft brought forth', i.e. monastic orders, whose members vowed chastity, propagated quickly and mother-houses had numerous offspring (and here indecency, or at least bad taste, can hardly be excused by Marvell's antipapist zeal). Passing over many other instances, we arrive at the oaks on Billbrough Hill, which have Lady Fairfax's name 'writ already in their Heart' before her husband carves it on their bark:

> For they ('tis credible) have sense,
> As We, of Love and Reverence,
> And underneath the Courser Rind
> The *Genius* of the house do bind.

Here we come very near to ancient mythology: the word '*Genius*' calls up Roman beliefs; and the poet proceeds to tell of the 'Discourses' the 'breathing Trees' hold with the 'flutt'ring Breeze'; thus these eloquent 'Okes' remind us of Dodona, and also of the Hamadryads. In 'The Garden' the Greek names themselves reappear for the laurel and the reed, but Marvell's purpose here is to protest against the anthropomorphism that has supplanted the primitive naturalism in ancient religion and poetry. Of course he has no foreknowledge of these pretentiously scientific terms, but by his poetic intuition he discovers this truth that Daphne and Syrinx should be loved not as 'Nymphs' but as plants. He refutes Boileau in advance, who was soon to exalt into a precept his own incapacity to feel the beauty of the ancient myths:

Echo n'est plus un son dont les bois retentissent,
C'est une Nymphe en pleurs qui se plaint de Narcisse.

In neo-Classical poetry nothing will remain of mythology but a *caput mortuum*, an inert phraseology; but with Marvell the fiery liquor that intoxicated the poets of the Renaissance has not entirely evaporated.

Whether traditional or original, the attribution to things of human feelings and the personification of abstract ideas are not, in spite of the number of examples one might quote, the most distinctive features of Marvell's poetry, and they can hardly be considered as obstacles to the reading of it. When the Nymph says to her fawn: 'this warm life-blood, which doth part / From thine, and wound me to the Heart,' she has recourse to an ellipsis rather than she arms the blood of the fawn, turned into a murderer, with a dagger that, to a Frenchman, would dangerously recall the blushing author of Pyramus' death in Théophile's notorious lines. When she speaks of her own 'unhappy Statue' she uses a concise Latin-ism for 'the statue of unhappy me'; true, the ambiguous epithet serves to bring in a conceit in which the statue quickens: 'For I so truly thee bemoane, / That I shall weep though I be Stone', but this *préciosité*, a mere variation on the myth of Niobe, sounds more trite than bold.

What element, then, in Marvell's poetry can surprise, puzzle, or shock and put off minds trained on the Augustans? It is neither the subtlety of the thought (real enough at times but infrequent when compared with Donne's), nor the diction, nor an almost absent mythological erudition, nor Arcadian animism contained within bounds, but rather the strange quality of the metaphors.

The great Spenserian comparison, luminous, full-blown, underlined by conjunctions—'as . . . so', 'such . . . such'—rarely occurs in Marvell's lyrical verse though it does so frequently in his political poems. We have referred to the flight of the kingfisher in the twilight on the Wharfe, near the end of 'Upon Appleton House', as a description both ample and detailed: it is the first term of a comparison; but the second term, Mary Fairfax's apparition, is drawn in two lines. After a very poetical picture this sketch may look bare: the poet seems to turn short. In fact he leaves it to the reader to apply to the girl the circumstances with which he has surrounded the bird. Such as it is, this instance of a sustained simile remains exceptional even in the descriptive passages. And no instance exists in the love poems or the religious poems.

Yet it happens that a piece is built wholly on an implied comparison, or rather a symbol since its two terms are indistinguishable and every phrase must be taken at once literally and figuratively. So it is with 'The Gallery', where indeed no straining is exacted from the reader's brain: the word 'imagination' witnesses to the resemblance, long-established in the language, between the activity of the mind and the art of the painter. The poet's originality here consists in rejuvenating and developing that worn-out, almost dead metaphor.

But the difficulty begins when Marvell hesitates between comparison, which distinguishes, and symbol, which fuses, as he does, for instance, in his meditation 'On a Drop of Dew'. The *ordonnance* of this piece is classical, as we have said: the first eighteen lines depict the natural phenomenon, the dew drawn up by the sun to the sky; the next eighteen lines, introduced by 'so', depict the supernatural phenomenon, the soul drawn up by God to Heaven. Apparently the symmetry is perfect; in fact the poet introduces into each part epithets that properly suit the other. He gives the Drop human feelings: indifference ('careless of its Mansion new'), disdain ('it the purple flow'r does slight'), nostalgia ('with a mournful Light'), inquietude ('Restless it roules and unsecure'), while the Sun feels 'pitty'. Conversely the Soul is endowed with physical qualities that come under the senses: it is spherical ('circling . . ., wound . . ., round'), 'Dark beneath, but bright above', 'Moving but on a point below', it 'Shuns the sweat leaves and blossoms green'. This confusion becomes worse confounded in the last four lines, which aim at drawing the moral lesson. As regards rhythm these decasyllabics, coming after a series of octo- and heptasyllabics, are a fine success, a majestic finale:

Such did the Manna's sacred Dew destil;
White, and intire, though congeal'd and chill.
Congeal'd on Earth: but does, dissolving, run
Into the Glories of th' Almighty Sun.

To the eye of logic these lines are less satisfactory: they introduce belatedly a new image, that of manna, slightly different from that of the dew, and the coalescing of the two images defies analysis. The last line pursues this process to the making of a pun, since 'th' Almighty Sun' is also the Son of God. Marvell was by no means the first to play on the two words; innumerable precedents authorized this piece of wit, in which ages of faith saw no irreverence. But we apprehend here, in a poem that comes near perfection, the abuse against which the neo-Classical school was to react to excess. Yet this abuse results from the legitimate desire of giving abstract thought a concrete expression.[1]

In his less inspired moments or when he handles less exalted themes our poet indulges in other freaks: although each of the metaphors (symbols in miniature) introduced is usually brief, their accumulation renders their incongruity

[1] Perhaps I should have confessed here in 1928 that I could not unravel the metaphors entangled in the last six lines of 'To his Coy Mistress'; they were to me as unanalysable as any cluster of images in Shakespeare, and no less powerful. Since then many have tried to explicate those lines, with the result that I understand them less and less. The crowning instance (so far) of misused ingenuity and industry is John J. Carroll's 'The Sun and the Lovers in "To his Coy Mistress"', in *M.L.N.*, 1959, pp. 4–7, where the phoenix is introduced gratuitously to make matters worse. I dare not pronounce on Wolfgang Iser's *explication* in *Die Neueren Sprachen*, 1957, pp. 555–77, because it is written in particularly philosophical German, but fear it is unduly moral and religious. Anthony E. Farnham, 'Saint Teresa and the Coy Mistress', in *Boston University Studies in English*, 1956, pp. 226–39, contrasts Marvell's poem with Crashaw's famous hymn but does not suggest any relation between the two, only opposition in method and creed. The latest attempt, at the time of going to press, is Patrick G. Hogan, Jr.'s 'Marvell's "Vegetable Love"' in *Studies in Philology*, 1963, pp. 1–11: building on the unsafe foundations of Klonsky and other research-workers who have dug up Plotinus from under Marvell's poetry, he rears a mystical interpretation of this poem, unconvincing to gross sense. He agrees with John Wheatcroft, 'Andrew Marvell and the Winged Chariot', in *Bucknell Review*, 1956, pp. 22–53, up to a point, but does not admit that Marvell's coy mistress is merely his Muse. *Pace* both of them I still hold that she is nothing more nor less than a woman.—Since I was first to point to the sexual conceit on 'honour' (l. 29) I must state my disbelief in those later found in ll. 41–44, especially in 'gates': true the word was often used metaphorically for 'labiae', but then the epithet 'Iron' would have to be explained here.

still more outrageous. 'The unfortunate Lover' might be a
fragment of an allegory if the governing idea were alone
retained; but this almost disappears under the overloading
of the style. The life of this victim of love is represented by
a shipwreck, which threatened to swallow him even in his
mother's womb had she not 'split against' a rock 'In a
Cesarian Section'. This daring image makes the sweetishness
of the succeeding conceits more sickening: tears lent by the
sea, sighs by the winds had long been part of the Petrarchist's
stock-in-trade. Then the orphan was 'Receiv'd into their
cruel Care' by 'Corm'rants black', who 'fed him up with
Hopes and Air' but 'on his Heart did bill'. The next stanza
shows him apparently of age and rid of his 'Guardians' but
the prey of many other evils. If we try to put stanza vi into
prose, the sum of what we have to visualize is this: a duellist
fights, in the lists, under the eyes of a bloody sovereign,
against an invulnerable adversary, but at the same time the
malicious archer, who is also a tyrant, shoots at him; and
this happens on a rock amidst the raging seas, while lightning
strikes all around the wretch; lastly we are bound to call up
the epic memory of Ajax (not the son of Telamon but the
less famous son of Oileus) made the butt of Neptune's
wrath. Under the strain imposed on him the reader has
entirely lost sight of the spiritual meaning these gestures
should express.

Yet the allegory maintains in 'The unfortunate Lover'
a certain imaginative unity, which makes itself felt in spite
of many disparates. But in most pieces Marvell rejects this
restraint and indulges in a riot of heterogeneous comparisons. In 'Mourning' all the guesses at the cause of Chlora's
weeping are clothed in metaphorical garb; nevertheless this
piece, thanks to its refined malice, its icy politeness, remains
perfectly intelligible and avoids sheer extravagance. But
here is the parting of 'Daphnis and Chloe', after she has, too
late, confessed her love for him. Two stanzas express, in
their abstract form, the ideas that the lover will not owe to
his departure 'What [his] Presence could not win', and that
it is better not to increase his losses 'By a late Fruition'.
The next six stanzas present each a facet of those two ideas,
always through images: 'my Fate' becomes (silently) 'my

Executioner', and as such is entitled to the 'Jewels' worn by the executed person. Of course what we have to remember as historical, or be reminded of, came effortlessly to the mind of readers during the score of years that separated the beheading of the Earl of Strafford from that of Sir Henry Vane, with the Regicide in between. Then let us proceed: Fate turns from an executioner into a 'Cannibal' for whose dinner Daphnis refuses to 'be fatted up express'. Without warning the next stanza introduces a no less gruesome but entirely different image: Daphnis refuses to take advantage of Chloe's helplessness, because 'th' Enjoyment' of her 'But the ravishment would prove / Of a Body dead while warm'. After this evocation of Egyptian necrophilia, taken out of Herodotus (we may imagine) by the prurient humanist, what a surprise to find again the Puritan resting on the authority of the Bible! Religion and modesty resume their rights, unfortunately at the expense of clarity: the analogy between the 'lust' of the Hebrews punished for eating quails and manna (Exodus xvi) and the lust Daphnis could satisfy if he took advantage of the auspicious hour[1] remains very dim. Hardly have we accepted as a feature common to both an unresisted sensual temptation followed at once by the wages of sin, when we enter new obscurities. I should look, says Daphnis, like the wizard who gathers fern-seed at midnight to make himself invisible. This time we are lost irrecoverably, for the only point of contact between the two terms is the fugitive opportunity—and what then? Fortunately the next stanza brings us back to the light of day:

> Gentler times for Love are ment.
> Who for parting pleasure strain
> Gather roses in the rain,
> Wet themselves and spoil their Sent.

Here is, at last, an implicit comparison at once simple and poetic, but after what queer wanderings!

---

[1] Gallicè, 'l'heure du berger'. I cannot accept a suggestion lately made to me, viz. that 'quails' is a *double-entendre*: the word undoubtedly could be used to mean a woman, generally a prostitute; but then what ambiguity shall we find in manna? No more sexual appears to me the 'Seed' in the next stanza. The gathering of 'roses' had of course been symbolical at least since Jean de Meun and Marvell may have had this symbolism in mind, but the metaphor in stanza XXIII does not require it, in fact is the better without it.

Nothing is less classic, and also less Puritan, than this striving for the concrete and sensuous expression of feelings. Without going so far as to make of Marvell an unconscious Ritualist, we note how this tendency of his mind is allowed free play when, in 'Upon Appleton House', he describes the joys of monastic life. Naturally he does not speak in his own name but places this long panegyric on the lips of a 'Suttle Nunn', who wants to 'suck in' a wealthy heiress for her order. Yet the poet's imagination runs away with him and he uses all the resources of his art to tell of the charm of the cloister. Now and then there peers out indeed the Protestant prejudice that sees behind the pious setting mere hypocrisy, avarice, and lecherousness. But it would be a mistake to ascribe a burlesque intention to such images as these:

> Our *Orient* breaths perfumed are
> With insense of incessant Pray'r.
> And Holy-water of our Tears
> Most strangly our Complexion clears.
> Not Tears of Grief; but such as those
> With which calm Pleasure overflows;
> Or Pity when we look on you
> That live without this happy Vow.

In defence of the first couplet the *Song of Songs*, with its mystical interpretations, may be invoked. The second appears less defensible, yet Marvell does not sneer at this beauty-wash, since he proceeds with a dignity and feeling worthy of 'Eyes and Tears'. Later indeed we find ourselves sinking into bathos—or irony—with the religious confectionery of the nuns:

> Here Pleasure Piety doth meet;
> One perfecting the other Sweet.
> So through the mortal fruit we boyl
> The Sugars uncorrupting Oyl:
> And that which perisht while we pull,
> Is thus preserved clear and full.

Better not go any further in this account of Marvell's stylistic vagaries. When all has been said of their bad taste or obscurity those faults must be recognized as the price of originality: he wants to renew the traditional stock of images from which too many poets draw without ever adding to it.

Negative criticism must henceforth yield to the appreciative study of preferences. Where will Marvell turn most readily to provide himself with comparisons? To Nature, the universal magazine? Yes, but, as our study of his descriptive technique has shown, he is not content to perceive through the senses that vast aggregate of appearances, colours, sounds, and perfumes; he will interpret it by means of the intellect; so doing he follows in the footsteps of the man of science, genuine or bogus. Whence it follows that his metaphors will derive not from the direct observation of natural phenomena but from the theories to which they have given rise, from what books have said.

The fanciful zoology and botany that had given Lyly's euphuism its most obvious characteristic has left some vestiges in Marvell's poetry. But these at most prove the survival of an antiquated fashion. Whether he believed or not in those fables he did not find in them that explanatory quality his mind chiefly sought.[1] The physical sciences, which already went beyond mere observation and description, pleased him better.

Chemistry and alchemy, now confounded now distinct, had provided Donne with numerous metaphors and one title. In an early piece, where his master's influence is felt most strongly, Marvell quaintly compares the grief of Aesculapius, who has failed to cure Hastings, carried off when he was about to show his full worth, to that of 'some sad *Chymist*, who, prepar'd to reap / The *Golden Harvest*, sees his Glasses leap'. After the Fire of London, the satirist was to compare the City trying to rebuild itself to 'vain Chymists, a flower from its ashes returning'. Later still the intolerant Anglican bishops 'would like Chymists fixing Mercury / Transfuse Indifference with necessity', that is, compel the Nonconformists to accept as articles of faith the least points of ecclesiastical discipline and ceremonial.

Physics, as still taught at that time, was even more than chemistry caught up in the cobwebs of the Schools. Reified

---

[1] In 'The Loyall Scot', ll. 77–78, he will use this incapacity of the naturalist as a term of comparison: 'Anatomists may sooner fix the Cells / Where life resides or Understanding dwells.' Of course these are 'cells of the brain' in a pseudo-scientific sense (*O.E.D.* 11c).

abstraction reigned there, notwithstanding the efforts made by some great innovators to dethrone it. Bodies, in spite of Hobbes's sarcasm, still flew up when 'rarefied': such is the fate that threatens Flecknoe as a consequence of his fastings, no less prolonged than involuntary. On the other hand, the 'compactness' of the famished poetaster's 'Chamber' is such that into it 'there can no Body pass / Except by penetration', an operation that involves the replacement of one thing or person by another, while it still retains its original place. Now does Nature admit penetration? A grave question on which doctors disagree. Marvell settles it negatively in the 'Horatian Ode': Nature 'Allows of penetration' even less than of 'emptiness', which it 'hateth' (our poet had not heard of Pascal's experiments, already two years old). This last allusion to the most subtly vain physical theories still current proves that to him they are no mere butt for satire. Why has Cromwell destroyed the old monarchy? Not out of choice but out of necessity, because Nature, not admitting of penetration, 'must make room / Where greater Spirits come'.

Marvell occasionally distinguishes astrology from astronomy; but more often he confuses or blends them. Astrological comparisons occur so frequently in seventeenth-century poetry, even outside the metaphysical school, that their presence here or there has no special significance. More interesting are those where true science prevails over pseudo-science. In 'The Definition of Love' Marvell compares himself and his mistress to the two celestial poles; this figure would be no more noticeable than the current phrase 'poles apart' if he did not thence proceed deductively: they are not to be embraced by each other unless the vault of each celestial hemisphere should fall flat on the equatorial plane; the two poles, then fused into one, would become the centre of this 'Planisphere', as Marvell calls the resulting figure in a very concise, even obscure stanza. From this cosmographic and cartographic metaphor, we pass without transition[1] to a geometric comparison: parallel lines never

[1] So I thought in 1928; but see Dean Schmitter, 'The Cartography of "The Definition of Love" ', in *R.E.S.*, 1961, pp. 49–54 (including my comment). I should now say that Marvell passes from astronomy (the poles) to geometry (oblique and parallel lines) through cartography (the planisphere where the meridians are shown as straight lines intersecting at either pole).

meet and no more do the loves of the poet and his mistress, 'though infinite', while oblique lines as well as 'Loves oblique' always meet in an angle. The next, and last, stanza takes us to the field of astrology with the then familiar terms of 'Conjunction' and 'Opposition'. So that analysis reveals three distinct terms of comparison with the poet's unhappy love; the piece nevertheless preserves a striking unity, due to its atmosphere, abstract, scientific, stripped of any sensuality, or even sensuousness, in the expression of a passionate ardour.

Marvell's interest in mathematics does not appear only from the above mention of parallel and oblique lines and angles. Indeed his first biographer, Aubrey, tells us that 'John Pell, D.D.', one of the foremost English mathematicians of the age, 'was one of his [limited] acquaintance'. So we are not surprised to find a 'Compass' coming to the poet's mind when he admires that 'perfect Hemisphere', Bilbrough Hill, or to hear him sneer at those (Hobbes among them) who 'vainly strive t'immure the *Circle* in the *Quadrature*', while Appleton House has managed, thanks to its '*holy Mathematicks*', to contain 'Things greater . . . in less'. Some twenty years later Marvell gives new life to the well-worn astrological metaphor of 'influence' by introducing a geometrical notion into it: can Tweed by dividing England and Scotland also divide virtue from vice? An absurd supposition, for it would compel us to admit that a 'new Perpendicular does rise / Up from her Streams, continued to the Skies, / . . . And split the Influence of every Star'. Even in prose, mathematics will provide Marvell with conceits, e.g.: 'a straight line continued grows a circle,' and so infinite regal power becomes 'extended unto impotency'.

This enumeration of the sciences recognized by the seventeenth century would remain incomplete did we omit theology, then the alpha and omega of knowledge. It provided poetry, even of the most profane kind, with reasoning tricks and terms of comparison that now require a long commentary to be understood. Here again Donne leads, but Marvell scarcely follows him. The former had received a Roman Catholic education and the latter a more or less Puritan one: does that account for the difference? If so, it seems that the Bible should supplant the merely human speculations of the Schools in the mind of the son of the Lecturer of Trinity Church, Hull. Now Marvell's lyrical poetry contains few biblical allusions and they mostly appear, to the infidels or lukewarm Christians of this latter age, as rather irreverent. This impression is strengthened by the reading of his satires, where biblical allusions are far more numerous. That is not the least of the contradictions present in the complex character of our Puritan poet.

Shall we say that his preference for images drawn from the art of war, plentiful in his lyrical poetry, makes a Cavalier of him? True, when he despairs of resisting 'The Fair Singer's' charm, 'She having gained both the Wind and Sun'; or blames Daphnis, who, though an expert in amorous poliorcetics, 'Knew not that the Fort to gain / Better 'twas the Siege to raise' then Marvell's verse can hardly be distinguished from Suckling's or Lovelace's. But the Roundheads were not behindhand, whether in dealing blows or in parading military knowledge, and it is as an Ironside clad with the mystical armour described by St. Paul that our poet beats back the onsets of Created Pleasure. The arsenal of warlike comparisons supplied not one political party but a whole generation.

We have now reached the point beyond which analysis can scarce proceed.[1] Marvell's favourite modes of expression,

---

[1] Or could not in 1928. Since then criticism has dug deeper and deeper. Marvell would say it has found 'what depth the Centre draws'. References have already been provided in several footnotes, *supra*, but here are some more: M. F. E. Rainbow, 'Marvell and Nature', in *Durham University Journal*, 1944, pp. 22–27, and Joseph H. Summers, 'Marvell's Nature', in *E.L.H.*, 1953, pp. 121–35. On one point these two agree: Marvell is 'sophisticated'. Somewhat more helpfully H. W. Smith, 'Cowley, Marvell, and the Second Temple', in *Scrutiny*, 1953, pp. 184–205, studies the seventeenth-century development of the concept of Nature, in gardening and architecture as well as poetry. Jim Corder, 'Marvell and Nature', in *N.Q.*, 1959, pp. 58–61, restates my views on the poet's acceptation, apart from the Mower poems, of the formal garden and on his own formalized descriptions of it (*v. supra*, p. 44 sqq.); but the American critic does not avoid exaggeration. Fresher and more entertaining in its free composition and its occasional extravagance is 'Evening in the Botanics: A Tropical Essay', by Patrick Anderson, in *The Cambridge Journal*, 1952–3, vol. vi, pp. 546–60, where Marvell, seen from Singapore, plays the leading part. Renato Poggioli, 'The Pastoral of the Self', in *Daedalus, Journal of the American Academy of Arts and Sciences*, 1959, pp. 686–98, sees things from a great height, which enables him to draw together the 'chief bucolic episode' in *Don Quixote* (1. x) and 'The Garden', arbitrarily called a pastoral. Yet the article is readable and stimulating.

chiefly in their relation to his imagination, lie before us, numbered, labelled. And yet we feel that the same elements might combine in a wholly different style; there is in their blending an indefinable something that makes them poetic instead of comic. The neo-Classics will soon deliberately separate laughter and tears. Then the Romantics, no less consciously, will contrast the sublime and the grotesque. With Marvell as with his contemporaries there seems to be rather lack of distinction than deliberate blending. Among the many images we have quoted almost everyone stands in the disputed territory between the serious and the burlesque. One instance will suffice to show how easily the limit is crossed between these two literary provinces. In one of his most inspired moments, when the poet describes his communion with the life of birds and even of plants, he follows up the idea with an alternative wish: 'Give me but Wings' as the birds, 'and I . . . shall fly' (there is nothing there to shock us, unless the psycho-analyst intrudes with his dirty hands),

> Or turn me but, and you shall see
> I was but an inverted Tree.

This pulls us up sharply, perhaps because[1] we at once remember Swift's 'Meditation upon a Broomstick': this instrument, says the English classic *par excellence*, is 'a tree turned upside down', and at the same time it symbolizes man: 'But a broomstick, perhaps you will say, is an emblem of a tree standing on its head; and pray, what is man but a topsy-turvy creature . . .?'

We must, therefore, in order to enjoy Marvell's fancy without embarrassment, forget for the nonce what his successors have taught us; we must also see every image not in itself but in the movement of a larger unit. The most convincing test is the reading of 'Eyes and Tears', Marvell's most ornate poem, the one most thickly sown with metaphors, apparently the most immobile. Here the variety of

---

[1] First because we have forgotten Aristotle. See my note in *André Marvell* (iii. 262). I had since procured the Aristotelian references from M. Pierre Louis, my *Recteur* and the greatest living French authority on the Stagyrite. But I see now that I have been forestalled by A. B. Chambers's article in *Studies in the Renaissance*, viii. 291–9 (1961). Indeed he even derives the metaphor, less closely, from Plato.

images defies classification. The sciences are indeed well represented—by trigonometry and oceanography (stanza II) and chemistry (VI). The military art may claim the well-worn metaphor of 'The sparkling Glance that shoots Desire' (x). The incense comes from the Bible, more precisely from the Old Testament, since the Puritan reveals himself in the tense of the verb: it 'was to Heaven dear' (XI). But how many other comparisons come from hitherto unmentioned fields! Shall we wonder that all do not seem equally felicitous? We moderns may try (and fail) to visualize tears as 'Pendants of the Eyes' in which jewels 'melt' (IV), an unexpected transposition of the legendary ear-pendants that Cleopatra melted in vinegar. In our days[1] Prudery averts her eyes from 'the chast Ladies pregnant Womb' and Sterility thinks it ridiculous (IX). On better grounds we may censure the over-ingenious mythological designation of the full moon: '*Cynthia* Teeming' (IX) or object to the Christian God's being called 'the Thund'rer' (x), or deem it mawkish gallantry when repenting Magdalen is given 'captivating Eyes', like any 'Phyllis en l'air'. The conceit that turns the 'Dew' of the Eyes into a medicinal lotion to bathe them with hardly appeals to us; it even shocks us because it follows two lines, simple and classic in form though romantic in feeling:

> Yet happy they whom Grief doth bless,
> That weep the more, and see the less:

But, all reservations made on such details, beauty and charm remain. And what is true of this poem is true *a fortiori* of many others less heavily decorated. Even for one who does not relish the queer or the bizarre Marvell's style compels esteem and even admiration because it rarely falls into *précieuse* triviality but often offers unique felicities.

His versification on the whole shows far less originality than his style, and his lack of craftsmanship, or rather his amateur's insouciance, makes itself felt more often, while brilliant successes are fewer.

His prosody, in the stricter sense of the term, illustrates the transition between the end of the Renaissance and the

---

[1] Meaning the twenties.

neo-Classical age, but stands very close to the latter. The trisyllabic element appears only in the most unobtrusive manner. Like his contemporaries, but rather less than most, Marvell uses the apostrophe (as the sign of elision, contraction, or apocope) to disguise as an iamb an anapest that a modern poet would rather parade. Most of his poetry having been published posthumously it is difficult to assess responsibility between the poet and the printer; and inconsistencies abound, the same word (counting for the same number of syllables) taking and not taking the apostrophe in two consecutive lines. But, apostrophated or not, extra syllables in Marvell's staple foot are such as can be slurred by any reciter aiming at regularity. Among the few that today resist compression are 'it' as subject, 'to' before a vowel, '-ing' after a 'y', '-est' after a consonant; and the word 'violet' would lose its fragrance if reduced to two syllables by the omission of the 'o'. As a rule Marvell's thought is cast easily in the iambic mould, maybe because it seldom achieves the same compactness (or crabbedness) as Donne's.

He rather avails himself of the opposite sort of traditional prosodic licence: of two pronunciations of a word he will prefer the older one, with diaeresis, as in 'militiä', 'fruitiön', 'sectiön'. And he will use the flexional endings '-ed' often, '-eth' sometimes, to provide unstressed syllables. On the whole he resembles Spenser rather than Donne in this respect; whether deliberately or instinctively he seeks harmonious easiness, even at the cost of monotony, rather than rough and nervous concision.

The same remark applies to stress. The substitution of the trochee for the iamb seldom occurs save, quite normally, at the beginning of a line or after a pause. One of Marvell's most famous single lines contains a signal instance of each:

$$\text{Lílies} \mid \text{without,} \parallel \text{Róses} \mid \text{within.}$$

The way the rhythm rears twice underlines the opposition in the meaning, most happily. Another equally famous line is built on the substitution of a pyrrhic followed by a spondee for two iambs, in each hemistich:

$$\text{To a} \mid \text{green Thought} \parallel \text{in a} \mid \text{green Shade.}$$

It is impossible not to stress 'green' as well as 'Thought' and 'Shade', so as to obtain similarity in difference. Both instances illustrate the middle pause, frequent in Marvell's octo-syllabics but seldom so significant.

He respects the rhythm of the language; twice only is he clearly guilty of 'wrenching the accent' in order to rhyme: 'a reforming eye/Presbýterý'; 'Return/*Satúrn*'. Inside the line matters are not so easy to settle, yet Donne's disregard of feet rarely reappears in his disciple. Some octosyllabics indeed fall naturally into three divisions, including such a fine one as this:

> Let us roll | all our Strength, | and all
> Our sweetness, . . .

Even here we can obtain four feet by stressing the first 'all' (like the second), thus making 'roll all' a spondee (after a pyrrhic?).

> Let us | roll all | our Strength, | and all
> Our sweetness, . . .

But what of this?

> its foot more soft,
> And white, (shall I say then my hand?)

'shall I' might pass for a trochee after the pause, but 'say then'? These instances and a very few others do not suffice to link Marvell's prosody with Donne's. The two poets are more alike in the use of monosyllables, even to the exclusion of longer words in single lines. 'Clorinda and Damon' offers some bad instances, and even among the grass of 'The Garden' the rocky soil appears here and there: out of seventy-two lines seven consist wholly of monosyllables, not all exceptions to the rule that condemns this sort of line in the name of euphony. Only in 'The Definition of Love', a sombre and hard poem where Donne's influence is printed deep on the thought and the metaphors, has Marvell used monosyllabic lines to good effect:

> (Though Loves whole World on us doth wheel)

is heavy indeed, but with an energetic weight suiting the matter. Nevertheless, considering Marvell's lyrical poetry as a whole, we must admit that a certain arhythmia is the price paid for the simplicity we have praised in his diction. Both the quality and the fault make him the very opposite of Milton, whose infallible harmony is too often paid for by a pedantic vocabulary. These two poets illustrate English poetry's Scylla and Charybdis, arising from the very nature of the language.

In spite of occasional monosyllabic harshness Marvell's prosody is characterized on the whole by a softness that may become monotonous and sometimes limp. This impression is strengthened when we pass from the study of feet to that of metres.

In Marvell's lyrical pieces lines of 12, 10, 8, 7, 6, 4, and 2 syllables are found. Of these seven metres, four never appear alone and therefore need no separate examination. The three that must be considered are the decasyllable, the octosyllable, and the heptasyllable, each found either alone or in conjunction with other metres.

The decasyllable, which arithmetic would place second, comes last as regards interest. Of the six isometrical pieces it provides, four are occasional, and more important biographically than artistically. The other two, curiously enough, are 'The Fair Singer' and 'Musicks Empire': why has the poet chosen the least lyrical of metres to praise the art with which lyrical poetry is etymologically and traditionally associated?

The octosyllable and the heptasyllable, very closely akin and yet different enough, are seldom used by Marvell in the same piece. Here again the versifier sacrifices variety to regularity.

The octosyllable predominates in his lyrical poetry; first by mere amount (three-fourths of the total) but also because of the superior quality of the pieces in which it is found alone: 'To his Coy Mistress', 'The Nymph complaining for the death of her Faun', 'The Garden', 'Bermudas', to name only the best known. In it are gathered almost all the beauties of Marvell's versification, but also, alas! its defects. These appear chiefly in the long, too long, poem 'Upon Appleton House'. Byron, ingeniously and not unfairly, once called the octosyllabic the metre 'of fatal facility': seldom was the definition more apt than when applied to Marvell's most ambitious attempt. If the manner has made us think at times of a rather childish babble, amusing but prolix, the fault, no doubt, lies partly with the octosyllable: it flows easily, often without a pause, and is almost inevitably end-stopt. Out of 776 lines some two dozen run on, and if the odd line sometimes runs on, the even one hardly ever does. Each couplet is either grammatically self-sufficient or else articulated with the next one, or two, or three. Marvell makes stanzas of a sort with groups of four couplets separated by roman figures. These units have little to do with the art of versification; at best they answer to the desire of dividing the movement of thought into equal time-lengths. They are also found in 'Bill-borow', 'The unfortunate Lover', 'The Gallery', 'Damon the Mower', and 'The Garden'. This last poem comes so near perfection that one hesitates to disparage the metrical pattern on which it is built and the poet who probably preferred this pattern to all others. Yet one may confess to a preference for the undisguised couplets of 'Bermudas' or 'To his Coy Mistress', and find a greater technical interest in 'The Nymph complaining for the death of her Faun', the only poem in which the meaning refuses to be shut up in any metrical frame, whether line, couplet, quatrain, or octave. The proportion of run-on lines rises to one in six (instead of the one in thirty in 'Upon Appleton House'). And those run-on lines are not evenly distributed through the poem: scarce in the middle section where the Nymph recalls the sad or merry past with a restrained emotion, they abound in the first twenty-four lines where her grief and indignation burst out like sobs. Though figures here may seem impertinent and every reader should judge for himself (the personal equation plays a large part in statistics of enjambments) we shall venture to say that nearly half of the lines (eleven in our count) run on, and three couplets are enjambed ones. And the end of the poem, where immediate pathos again prevails with the present death of the fawn, offers the same metrical feature, hardly less marked. Marvell then was fully aware of the dramatic quality of run-on lines; if confirmation were wanted it would be found in the fact that almost the only passages in 'Upon Appleton House' where they occur are the nun's speech and the lover's soliloquy.

Neither was Marvell ignorant of the effects the alternation of the octosyllable and the heptasyllable could produce; he proved it in a metrically remarkable piece, 'A Dialogue between the Resolved Soul and Created Pleasure'. The preamble, in which the poet exhorts his Soul to constancy, and all the Soul's speeches consist of octosyllables; as also do the two choruses, angelic or at least pious, which mark the middle and the end of the poem, save that the former of the two concludes with a decasyllabic couplet enhancing its gravity. But Pleasure uses the heptasyllable, in the former half of the piece alone in quatrains or sizains (i.e. groups of two or three couplets), in the latter alternating in quatrains with the hexasyllable. Pleasure thus produces an impression of voluptuous instability that contrasts dramatically with the Soul's immutable resolution. The absence of the anacrusis imparts to the heptasyllable a trochaic rhythm exactly opposite to the iambic rhythm of the octosyllable. While this one is sedate and even, that one is lively and skipping, or else vehement and passionate. Unfortunately Marvell never again took the same pains. In 'Clorinda and Damon', the theme of which so much resembles that of 'A Dialogue between the Resolved Soul and Created Pleasure', the sensual shepherdess like the virtuous shepherd observes the iambic rhythm; and this piece of thirty lines manages to seem monotonous to the ear. In 'Thyrsis and Dorinda' metrical variety does exist, but the lines of seven, eight, and ten syllables are divided so capriciously between the husband and the wife that this (early) piece, enigmatic as regards matter and textually uncertain, becomes still more obscure.

In four pieces the heptasyllable reigns without a rival. The choice of this metre is easily explained for 'Daphnis and Chloe', that libertine pastoral, and even better for 'Ametas and Thestylis making Hay-Ropes', a lovely trifle in which Created Pleasure triumphs with little difficulty over a Soul well-informed indeed but not 'Resolved'. In 'Young Love' the heptasyllable, through its alertness, enables the inherent sensuality of the theme to pass almost unnoticed. Lastly, if meeting this rhythm, more lively than sober, in the translation of a moralizing chorus from Seneca's *Thyestes* causes some surprise, its use may be accounted for by the desire to preserve the lyrical cadence of the original glyconics. Anyhow, Marvell is almost as fond of the heptasyllable as Herrick.

Yet the octosyllabic, easier to handle, remains his favourite medium; and to measure the distance that separates his average versification from the summits of that art it suffices to read 'Upon Appleton House' and then read again 'L'Allegro' and 'Il Penseroso'. In the Miltonic diptych, to which we have already referred as a convenient term of comparison, the triumph of concision is achieved notwithstanding the facility of the metre. Marvell never attains to such terseness, not even in 'Bermudas' or 'To his Coy Mistress'. However, it must be granted that he has, especially in the last-named piece, drawn unexpectedly sonorous notes from his pleasant instrument, the stock instance being:

> But at my back I alwaies hear
> Times winged Charriot hurrying near:
> And yonder all before us lye
> Desarts of vast Eternity.

(pronounced 'Etarnity'). In view of Marvell's sublime achievement here it sounds ungracious to insist on what yet remains generally true, viz. that he is too often casual in his choice and use of metres.

He is not more fastidious in his way of rhyming (but what English poet is?). Allowing for all the changes in pronunciation since the mid-seventeenth century, a fairly long list could be made of his lax rhymes. He occasionally ventures into assonance veiled by spelling: converse/hers; chase/rase; and he even defies both ear and eye in sigh'd/night.

He does not often indulge in rhyming syllables that bear only secondary stresses; as turnaments/ornaments; enemy/harmony; leviathans/hurricans; conspiracies/prophecies. And Waller in his 1645 volume of verse also has two of these rhymes. But what Marvell does frequently is to rhyme a syllable bearing a main stress with one bearing a secondary (and more or less fictitious) stress. Granted that such rhymes, used discreetly, may soften the harshness of the normally stressed ones, their abuse enervates the verse. And Marvell's lyrical poetry, averaging one such in twelve, as compared with one in twenty in 'L'Allegro' and 'Il Penseroso', and one in fifty in Waller's volume, tends towards laxity. Besides, Marvell often attributes to the syllables thus promoted an arbitrary vocalic quality or quantity. From a permissible rhyme like frustrating/king we pass to survives/Donatives, lye/Eternity, try/virginity, seas/deluges, wear/executioner, war/Oliver, home/Elizium (while this word, a little later, rhymes less strangely with come), will/Pinacle/still. So that one octave of 'Upon Appleton House' presents these rhymes : fierce/Universe, try/Germany, prophecy'd/ride, in succession, the last one (kept/intercept) just bringing us back to normal.

Curiously enough, Marvell, so free as regards stress, accepted on other points the restrictions enforced by the neo-Classical school. The feminine rhyme appears three times only in his lyrical poetry, as against ten in 'L'Allegro' and 'Il Penseroso' alone. Even Waller, at any rate in 1645, admits it more liberally. The same remark applies to the identical rhyme,[1] of which we find only two instances. Equally exceptional are the rhyme of the simple with the compound word, and the broken rhyme.

Marvell's rhymes seldom achieve originality; we cannot blame him for it since we have praised the plainness of his vocabulary, yet we may note the too frequent occurrence at the end of lines of such couples as heart/art or art/part. Such an unexpected rhyme for 'hands' as '*Deodands*', very aptly brought in, remains isolated in his lyrical verse.

Marvell also resembled the neo-Classics in the limited number, and the simplicity approximating to poverty, of the stanza-forms he uses. Only three pieces are anisometrical: 'The Mower's Song', in which it has been noted that the burden, a final alexandrine, following upon five octosyllabics, 'suggests the long regular sweep of the scythe'; 'The Mower against Gardens', in which decasyllabic and octosyllabic lines alternate, giving a shorter version of the Latin elegiac distich (here Marvell follows Ben Jonson);

[1] Condemned by Cowley, in note 2 to his ode 'To Dr. Scarborough' (*Poems*, ed. Waller, p. 200).

'An Horatian Ode', where he aims at a resemblance, perforce superficial, with stanzas used by Augustus' poet, not, however, in the ode glorifying the victory at Actium but in more intimate pieces (the alcaic stanza or the asclepiad B).[1]

The rhyme-scheme of Marvell's lyrical poems, whether iso- or aniso-metrical, reveals the same lack of variety: a long way after the couplet comes the quatrain with alternate rhymes. In this well-tried form (the long measure of the hymn-books) the poet meets, to our mind, his greatest metrical successes, e.g. the final stanza of 'The Definition of Love':

> Therefore the Love which us doth bind,
> But Fate so enviously debarrs,
> Is the Conjunction of the Mind,
> And Opposition of the Stars.

He was also content to use instruments provided by his predecessors in 'The Fair Singer' (the sixain of *Venus and Adonis*) and in 'Daphnis and Chloe' (the quatrain with embraced rhymes).

In only two pieces do the two elements of a truly lyrical stanza combine: unequal metres and a complex rhyme-scheme. 'The Match' calls for no comment since it uses the ballad metre (or common measure). But the stanza of 'Little T.C.', more intricate, might well be Marvell's single innovation; the pattern, $abaccb^8d^4d^{10}$, seems to have been taken up by no later poet either: indeed the effect produced on the ear is pleasant and nothing more.

Less original metrically but far finer are the two pieces written by Marvell in what we may call free verse, i.e. without any set pattern of rhyme or metre. Jack Donne had provided precedents, notably in 'The Apparition'. The pious Rector of Bemerton had sanctified this revolutionary venture in one of his strongest pieces, 'The Collar'. Then Milton had surpassed both his predecessors, in sonority; but though Marvell knew 'Lycidas' he took Herbert for his model in

---

[1] I thought Marvell had innovated there, but William Simeone, 'A Probable Antecedent of Marvell's "Horatian Ode" ', in *N.Q.*, 1952, pp. 316–18, showed that Richard Fanshawe had anticipated him in a poem written twenty years before but still unpublished in 1650. Marvell may have devised the stanza independently but he may well have been acquainted with Fanshawe.

'On a Drop of Dew' and 'The Coronet'. The former of these two pieces offers the greatest metrical variety: lines of four, six, eight, and ten syllables, with an infusion of heptasyllabics, which entitle it to be called not only ani-sometrical but also anisorhythmical. As to the rhymes we find beside the usual arrangements the rarer and more artistic, if not artificial, abcabc. Reading 'On a Drop of Dew' aloud one may come to the conclusion that Marvell, re-maining well on the hither side of Herbert's audacity, made good use of freedom; often perilous for other poets, it was less so for him than the regularity of the octosyllabic couplet. It seems a pity he did not reverse the proportion of the one to the other metrical forms in his lyrical poetry.

Fully realizing, however, that such analysis as we have given proves even more inadequate for versification than for style, even though the poet might have subscribed to all the rules we have invoked, we ought at least to mention the unconscious element: as in the composing, so in the enjoy-ing of poetry. For want of a better word we should call that element the 'musicality' of the verse and illustrate our meaning from some of Marvell's deservedly less-known poems. Never mind what Hastings was, but listen to this description of his celestial home:

> Before the *Chrystal Palace* where he dwells,
> The armed *Angels* hold their *Carouzels*;

Let us forget the moralizing platitudes of 'Clorinda and Damon', and cull, among those harsh monosyllabic lines, this melodious couplet:

> Near this, a Fountaines liquid Bell
> Tinkles within the concave Shell.

In 'Mourning', just before the parting shot, given by us as an instance of polite malice, one stanza takes us very far away from society scandal, but the beauty of the image could not operate this removal without the magic of sound:

> How wide they dream! The *Indian* Slaves
> That sink for Pearl through Seas profound,
> Would find her Tears yet deeper Waves
> And not of one the bottom sound.

In 'Damon the Mower' we are indebted to Juliana's

conventional cruelty to her lover for this reminder of his gifts to her:

> To thee *Chameleons* changing-hue
> And Oak leaves tipt with hony due,

and for this boast of the love Aurora bears him:

> On me the Morn her dew distills
> Before her darling Daffodils.

When one has noted the double alliteration, of *m* and of *d* (beginning five syllables, four of them stressed), has one fully accounted for the appeal of this couplet to the ear? Better acknowledge in these exquisite passages the presence of a *je ne sais quoi* and linger over them sensuously.

Unfortunately, such a technical study as ours, based on the whole and not on exceptions, calls for a more judicial, and therefore sullen, conclusion. To the historian of English versification Marvell, we must repeat, stands near to the neo-Classical age, already accepting the proscription of feminine rhyme and enjambment, no longer feeling the urge, so characteristic of the Renaissance, to create metrical forms. Considered in itself, his versification offers few attempts at novelty, and these not specially successful, side by side with some fine successes devoid of originality.

An open-minded but lazy poet, Marvell did not use his natural gifts to the full. In so limited an output one wonders at the high proportion of careless improvisation. Yet the lack of steady diligence is partly compensated by his sound classical education. This and his wide adult reading place him above 'the mob of gentlemen that wrote with ease', though some critics in the past have confounded him with them. He never falls so low as Suckling or Lovelace. On the other hand, his nonchalance no less than his taste saves him from Donne's worst contortions. Less than Crashaw or Vaughan is he the plaything of a seemingly external inspiration, of an enthusiasm that lifts the poet high up to Heaven only to drop him heavily the next minute. He could, if he would, have pruned his luxuriance, and polished his style and verse; whenever he tried he succeeded worthily. With very similar but less delicate gifts Dryden slowly reached a position in English poetry that Marvell might have filled with as much majesty and a spontaneous charm rarely found in the laureate of Charles II.

But regrets avail little and recriminations even less. We must thank Marvell for what he was and did. Alone among Donne's followers he presents a personality comparable to the master's in variety and even strength; and in his best poems he reaches a humaneness, a cordiality, he expresses in a way at once widely accessible and refinedly artistic, universal feelings that Donne only vents on very rare occasions. He remains and will remain the metaphysical poet of the open air, and this aspect of his work alone could secure his fame. But he sometimes rose above the fashion of his time;[1] and then he gave poetic expression to some aspects of Nature so happily or intensely that for most readers, whatever the critic may say of this generalization, he will remain the forerunner of Wordsworth, Shelley, and Keats, the poet who noted 'the hatching Thrastles shining Eye', perceived the perfume of flowers as music, nay, on a mossy bank in the shade of old trees, fainted with a sensuous ecstasy in which neither God nor woman played a part. And if a man is defined by his supreme gift and achievement, this image of Marvell, however simplified, may well be the most faithful.[2]

[1] And of ours.

[2] Perhaps the most balanced study of Marvell's lyrical poems in recent years is to be found in H. R. Swardson's *Poetry and the Fountain Of Light Observations on the Conflict between Christian and Classical Traditions in Seventeenth Century Poetry*, 1962. Chapter IV, entitled 'Marvell A New Pastoralism', suffers only from a tendency to carry a legitimate interpretation too far, for the sake of a general thesis. In most of Marvell's nature poetry, or love poetry at that, there is felt little sense of inner conflict; this is restricted to the properly religious poems, as we have seen.

Addition to n. 1 of p. 49: Maren-Sofie Røstvig, 'Benlowes, Marvell, and the Divine Casimire', in *Huntington Library Quarterly*, 1954, p. 31, says: 'Marvell has been praised for [introducing] real mowers into his landscape, but Benlowes did this before him in the pastoral parts of *Theophila*' (published in 1652, but according to that critic seen in manuscript by Marvell at Fairfax's); and she quotes four lines from Benlowes's 'dinosaur' (Canto XIII, Stanza ii) in support of this claim. These lines indeed contain one graphic touch: the mower has 'big swoln veins'.

Addition to n. 1 of p. 54: Maren-Sofie Røstvig, 'Andrew Marvell's "The Garden": A Hermetic Poem', in *English Studies*, 1959, pp. 65–76, also provides an esoteric interpretation of this poem. She makes much of the 'bi-sexual' character of the vegetable world. Her main argument, however, rests on what I consider a misunderstanding of the epithet 'amorous' applied to 'green'; I take it to have only the passive (obsolete) sense of 'lovely'.

IV

CROMWELL'S POET

MARVELL left the Fairfaxes about the end of 1652. We do not know why. Possibly, in spite of his declarations of love to Solitude, he regretted London. Very soon after his return there he was to deride the Dutch, those 'Bores' (boors) who had chosen for their capital The Hague, a mere 'Village'. Anyhow, in February 1652/3 he was applying for an official position. Then he was (to use a French nineteenth-century term) a *rallié* to the Commonwealth. How long had he been such? Here we meet not lack of evidence but sharply conflicting evidence, and a so far unsolved problem.

On 13 November 1650 died Thomas May, a playwright and poet favoured by the Court before the Civil War, afterwards the official historian of the Long Parliament, praising the Presbyterian Earl of Essex first, and then the Independent generals, Fairfax and Cromwell. His sudden death in his sleep, a drunken sleep the Royalists specified, was of course looked upon as a visitation of Heaven on a mercenary renegade. What surprises us is that Marvell should have adopted this view unreservedly. Moreover, in a satire entitled 'Tom May's Death', he included in his denunciation all the Parliamentarians collectively, under the then highly discreditable name of 'Spartacus'. And he even went out of his way to call Brutus and Cassius 'the Peoples cheats', using, it is true, Ben Jonson as his mouthpiece and also imitating Dante, two determined monarchists,[1] but no doubt expressing his own Royalist fervour. How can we reconcile this with the 'Horatian Ode', written five months before?

And if we did, it would not help much since another chasm stops our progress: three months at most after having written 'Tom May's Death' Marvell addressed in clever and flattering Latin verse one of the leading men of the

[1] A third one is Davenant, whom Marvell praises (ll. 57–58).

Commonwealth, and one of those the Royalists hated most, Oliver St. John, Chief Justice of Common Pleas. True, the occasion of those eight distichs belongs not to home but to foreign politics.

St. John, along with another Puritan, Walter Strickland, M.P. for Hedon, a borough not far from Hull, had been chosen on 14 February 1650/1 as Ambassador to the United Provinces. Marvell plays on the Christian name Oliver, derived from an emblem of peace,[1] and the surname St. John, which recalls the apostle in his angry mood (Mark iii. 17); in diplomatic language he interprets the message brought by the Ambassadors as an ultimatum: either a perpetual alliance, such as the one lately enforced upon the Scots, or open war, at once. To Marvell, who knew the country, the Dutch answer allowed little doubt: even the peaceful merchants who governed the United Provinces almost without any check (the future William III being only two months old and an orphan) could not accept such vassalage as this unequal alliance would have amounted to.

Even if Marvell's chief inducement to write this piece lay in the double conceit that offered itself, no such explanation will serve for his next poem, an English poem, 'The Character of Holland', full though it is of puns and quibbles. Here Marvell openly supports the war policy of the Commonwealth against a country that sheltered many of the exiled Royalists; this hospitality does not indeed appear in the poem as one of the causes of the war, but Marvell's conclusion leaves no doubt of his newly acquired republican faith:

> For now of nothing may our *State* despair,
> Darling of Heaven, and of Men the Care;
> Provided that they be what they have been,
> Watchful abroad, and honest still within.

Like many an honourable convert before and since, Marvell went over to the new régime on the occasion of a foreign war. Yet we cannot but note that this praise of the Commonwealth (written at the end of February 1652/3 or little after)

---

[1] *Pace* Carl E. Bain, 'The Latin Poetry of Andrew Marvell', in *Philological Quarterly*, p. 445, who inverts the significance of the two names. The more common usage of 'hoc' and 'illo' (l. 9) is on my side.

coincides with his first known attempt to obtain official employment. Fortunately for his moral reputation he did it through Milton.

We do not know when the two poets had become personally acquainted; probably not long before the older one dictated a letter of recommendation (dated 21 February 1652/3) to Bradshaw, then President of the Council of State, since it invokes 'report' no less than 'the converse' Milton has 'had with him' to guarantee 'Marvell's singular desert', and grounds its belief in his being 'of an approved conversation' on his late position of trust at Lord Fairfax's. Yet a curious document seems to show that already in 1653, or 1654 at latest, the friendship between the two poets incurred the reprobation of the Royalists and was thought to date back to the writing of *Eikonoclastes* (1649). The charge, an utterly incredible one, that Marvell had helped Milton to write that regicide pamphlet, was made by a credulous old lady, Mrs. Anne Sadleir, sister to Bridget Skinner and aunt to Cyriak Skinner, Milton's disciple and admirer from 1647 at least. Since Mrs. Sadleir had had a sermon dedicated to her by the Reverend Andrew Marvell in 1627, she must have written of his son's shameful perversion in sorrow no less than in anger. We shall shortly see that other adherents to the Stuarts' cause considered Marvell's political behaviour in those crucial years as utterly unscrupulous. There may be more in this reprobation than we now know.

Milton states clearly in his letter what kind of employment Marvell aimed at; he himself had been since 1649 'Secretary for the Foreign tongues', and in fact had, by his own choice, become 'Latin secretary' only. Yet he praises Marvell to Bradshaw for his command of Dutch, French, Italian, and Spanish, in addition to the classical languages, and proposes that Marvell should be made his assistant, filling a vacancy in the staff. He confesses that his own 'condition' makes him unfit for part of his duties; by the word 'condition' he means his blindness, complete for nearly a year by then: he may well never have seen Marvell.

Marvell did not obtain the post at this time; his application to the regicide *par excellence* (Bradshaw had presided over the Commission that had sentenced Charles I to death, the very tribunal that Lady Fairfax had upbraided, and from which Oliver St. John had kept away) nevertheless marks a decisive turn in his career.

On 20 April following, the day of Pride's Purge, Cromwell dissolved the Council of State despite Bradshaw's solemn protest. Milton for the nonce proved less of a doctrinaire, and preferred religious freedom, which he thought safer with Cromwell, to such legitimacy as the Rump still commanded. Marvell for his part seems to have seen without regret the civil power supplanted by the victorious General, with whom he came in contact about that time, perhaps through St. John whose second wife was Cromwell's first cousin. She having died, he had married, in 1645, Elizabeth Oxenbridge, sister of the Reverend John Oxenbridge, now a fellow of Eton. St. John may have recommended his brother-in-law to Cromwell who was looking for a godly family in which to place a young protégé of his, William Dutton; in addition he may have suggested Marvell as a tutor for the boy. At any rate, we find Marvell writing to Cromwell on 28 July 1653 from the Oxenbridges' house at Eton, very soon after having begun this new tutorship. His letter, in which God is named twice, shows deep respect without servility, and diplomatic caution; he insures against failure with a pupil whose health and wits did not apparently promise brilliant success; and he will not spoil his chance of more congenial service under the ruler of England.

Cromwell's interest in William Dutton, the son of a Cavalier who had died in 1646 after fighting bravely for the King, reveals less the statesman than the father in him; he had entered into an agreement with the boy's uncle and guardian, John Dutton, 'a learned and a prudent man, and as one of the richest, so one of the meekest, men in England': William would marry Frances, Cromwell's youngest daughter, on the condition of inheriting the ancestral estate of Sherborne, which, since John had daughters only, could shock no one, apart of course from his sons-in-law. Though William was not to become Cromwell's legal ward before John's death in January 1656/7, it appears that the Lord General at once took the boy's education in hand; he wanted his son-in-law elect to live in a Puritan atmosphere, whereas the orphan's surviving relatives remained Anglicans at heart.

The Oxenbridges answered Cromwell's requirement very well. The husband had been deprived of a tutorship at Magdalen Hall, Oxford, by Laud in 1634, had married Jane Butler, of gentle blood, and made with her two long sojourns in Bermudas. In 1641 he had returned to England so as to participate in the reformation of Church and State, and after having 'tumbled about' for over ten years, had settled at Eton before the end of 1652. His wife 'preached in the house among her gossips', as Anthony à Wood malevolently puts it; Marvell, in the Latin epitaph he was to write for her in 1658, relates the same fact with reverent nobility: 'Ipsa . . . antiqua modestia eandem animarum capturam domi, quam ille foris exercens. . . .' Still more than her husband she had been 'the first groundwork of the faction' of the Independents in Bermudas. After their return to England they had kept up their solicitude for the spiritual welfare of the islanders, and on 25 June 1653 he was made one of the seventeen commissioners entrusted with the government of the colony, from the metropolis of course.

The Oxenbridges would, no doubt, tell Marvell wonderful stories of the Bermudas, but these islands had already made their appearance in literature and the famous piece he wrote on them combines oral information with the descriptions in Edmund Waller's 'Battle of the Summer Islands' (1645). However, this laboured badinage in two cantos, on a fight between the colonists and two stranded whales, is very tiresome today; while Marvell's 'Bermudas' gives us in forty octosyllabics a model of nervous concision. This poetry does not describe for the mere pleasure of describing; through it breathes the Puritan spirit, wholly intent on God but here almost freed from the surliness to man that too often spoils it, and, far from its persecutors, reconciled with the Creation, with the luxuriant beauty of a land of sunshine, attaining joy.

The happy union of formal beauty and religious fervour here lies beyond question and has ensured a place for 'Bermudas' in almost every anthology since Thomas Campbell's in 1819. The trouble begins when the historian tries to check the poetic description of the islands point by point. Marvell's flora coincides with Waller's and lies open to the same doubts. What matters more, the spiritual condition of the islanders undergoes transfiguration; ever since Oxenbridge's arrival the inhabitants had been at loggerheads with him and one another, for persecution had not taught him tolerance: in June 1639, at the local assizes, one Vincent Sedgewicke was tried for having 'slanderously reported that Mr. John Oxenbridge should speake false Latine in the pulpitt'. Though a solecism in a learned language then affected a man's, and a clergyman's, reputation worse than it would now, this prosecution seems to denote a lack of humour as well as charity in the plaintiff. To preserve its significance 'Bermudas' should be heard from a great height. Thus Oxenbridge's individual adventure broadens so as to include the exodus of all the Puritans that left for America under James I and Charles I. Then the islands, rent by discords similar to those of the mother country but petty in proportion to their smallness, become a Utopia, not unlike the *Oceana* that a friend of Marvell's was soon to fashion, and adorned with recollections of the Golden Age. Who has worked the metamorphosis: the enthusiastic minister, deaf and blind to the protests of human weakness, or the dreamy poet for whom facts have only a symbolic value? At any rate this lyrical piece encloses in its coloured crystal the legend of Puritan emigration.

At no other time in his life do we find Marvell so much of a Puritan. Yet even then he was too versatile and open-minded to feel quite happy in the company of the Oxen-bridges unless he enjoyed an occasional break. He discovered the indispensable complement in the person of John Hales, the 'Ever Memorable' witness of the striving within the Anglican camp towards a broader comprehension and greater charity. His long career had begun thirty-five years before at the Synod of Dort where the Arminians had been crushed under the numbers rather than the arguments of the Gomarists. Leaving Dort, Hales had 'bid John Calvin good-night'. But unlike the Laudians he had seen in Arminius and Grotius's doctrine not an oppressive orthodoxy but a liberating aspiration. He had, indeed, according to his enemies, found an inspiration in the works of Socinus, whose bold spirit still worked as a ferment, more or less clandestinely, alike among the Catholics and all the Protestant Churches. Hales's audacity in a hitherto unpublished *Tract concerning Schism and Schismaticks* disturbed Laud, who summoned him to Lambeth. However, the explanation resulted in Hales's being made the Archbishop's chaplain. When the Press became free (for a short time) in 1642 the treatise appeared anonymously, and perhaps against the author's will. The true schismatics, Hales closely argues, are those who try to compel others of the faithful to act against their consciences, and thus make them leave the Church. Soberly written, with here and there a striking image, this treatise of sixteen pages nourished the controversies of a generation. We shall see Marvell transcribe it almost whole in one of his own pamphlets (1672). But the comment he then added proves that Hales's teaching did not come to him through the printed page alone: 'I account it no small honour to have grown up into some part of his acquaintance, and convers'd a while with the living remains of one of the clearest heads and best-prepared breasts in Christendom.'

Hales, when Marvell met him, had been deprived by the Parliamentarians of a fellowship of Eton College and a canonry of Windsor. He was compelled to sell his books at less than a third of what they had cost him, but it did not matter so much since he was himself 'a walking library', having published little but read continuously, and having a prodigious memory. Being as charitable as he was learned, he found himself short of ready money and accepted in 1653 a salary of £25 a year 'with his diet, in the family of one Madam Salter (sister . . . to Dr. Duppa bishop of Sarum) who lived near Eaton, purposely that he should instruct her son Will. Salter; but he being blockish, Hales could do nothing upon him'. This was at Ritchings, near Langley, a few miles north-east of Eton. Here probably[1] Marvell paid some visits to the sage, with William Dutton since

[1] Rather than at Eton, as I thought in 1928: see E. E. Duncan-Jones's letter in *T.L.S.*, 20 June 1958. On the other hand, Marvell's place of residence continued to be Eton, as confirmed by Noel Blakiston in his letter to *T.L.S.*, 8 February 1952: he signed leases of College houses there on 3 August 1654.

the boy's aunt by marriage, Mrs. Anne Dutton, John Dutton's wife, stayed in the house with her brother, Doctor Henry King, Bishop of Chichester (of course expelled from his See) and, what appealed more to Marvell, in his youth Donne's friend and poetical disciple. Ritchings was an Anglican stronghold where Marvell does not seem to have felt ill at ease. Hales was to leave it in November 1655 after Cromwell had issued a proclamation against harbouring malignants: he would not bring Mrs. Salter into trouble. He withdrew to the house of a former servant of his at Eton and died there on 19 May 1656. Marvell, as we shall see, had left England not later than January 1655/6 and could not attend the funeral, as did a small band of loyal friends.

Beside his breadth of theological outlook Hales may have imparted to Marvell his own one worldly taste; Aubrey uses almost the same words of the former biographee—'He loved Canarie; but moderately, to refresh his spirits'—as of the latter—'He kept bottles of wine at his lodgeing, and many times he would drinke liberally by himselfe to refresh his spirits and exalt his muse.' That Marvell's favourite wine, here unnamed, was also Canary may be inferred from lines in a poem he wrote the year after Hales's death, where the Canary Isles are described as 'the best of Lands':

> There the indulgent Soil that rich Grape breeds,
> Which of the Gods the fancied drink exceeds;

Aubrey indeed had jotted down a previous note: 'though [Marvell] loved wine he would never drink hard in company, and was wont to say that, *he would not play the good-fellow in any man's company in whose hands he would not trust his life*'; which implies that the taste developed in the disciple somewhat beyond the master's moderation. But this development probably took place near the end of Marvell's life when he had more powerful enemies in London than trusty friends. We are not surprised then to see one of those enemies call him, after his death, a drunken buffoon, 'temulentus scurra'. In the same year when this slander was published (1726) the editor of his *Works*, Thomas Cooke, thought it necessary to insert an attestation of temperance in the introduction, probably at the request and on the authority of Marvell's 'nieces' (probably great-nieces).[1]

Yet neither wine nor divinity, of whatever vintage or brand, could engross Marvell so completely that he did not continue to take a lively interest in politics. The winter of 1653/4 saw him again serving Cromwell's foreign policy with his Latin pen. The most important of three related pieces takes the form of a verse-letter to Nathaniel Ingelo, a fellow of Eton like Oxenbridge but of a very different temper. Marvell seems to have made his acquaintance at Eton, too late as he deplores in elegiacs. They had a common friend, Benjamin Rogers, a composer, and the love of music bound the three together. Rogers had been a 'singing man' of the royal chapel, and both he and Ingelo were to welcome the Restoration, for which they would compose an *Hymnus Eucharisticus*. But for the present they made the best of the Commonwealth. In September 1653, two or three months after Marvell's settling at Eton, Ingelo had agreed to accompany, as chaplain and *rector chori*, Bulstrode Whitelocke, one of the three Commissioners for the Custody of the Great Seal, and also Constable of Windsor Castle, when he was sent by the new Council of State, at Cromwell's suggestion, on an Embassy to Sweden. While Marvell's distichs begin and end with a lament for Ingelo's absence from the banks of the Thames—'Nos sine te frustra *Thamisis* saliceta subimus'—the greater part of the poem is devoted to an encomium of Queen Christina suitable to be shown, by Ingelo, if not by Whitelocke himself, to the young but prodigiously learned sovereign. Marvell, like the Ambassador, aims at proving that a Puritan can possess all the graces of a Cavalier. Whitelocke's skill as a dancer finally convinced the Queen. But the musical talents of his attendants had prepared this conversion and it may be that our poet's flattery had its share in it. In his verse the English Puritan spirit, before preaching a crusade, under the new Godfrey of Bulloigne,

---

[1] Marvell himself feared less for his reputation and jocularly alluded in his letters to the probable effect on him of gifts of liquor. See, for instance, the newly discovered letter to Sir Henry Thompson of 14 November 1676 in *T.L.S.*, 20 March 1959.

of all Protestant states against Popery and the Hapsburg
dynasty, grows gallant, even roguish; mythological comparisons make it possible boldly to extol Christina's charms
from her portrait; regretfully the poet abstains from unveil-
ing what the painter has hidden, and yet her *décolleté* appears
to have been fairly liberal since he only complains that he
can hardly see the whole of the Queen's 'Pectora'.

Not only in his own name does Marvell court Christina.
As Voltaire relates in his *Dictionnaire Philosophique*, when
Cromwell 'eut outragé tous les rois en fesant couper la tête
à son roi légitime, il envoya son portrait à une tête couronnée;
c'était à la reine de Suède Christine. Marvell, fameux poëte
anglais, qui fesait fort bien des vers latins, accompagna ce
portrait' with four elegiac distichs, the meaning of which
appeared 'hardi' to Voltaire (who thought that Cromwell
had corrected them!). Today we are impressed by their
audacity less than by the preciosity of the final conceit.
Cromwell, by this time Lord Protector, *loquitur*:

> At tibi submittit frontem reverentior *Umbra*,
> Nec sunt hi *Vultus* Regibus usque truces.

Marvell no doubt took his cue from the godly but crafty
Council of State; and he played his part in the diplomatic
campaign without constraint, thanks to his double nature
of wittily tender poet and earnest Protestant.

In his answer Ingelo could tell his friend that, after Cromwell, the most famous Englishman in Sweden was Milton:
not indeed the poet of *Comus* and *Lycidas* but the formidable
pamphleteer of the *Defensio pro Populo Anglicano*. And Marvell may have reported to Milton, from Ingelo, a compliment paid to that pamphlet by the Queen, which led to
the insertion of extravagant praise of great Gustavus'
daughter in the *Defensio Secunda*, then composing and to be
issued in May 1654. Among the first to receive presentation
copies were Bradshaw, Oxenbridge, and Marvell. To the
last-named Milton entrusted the delivery of Bradshaw's copy
since the former President of the Council of State now lived
at Eton, having voluntarily withdrawn from the management of public affairs. An unbending republican, he believed
that the ignominiously dismissed Rump still represented the

people of England. Cromwell, always conciliatory, would
have liked to win over such republicans to the Protectorate.
Milton, no less a republican than Bradshaw, tried to persuade him that a strong executive formed a necessary
counterpart to a legislative assembly. He wanted Marvell to
report how the recipient of the copy had taken the gift. It
appears that a first letter failed to tell the author—emphatic-
ally one of the *genus irritabile*—all he would know, so Marvell
wrote a second, dated 2 June 1654, which has been preserved and shows him as diplomatic with Milton as he had
been a year earlier with Cromwell. In case Bradshaw's rather
reserved reception of the book did not satisfy Milton, Marvell adds his own thanks 'with all Acknowledgement and
Humility'. He continues:

I shall now studie it even to the getting of it by Heart: esteeming
it according to my poor Judgement (which yet I wish it were so
right in all Things else) as the most compendious Scale, for so
much, to the Height of Roman eloquence. When I consider how
equally it turnes and rises with so many figures, it seems to me
a Trajans columne in whose winding ascent we see imboss'd the
several Monuments of your learned victoryes. And Salmatius and
Morus make up as great a Triumph as That of Decebalus, whom
too for ought I know you shall have forced as Trajan the other,
to make themselves away out of just Desperation.

Let us hope this letter contented the touchy great man's
thirst for praise. At any rate it shows us, under the conventional humility of epistolary form, the genuine respect
with which Marvell regarded Milton, less famous then in
his own country than abroad. Milton's nephew, Edward
Phillips, in his *Life* of his uncle (1694) lists the visitors who
between 1652 and 1660 frequented the house in Petty
France: Lady Ranelagh receives due precedence, followed
by 'all learned Foreigners of note' but Andrew Marvell
comes first of the English commoners, 'particular friends
that had a high esteem for him'; the others are 'young *Lau-
rence* (the son of him that was President of Oliver's Council)'
and 'above all Mr. *Cyriack Skinner*', whose genuine devotion
to the great blind man was rewarded by him in sonnets.
Unfortunately they are separated on the list by 'Mr *Marchamont Needham*, the writer of [*Mercurius*] *Politicus*', a rather

contemptible person as we have seen. Yet Milton must have believed in the lasting quality, if not in the high-mindedness, of Needham's republican faith. The confidence proved to have been misplaced, for the venal pen was to write for the Danby administration, some twenty years later, when it received from Marvell a severe but well-deserved rebuke. Nevertheless, this unlucky association between the two honest supporters of the Protectorate and a self-seeking one long remained a weapon in the hands of their enemies. As late as 1718 the Tory historian Lawrence Echard took advantage of Marvell and Needham's having died in the same year to connect them in one obituary: 'both pestilent Wits, and noted Incendiaries. But Mr. *Marvel*, having an Appearance of more Honesty and steadiness, is first mentioned'.

On 16 December 1654 Cromwell celebrated the first anniversary of his election, so called, to the Protectorate. For this occasion Marvell wrote a dithyrambic poem in English, his first effort on a large scale as Court poet. As in all his longer works the general composition is weak: this should be an annal of 1654, in itself a subject lacking unity of action, and Marvell does not keep within it at all strictly. Each paragraph, narrating a separate incident or developing an epic simile, flows well; it opens and closes with one or two forcible and high-sounding lines. But the transitions are either missing or clumsy. The order, now logical, now chronological, entails iteration.[1] Actually the matter of the poem falls into two divisions: one part looks abroad, the other looks at England.

As regards foreign affairs it enlarges upon the ideas expressed in the epistle to Ingelo. Having made peace with

---

[1] James F. Carens, 'Andrew Marvell's Cromwell Poems', in *Bucknell Review*, 1957, pp. 41–70, who devotes most of his space and energy to 'The First Anniversary', discovers in it 'an intricately patterned metaphysical imagery', so that 'all the elements of the poem . . . are drawn together and fused by an imagery that is completely in the poet's control' (pp. 55–56). Less hazily J. A. Mazzeo, 'Cromwell as Davidic King', in *Reason and Imagination*, 1962, pp. 29–55, also tries to provide a central motif for 'The First Anniversary'; his interpretation of it is a worthy continuation to that of 'An Horatian Ode' (see p. 17, n. 1), no less lucid and vigorous but also somewhat forced. An unfortunate confusion between Gibeon and Gideon (p. 52) does not, however, affect his demonstration materially.

Holland and tightened as much as possible the bonds between England and Sweden but failed to organize a Protestant Crusade, Cromwell has decided to attack Spain, and to do so in the most vulnerable part of her empire, the West Indies. This enterprise, most questionable morally and politically rash, rouses Marvell's enthusiasm. And he seems to have privileged information of the Protector's design, still wrapped in mystery, since he symbolically calls up in the New World General William Penn's fleet, which was to sail three days later from Portsmouth with sealed orders, while the attempt on San Domingo would be known to Englishmen as well as to other Europeans only in March 1655. Marvell congratulates Cromwell because 'He Secrecy with Number hath inchas'd', which means in plain English that he has begun hostilities with great armaments without declaring war (doubtless on the old principle: 'no peace beyond the Line', Pope Alexander VI's Line). No poem of Marvell's contains more biblical allusions and quotations, chiefly from the Old Testament and Revelation, which is typical of the Puritan; no poem of his breathes a more bellicose spirit, none is, to borrow the language of the nineteenth century, more imperialistic.

If the poet chides foreign monarchs with great confidence he lectures his fellow-countrymen even more harshly, and the choice of the English language shows that the poem is really aimed at them. He wants to convince them of the superiority of the Protectorate over all other forms of government; the attacks on kings, though aimed at foreign princes, probably Louis XIV of France and Philip IV of Spain, also hit the Stuarts. The political propagandist does not even scruple to wrench Scripture slightly in a comparison between Charles I and Ahab: both uxorious husbands of idolatrous wives (but that is implicit) they neglected the 'small cloud like a Mans hand' in the sky, which eventually 'wet' both kings. In fact Ahab had listened to Elijah for the nonce and taken shelter (1 Kings xviii. 44–46) while, applied to the Royal Martyr, the metaphor sounds somewhat of a euphemism.

Yet those dissuasives addressed to the persistent Royalists may come in here chiefly for the sake of political balance:

Marvell's chief concern is with the Protector's other enemies, those who do not forgive him the dismissal of the Rump. Three times does the poet justify this illegal but necessary step. He derides the 'tedious Statesmen' who 'many years did hack—Framing a Liberty that still went back'; he denounces the avarice of those

> Whose num'rous Gorge could swallow in an hour
> That Island, which the Sea cannot devour:

Military dictatorship is vindicated by a biblical precedent, Gideon's suppression of Penuel and Succoth. Then a nautical comparison assimilates Cromwell to the 'lusty Mate' who, in a tempest, 'The Helm does from the artless Steersman strain', and takes the ship away from 'the fatal Shore'.[1] What matter if the 'giddy' passengers 'a while . . . grumble discontent'?

After rightful violence against a spurious liberty there has come a constructive policy. Amphion-like, Cromwell has raised from the earth a new city where religion of course occupies the first place. Uniformity is unnecessary provided each one keeps his place; 'the crossest Spirits' consolidate the fabric through their very opposition, but the true pillars of the State are 'the most Equal', possibly recruited from among the constitutional monarchists; 'a Senate free'—an unconsciously ironic appellation for the Protector's first Parliament—serves as a basis. The English enjoy all possible liberty 'but more they vainly crave'. The Levellers, did not Cromwell keep them in awe, would soon, like Jotham's brambles, have devoured the cedars. Worst of all, religious sects swarm and their impudence knows no bounds. The poet, satirical even in the dithyramb, rails at those Puritans guilty of a *reductio ad absurdum* of the very principles of Puritanism; he loses his temper and no lines of his later satires will surpass in violent abuse the tirade beginning

> Accursed Locusts, whom your King does spit
> Out of the Center of th' unbottomed Pit;

[1] John M. Wallace, 'Marvell's "lusty Mate" and the Ship of the Commonwealth', in *M.L.N.*, 1961, pp. 106–10, tells the rather confused history of this simile from *Vindiciae Contra Tyrannos* to Marvell, who applies it in an entirely original manner. Wallace may be right in interpreting it here as an attack on Barebone's Parliament, but this was officially supposed to have withdrawn spontaneously.

There are united in the same reprobation the Anabaptists, the Fifth Monarchy men, the Adamites, and even the Quakers who 'Tremble one fit more' because of the Protector's recovery after the accident in Hyde Park, when his team of six horses upset the coach he was himself driving. Though three months old and already sung by several poets, friendly or hostile, this event could not be left out by Marvell, and in fact it holds an important place in his poem, where it assumes a symbolic value: the sins of the English people, their intractability, almost brought down on them the worst of calamities: the loss of their master.

Yet Cromwell will not be king. So at least thinks Marvell, who praises him for it, with Jotham's apologue again as his text, and with a pun on the olive-tree, which refused to reign over the trees. In a clever antithetic couplet the poet seeks to persuade his fellow-countrymen that the Protectoral régime conciliates the necessity of upholding the prestige of England and the respect for republican principles:

> Abroad a King he seems, and something more,
> At Home a Subject on the equal Floor.

Here, after a complete blank for the year 1655, intervenes an episode in Marvell's career that opens most interesting vistas. Unfortunately he has not left the least record of it himself; and, since it came to our knowledge, thirteen years ago, patient research has yielded just enough fruit to tantalize us.[1] Marvell and Dutton are found in France, at Saumur on the Loire, in 1656, still in their relation of tutor or 'gouverneur' and pupil. By this time William may have been sixteen years old, hardly ripe to attend the courses of the famous Protestant Académie (a university without the name, and limited to the Arts, Philosophy, and Divinity); even his admission, for less than a scholastic year, into the Collège (grammar-school) subordinate to the Académie appears improbable, though foreign pupils and students came to both from all over Europe, including England. But the intellectual atmosphere of the town was strongly Protestant,

---

[1] The discovery itself and most of the subsequent research are due to E. E. Duncan-Jones; see her letters to *T.L.S.*, 2 December 1949, 13 January 1950, 31 July 1953, 20 June 1958.

even though the Protestants were in a minority. On the other hand, Saumur lies just west of Touraine, where the best French was supposed to be spoken. Lastly the local wine already enjoyed a high reputation. Marvell may have passed or even stayed there during his first visit to France and recommended it when Cromwell decided to send his prospective son-in-law abroad. This marriage scheme, by the way, was so well-known to the French that, as an English Royalist, James Scudamore, tells us, they called Dutton 'le genre [*sic*] du Protecteur' by anticipation.[1] This put Marvell very much in the public eye but made his position delicate, for all French Protestants had professed, and most felt, indignation at the Regicide. The Académie of Saumur particularly had seized this opportunity of reiterating its unconditional loyalty to the French monarchy; even if it conceded to the English Presbyterians, closest in every respect to the French Réformés, that the English monarchy had from time immemorial been limited by the rights of Parliament, the Académie, and especially its most renowned divine, Moïse Amyrault, had denounced the usurpation of the Independents and its bloody consequences. Marvell must have been hard put to it to defend his patron on this count, but he did not shirk discussion if, as looks most likely,[2] he is the friend of Milton's who passed round the learned circles of Saumur a copy of the *Pro se Defensio*, published the year before and consisting of coarse personal invective, in choice Latin, against the Scoto-French minister Alexander Morus. The friend reported that it was well received, which made Milton send several copies the next year, through Henry Oldenburg, for free distribution; but Marvell (if it be he) must have been unduly sanguine since Oldenburg had to confess to Milton that he had thought it wiser not to present the copies. Yet this coolness may have resulted from a disinclination to pursue a controversy that had become tedious.

[1] Marvell himself, James Scudamore calls 'a notable English Italo-Machavillian'. Curiously enough Joseph E. Mazzeo (*v. supra*, p. 17, n. 1) does not quote this appreciation. Scudamore, a disreputable character, may have used the phrase irresponsibly; yet it confirms our impression that Marvell, soon after leaving Fairfax's household, had done something more than merely tutoring Dutton to disappoint and anger the Cavaliers.

[2] See E. E. Duncan-Jones's letter to *T.L.S.*, 31 July 1953, p. 493.

At any rate we know for certain that a comparatively charitable temper prevailed at Saumur; Protestants and Roman Catholics there maintained courteous, nay friendly relations. The Oratorians, progressive in education and philosophy, and tolerant in religion, had not only a Collège for boys in town but an Institution, i.e. a sort of higher seminary, just outside Saumur, at Notre-Dame des Ardilliers. There is some reason to think that Marvell became acquainted with the Father Superior, Abel-Louis de Sainte-Marthe, the not unworthy descendant of learned ancestors, who was to become, before Marvell's death, the General of his Congregation.[1] And even in the absence of any document we consider it as probable that the English visitor met a local physician, Doctor Louis de la Forge, remembered today as a pioneer of Cartesian philosophy, which he tried, not without success, to plant at the Oratorians' house and which, though himself a Roman Catholic, he was to help to triumph at the Protestant Académie a few years later. One last conjecture: Marvell may have met, at a small manor-house called Château des Réaux, a few miles from Saumur, Tallemant, the collector of *Historiettes*, a Protestant by birth and education but by temperament a *libertin* and *bon vivant*. They may have discussed Rabelais and bandied jolly stories, which, after the sobriety of Saumur, must have proved a welcome relaxation for Dutton's tutor.[2] All these various influences must have begun to qualify his Puritan fervour, apparently at its highest when he left Eton for France.

How long did Marvell and Dutton stay on the banks of the Loire? They had arrived by the end of January 1655/6; they were still at Saumur in August 1656; probably they

---

[1] See 'Marvell and "the two learned brothers of St. Marthe"', in *Philological Quarterly*, 1959, pp. 450–8. This article is an offshoot of a lecture (first given at Princeton in 1957 and yet unpublished) on 'Saumur as Marvell saw it'.

[2] See 'La Purge de Gargantua ou Marvell et Tallemant des Réaux', in *Études Anglaises*, 1953, pp. 236–8. For a possible introducer of the Englishman to the Frenchman see E. E. Duncan-Jones, 'New Allusions to Marvell', in *T.L.S.*, 20 June 1958, p. 345. Since then Mrs. Duncan-Jones has found evidence pointing to a possible connexion between Marvell and Tallemant through Williamson (later Sir Joseph), the London bookseller Humphrey Robinson, and the Saumur bookseller Lerpinière.

left in September when the academic year ended. But of
Marvell's whereabouts for the next twelvemonth we know
nothing. Yet it appears likely that he had returned to England, still in Dutton's company, when he wrote his next
official poem in June or July 1657: 'On the Victory obtained by Blake over the Spaniards, in the Bay of Santacruze,
in the Island of Teneriff'. Our poet had a fine opportunity,
of which he made little. Not for lack of patriotic fervour,
nor of interest in maritime affairs, since in his poem preceding this he had written: 'The Ocean is the Fountain of Command', a thought less trite then in England than it became
soon after. But in addition to puns and conceits unworthy
of the occasion this poem has a faint obsequious reek. The
real conqueror, though named in the title, withdraws into
the background. Marvell has eyes only for Cromwell; he
repeats again and again that his genius wins battles from
afar, and the last line shows us Fame blowing her trumpet
to praise Cromwell. Spain is charged, in the face of patent
facts, with having broken the peace, and the Puritan does
not scruple to recommend, no doubt as an indemnity, the
annexation of the Canaries:

> The best of Lands should have the best of Kings.

The Protector had just declined a new proposal to assume
the Crown, and this refusal was to prove final. But now
Marvell ranked himself among those who wished and hoped
to see Oliver accept kingship. He did not hesitate to give
him a title that was ostensibly unwanted.

That same year Marvell at last obtained the post he had
vainly applied for in 1652/3 and was made Latin Secretary.
When, under the Restoration, he was upbraided for having
served the Usurper, he answered, not without mental
reservation:

I never had any, not the remotest relation to publick matters, nor
correspondence with the persons then predominant, until the
year 1657, when indeed I enter'd into an employment, for which
I was not altogether improper, and which I consider'd to be the
most innocent and inoffensive toward his Majestie's affairs of any
in that usurped and irregular government, to which all men were

then exposed. And this I accordingly discharg'd without dis-
obliging any one person, there having been opportunity and
endeavours, since his Majestie's happy return, to have discover'd
had it been otherwise.

The words 'relation' and 'correspondence' are here used by
Marvell in a singularly restricted sense, and his explanation
of his choice of that particular official employment looks
very much like an afterthought. In fact he had developed
gradually not only admiration but love for Cromwell.

The administrative occasion of Marvell's appointment
does not clearly appear but we know that it took effect from
2 September 1657. Though they both drew—with long
delays—the same salary, viz. £200 a year—Marvell's position never equalled Milton's, as regards either fixity of
tenure or independence from Thurloe, the Secretary of State
and Cromwell's right-hand man. Nor did he attend the
sittings of the Privy Council as Milton had attended those
of the Council of State. No document even shows that he
attended those of the select Committee for Foreign Affairs.
But a few hints of the sort of work he was entrusted with
have come down to us. For instance, the Scottish 'Guinea
Company' had petitioned the Council against ill-treatment
by the Portuguese governor of San Tome; Thurloe an-
notates: 'Mr Marvill. I desire you to write a Letter upon this
petition to yᵉ K. of Portugall.' Lovelace's quondam friend
was also marked out by the elegance of his manners no less
than by his attainments as a linguist to attend foreign
Ambassadors or Envoys on their arrival in England, and
a despatch from one of these to his government, Their High
Mightinesses the States General of the United Provinces,
mentions him in that capacity. Once he received at the
Secretary's office the agent in London of the Elector of
Brandenburg, but only because of his chief's pretending
illness in order to avoid giving an answer, the Protector
himself then being in the throes of death.

Marvell's duties, modest so far, enabled him to obtain
a working knowledge of political affairs. In opposition under
the Restoration he was to judge those in power severely,
because he had been acquainted at first hand with an

executive that administered and governed incorruptibly and efficiently.

And he came closer and closer to the Protectoral family. He sang in verse the marriage of Mary Cromwell, Oliver's third daughter, with Thomas Belasyse, Viscount Fauconberg, solemnized on 19 November 1657. This nobleman, of a Royalist family but too young to have taken part in the Civil War, had easily obtained the hand of the quasi-princess, not at all Puritanically inclined. But poetic convention as well as Marvell's admiration for the Protector demanded that the suitor's humility and the boldness of his suit should be exaggerated. Using the names of Endymion and Cynthia (but reversing the position of the two as regards initiative in love) Marvell shows us the 'mortal', the 'shepherd', rebuked by the scornful goddess. But Endymion expresses such glowing thoughts, reminiscent of Donne, that Cynthia begins to relent. The Chorus encourages the suitor by quoting a precedent:

> *Anchises* was a *Shepheard* too;
> Yet is her *younger Sister* laid
> Sporting with him in *Ida's shade*:

For Frances Cromwell, once William Dutton's *fiancée malgré elle*, had succeeded in marrying, eight days earlier, young Robert Rich, the Earl of Warwick's grandson (after taking, it seems, the boldest step in order to make this marriage necessary). Marvell does not seem to have his former pupil's disappointment very much at heart.

Eventually, not only is Cynthia persuaded but also Jove, alias Oliver; he gives his consent,

> For he did never love to pair
> His Progeny above the Air;

rather surprising of Jove, but a possible allusion to the King of Scots whom gossip represented as having been ready to marry the lively Frances Cromwell in order to regain the throne of the Royal Martyr.

That pastoral dialogue, with a Chorus, and another one composed for the same occasion, belong to the same revival of interest in the drama as Davenant's *Entertainment at Rutland House* (May 1656): it is also an attempt, though on a much smaller scale, to reconcile Puritanism and the stage, on the lines laid down by *Comus*, with music as an excuse for acting. The Restoration was to put an end to that sort of compromise, and to Marvell's dramatic efforts as well, though he, unlike the true Saints, did not scruple to attend performances and borrow jests from plays, even from licentious comedies, as his own prose pamphlets testify.

But the Protectorate, apparently so well-established, was drawing to its end. On 3 September 1658 Oliver, not yet sixty, died. Marvell, moved by sorrow, wrote the last and finest of his official poems, if the epithet 'official' can be applied to a piece so touching, so heart-felt, and so free from the political preoccupations that filled the preceding ones.

True, neither the satirist nor the wit are quite silenced by grief. The former again hits out at the extreme Puritans, more difficult to rule than 'the worser sort', i.e. the unregenerate masses; for 'to the good (too many or too few)— All law is uselesse, all reward is due'. The latter brings in a few hyperbolical conceits, as:

> Numbers of *Men* decrease with pains unknown,
> And hasten not to see his Death their own.

But mythology hardly appears; and the Bible, though sometimes used for comparisons, occupies no such position here as in 'The First Anniversary'. Marvell writes less as the admirer of a great man than as a friend mourning for a friend.

In 1654 when the poet praised Cromwell's mother, just deceased, he expressed himself with banal elegance. In 1657 a more personal accent was already heard in his rejoicing at Mary Cromwell's happiness. This time Oliver's favourite daughter Elizabeth and her children are mentioned as by one who knew them. Marvell, a lover of music as we know, probably attended those family gatherings in which 'Francisca faire . . . with soft notes' sang her father's 'cares asleep'. At any rate the Latin Secretary, among other observant courtiers, attended the Protector's levee; he beheld 'that awfull state . . . always temper'd with an aire so mild,—No April sunns that e'er so gently smil'd;' he now laments that 'we'

> No more shall heare that powerful language charm,
> Whose force oft spar'd the labour of his arm:
> No more shall follow where he spent the dayes
> In warre, in counsell, or in pray'r and praise;
> Whose meanest acts he would himself advance,
> As ungirt David to the arke did dance.
> All, all is gone of ours or his delight
> In horses fierce, wild deer, or armour bright;

Here is a simple and pleasant picture, drawn by an eye-witness of Cromwell's daily life.

From the start the victorious soldier and the head of the State are deliberately thrown into the background; in the foreground shines the father of a family, kind and even tender, religious without any political ulterior motive, 'whom Nature all for Peace had made', and who

> Deserved yet an End whose ev'ry part
> Should speak the wondrous softness of his Heart.

He 'impetuously' follows in death his daughter 'Eliza' (departed on 6 August) since his own life was 'suspended by her breath'.

Nature now expresses her grief by classical convulsions. The stars choose for the fatal day the anniversary of Dunbar and Worcester, a choice that occasions a brief retrospect of the career of the hero who was also a saint. But nothing arrests us so much as the personal note:

> I saw him dead, a leaden slumber lyes,
> And mortal sleep over those wakefull eyes:
> Those gentle rays under the lids were fled,
> That through his looks that piercing sweetnesse shed;
> That part which so majestic was and strong,
> Loose and depriv'd of vigour, stretch'd along:
> All wither'd, all discolour'd, pale and wan,
> How much another thing, no more that man?

The Virgilian echo in the last line should not make us consider the grief as conventional.

Several poets extolled the Protector when alive and mourned for him at his death. Among them Marvell passed almost unnoticed; alone his 'First Anniversary' was printed (anonymously) at the time. One or two other pieces may have been read to Oliver or Richard Cromwell, but neither the father nor the son nor the general public would have thought of weighing them against Waller's, whose reputation as a poet then reached its zenith, though his character was justly despised. Yet, cowardly as he had shown himself to be, Waller clearly and strongly felt England's greatness under Oliver, and he knew how to express it in a manly style. His 'Panegyrick To My Lord Protector' (1655), which corresponds to Marvell's 'First Anniversary', surpasses it in loftiness and concentration. It voices national pride better, because in a simpler, broader way: an involved manner hardly suits a great commonplace. Waller's 'Of a War with Spain and a Fight at Sea' not only precedes 'On the Victory obtained by Blake' (it was not printed until April 1658, yet Marvell may well have seen it in a manuscript copy) but exceeds it in dignity; it treats the defeated enemy courteously and flatters the Protector less outrageously, doing more justice to the English sailors. But when Cromwell had relinquished both power and life Waller did not exert his poetic powers; 'Upon the late Storme, and of the death of his Highness Ensuing the same' has no other merit than conciseness. Its thirty-four lines served George Wither as a text for a composition twenty times that length; from its painfully prolix tittle-tattle a few lines survive to express, neatly if not vigorously, a judgement on Cromwell's role very similar to that found in the 'Horatian Ode', save that God takes the place of Fate:

> He had not gone,
> But that the work ordain'd for him was done.
> God rais'd him, by Destroying, to prepare
> A way for that which he intends to rear,

Dryden's 'Heroique Stanza's Consecrated to the Glorious Memory of His . . . Highness Oliver . . .', in a very different style, give Cromwell his due as a statesman, but their author had not enjoyed the same opportunities as Marvell of

appreciating the man, so that the 'Poem on the Death of O.C.'
easily surpasses the 'Heroique Stanza's', both as a document
and as the product of human emotion. We can leave out of
this poetic competition 'Pindaric Sprat', whose height of
thought and elegance of form may be judged from this one
couplet:

> A work which none but Heaven and thee could do
> Thou mad'st us happie wh're we would or no.

Yet this 'Pindarick Ode' had the honour of publication with
Waller's and Dryden's funeral poems under the collective
title of *Three Poems Upon the Death of his Late Highness Oliver
Lord Protector of England, Scotland, and Ireland*, London, 1659.
Marvell's poem was not included.[1]

With the help of Marvell's poems we have drawn the
curve of his feelings for Cromwell between 1650 and 1658.
Let us say at once that the inglorious collapse of the Protectoral régime did not cause our poet to renounce his hero.
He was to wear mourning for Oliver, not only on the day
of the funeral in six yards of black cloth allowed to him as
to Milton (but denied to 'Drayden') by the Privy Council,
but also in his heart all his life long, opposing England's
greatness under 'Old Noll' to her abjection under Charles II.
Starting with the 'Horatian Ode' from admiration in the
Latin meaning of the term Marvell passed to approving
admiration in 'The First Anniversary'; then in the funeral
elegy love adds its intimate note; when time has put the
object in perspective veneration subsists, but with an alloy
of anger against those who have undone what Cromwell had
done. Of these four modes of judging, neither the last, at
most hinted casually in one satire, nor the second, set forth
at length, belong to Marvell more than to several others.
On the contrary, the first and third modes are found in him

---

[1] Yet Hugh Macdonald, *John Dryden A Bibliography* . . ., 1939, pp. 3–4,
has revealed the interesting fact that Henry Herringman, the publisher, had
entered in the *Stationers' Register*, on 20 January, 'a booke called *Three poems
to the happy memory of the most renowned Oliver, late Lord Protector of this Commonwealth*, by Mr. Marvell, Mr. Driden, Mr. Sprat'. But Herringman gave up
this venture, and a little known 'printer', William Wilson, took it up, substituting Waller's poem for Marvell's.

only, at any rate in noble verse: the one owes its exceptional quality to the intelligence, the other to the feeling, informing them. How then can we account for the paradox that the 'Horatian Ode' has achieved popularity while the 'Poem on the Death of O.C.' survives only for those who haunt the by-ways of literature? But this victory in the public taste of reason over feeling was won only with the help of feeling: the average Englishman of the nineteenth century (and perhaps this remains true of the twentieth) saw in Charles I the hero of the 'Ode', and his emotions were aroused; he learnt by heart the three stanzas that describe the King's execution and read the rest listlessly. Besides, the formal beauty of the 'Ode' helps the reader to swallow its hard moral, even though this may be imperfectly understood. The funeral elegy, longer, more unequal, inflated here, short-winded there, discourages the ordinary reader who would relish its pathos. Yet it does not deserve this neglect; unique as the 'Ode' is in its approach, the elegy is of much greater value as a document on Cromwell.

It has been said of Marvell that he 'played the part of Laureate during the Protectorate', a phrase more ingenious than accurate. This might apply to 'The First Anniversary', where the poet writes as a panegyrist, but not to the 'Ode', where he writes judicially, nor to the funeral elegy, where he writes emotionally. Better leave the quasi-official title to Waller, or else (with Anthony à Wood) to 'Paganus Piscator', alias Payne Fisher, and call Marvell by a nobler title—Cromwell's poet. Even if he had composed nothing but the pieces on Oliver Cromwell, he would deserve no mean place in the poetry and history of England.[1]

---

[1] Perhaps this is the best place to mention Christopher Hill's 'Society and Andrew Marvell', in *The Modern Quarterly*, 1946, pp. 6–31, since this article purposes 'to consider the poetry of Marvell in relation to the age in which he lived' and limits this age to the Interregnum. This rather immature essay has since been republished, apparently unchanged, in *Puritanism and Revolution*, 1958, and again, under the title 'Andrew Marvell and the Good Old Cause' in *Mainstream*, January 1959, pp. 1–27. It contains a number of inaccuracies and many rash assertions in an attempt to fit Marvell's politics into the recognized pattern of Marxist 'dialectic'. Dennis Davison's 'Marvell and Politics', in *Notes and Queries*, May 1955, pp. 201*a*–2*b*, mostly reviews former estimates, some of them fantastic.

V

THE MEMBER FOR HULL

FROM 1659 to his death in 1678 Marvell sat for Hull in three successive Parliaments. This gives to the last twenty years of his life a relative unity, crossed by episodes like his voyage to Russia, complicated by an extra-parliamentary activity that assumed the form of writings anonymous or acknowledged; a unity sufficient nevertheless to make it preferable not to subdivide this period.

The two years that separate Oliver's death from the Restoration constitute for the historian either an epilogue or a prologue. This general duality is reflected in Marvell's life: he continued Latin Secretary for over a year but he also served in Parliament a three months' apprenticeship, instructive though compromising.

Some mystery surrounds Marvell's first election. According to Ludlow, a partial but honest witness, a majority of the burgesses were said to have given their votes to the candidate of the republican Opposition, Sir Henry Vane, who had sat for Hull in the Long Parliament; but the 'officers' of the new Protector, among whom we note Edmund Popple, Marvell's brother-in-law, then Sheriff of the town, 'refused to return him'. Various facts seem to give some substance to the rumour reported by Ludlow. And though the case for Marvell's retrospective unseating remains 'not proven' we can freely concede that he had as much official backing as any other governmental candidate, and that meant a good deal. But while he had spent little time at Hull for sixteen years his father's long services and moving death must have told in his favour.

However that may be, Marvell's loyalty answered to Richard Cromwell's expectations. The poet had hailed the new Protector at the end of his funeral elegy of his predecessor, in the most approved dynastic style. The Secretary now reveals, in a letter addressed (11 February 1658/9) to the English diplomatic agent at The Hague, George Downing, what the Member of Parliament thinks of the doctrinaire Opposition: 'They speak eternally . . . in all the tricks of Parliament', and, while admitting that 'they have much the odds' in eloquence, expresses this hope: 'our justice our affection and our number which is at least two thirds will weare them out at the long runne'. In a second letter (25 March 1659) he rejoices at a Government success in a division, yet expresses fear of forthcoming petitions in a way that shows him ready to make short work of the independence of Parliament and the rights of the subject.

Marvell's hopes in Richard were soon disappointed: the young Protector, under compulsion from the Army, dissolved his Parliament on 22 April. On 7 May the Rump resumed its sittings at Westminster, with Sir Henry Vane as its Member for Hull.[1] In June the Corporation of that borough sent the new régime an address of congratulation, thus disowning Marvell and making amends to his opponent, who was to the end of that year 1659 the most influential civilian in England. Be it said to his praise, he did not take advantage of his new power to revenge himself. While Thurloe drew aside for a while Marvell, like Milton, retained his position. He was even granted (14 July) lodgings in Whitehall. After 25 October, when the Council of State held its last sitting (the Rump had just been expelled again by the Army) and ordered its own servants to be paid their salaries due to date, Marvell's administrative fate, like Milton's, becomes obscure. But they may well have weathered the various political storms of the next Winter, though Milton's position at least must have become difficult when Monck compelled the Rump to readmit the Presbyterian royalists ejected by Pride's Purge (21 February 1659/60).

The polling at Hull for the Convention resulted in Marvell's return (2 April 1660) as the junior member, very far

---

[1] L. N. Wall has sent me a transcript of the letter, dated 10 May 1659, by which Vane informed his constituents that God had by his 'mighty and wonderfull hand, restored' the Rump; he admitted that in the recent election 'through the practises of some and the Influence of [the] Court party, The Major part went' against him. This partly confirms and partly refutes Ludlow's story. (Calendar of the ancient deeds, letters, &c. in the Archives of the Corporation. Kingston-upon-Hull, 1951, L. 635.)

behind John Ramsden, a friend of his, but just as far ahead of the candidate of the Good Old Cause, a republican Anabaptist colonel cashiered by Oliver for political reasons. Hull, it seems, adopted an expectant policy. But the Convention as a whole was ardently royalist, though at the start rather Presbyterian than Episcopalian. Marvell does not seem to have felt ill at ease there, for many of his fellow members had a more compromising political past than his. No document tells us what he thought at the time but he probably accepted the Restoration as the only possible solution of the crisis opened at Oliver's death. Nor did the Restoration inflict upon him any severer penalty than the task of composing a Latin answer to a letter of congratulation from the Elector Palatine, first cousin to the restored monarch (23 July 1660).

Yet Marvell had cause to fear, if not for himself, at any rate for Milton. That he exerted himself in favour of his friend and colleague we know, though how he did it remains doubtful. When Milton's life was no longer in jeopardy Marvell again intervened, this time openly in the House of Commons (17 December 1660), to have him released from prison without paying the extortionate fees demanded by the Sergeant-at-arms. The Attorney-General, Sir Heneage Finch, on whom Marvell was to retaliate in a satire, answered 'that Milton had been Latin Secretary to Cromwell, and deserved hanging', a retort that seems to have been meant to frighten Marvell, a sharer in this offence, since Finch might have proffered far more heinous charges against the author of *Eikonoclastes*.

In spite of these reminders, bantering or malicious, of his former official employment, Marvell's opinion seems to have carried some weight. He was for instance chosen by a select committee to report, favourably, on a Bill 'for erecting and endowing vicarages out of impropriate rectories' (15 and 27 November). On this moderate and yet far-reaching reform many Episcopalians were able to reach agreement with the Presbyterians, and the Bill indeed went up from the Commons to the Lords, but they allowed it to sleep until the dissolution (29 December) put an end to it. Even more characteristic of Marvell's interest in religious affairs was his acting as teller for the ayes in the decisive division on the 'Bill for enacting his Majesty's declaration' at Breda, promising indulgence to the Protestant Nonconformists. The Bill was defeated, though by a fairly narrow margin; the House of Commons thus showed itself less liberal than the King, with whom Marvell sided on this occasion. This incident prepares us to understand his action twelve years later in the same cause.

The interval between the Convention and the Cavalier Parliament provides a suitable resting-place for defining Marvell's position as Member for Hull, its advantages and its dangers.

Even if, as his first biographer in print asserts, he had 'a small paternal estate' left to him and neither 'diminished it by any extravagance' nor 'took . . . care to increase' it, he can hardly be described as of independent means at any time since his first acceptance of a tutorship. Now, under the Restoration, he is not known to have earned any money save his parliamentary stipend, or 'knight's pence'. Since this amounted only to 6s. 8d. per day, and that only when Parliament sat (the inter-sessions lasted longer than the sessions), most members gave up these emoluments as beneath their acceptance. Yet Marvell, contrary to a legend, was not the only member nor the last, to draw this modest remuneration,[1] called by his arch-enemy 'erogatam in pauperes Eleemosynam'. Even if we add to it occasional gifts of ale by the Hull Corporation we are still at a loss to know how Marvell lived: certainly he had never tried 'to live upon poetry' and failed, as a hostile pamphlet suggested in the last year of his life. We do know that his brother-in-law Edmund Popple had risen to a prominent position among the Hull merchants,[2] and that his favourite nephew, William Popple, first in London and from 1670 at Bordeaux, seemed on his way to do well also. As we shall see, Marvell had

[1] The whole problem is dealt with by R. C. Latham, 'Parliamentary Wages—The Last Phase', in *English Historical Review*, January 1951.

[2] Marvell was also connected with Humphrey Duncalfe, Mayor of Hull in 1668-9. See L. N. Wall, 'A Note on Marvell's Letters', in *N.Q.*, March 1958, p. 111.

dealings with other moneyed men in London or Yorkshire, more or less remotely related to him, and he may have received financial support from them, as a suspicious witness asserted after his death.[1] On the other hand, there is evidence, though only of a traditional kind, that the Government offered him a bribe if he would back their policy. The oldest form of the anecdote, and the least untrustworthy, shows Thomas Osborne, Earl of Danby, Lord Treasurer from June 1673, calling in person, by the King's command, on Marvell, 'who then lodged up two Pair of Stairs in a little Court in the *Strand*', and 'telling him that he came with a Message from his Majesty, which was to know what he could do to serve him'. Marvell answered first 'in his usual facetious way', and then seriously declined, on grounds of principle, to accept any favour from the King, either a place at Court or an order on the Treasury for a thousand pounds, 'tho, as soon as the Lord Treasurer was gone, he was forced to send to a Friend to borrow a Guinea'. This last detail, by the way, hardly agrees with the assertion, by the same editor and biographer, Thomas Cooke (1726), that Marvell always lived within his 'small patrimony'. Later in the eighteenth century legendary additions were made, including the famous dialogue between the incorruptible patriot and his servant-boy in the presence of the Lord Treasurer: 'Jack, child, what had I for dinner yesterday?' 'Don't you remember, sir? You had the little shoulder of mutton that you ordered me to bring from a woman in the market.' 'Very right, child. What have I for dinner today?' 'Don't you know, sir, that you bid me lay by the blade-bone to broil?' ' 'Tis so, very right, child, go away.' And Marvell draws the obvious lesson for the crushed Lord Treasurer. In the eighteenth century such honest poverty inevitably called up Curius Dentatus and his turnips. Today these vegetables and the blade-bone as well are relegated to the category of symbols. That the Government, and in particular Danby, Walpole's forerunner in this respect, should have tried to turn an annoying opponent into a useful supporter sounds most likely; that they must have failed is equally certain.

---

[1] In the lawsuit referred to *infra*, pp. 148–9. His name was John Farrington: he wanted to prove that Marvell had left no property.

In the later form of the anecdote Marvell's lodging becomes 'a garret'. This again looks more picturesque than accurate. He seems to have lived mostly 'in Maiden Lane, in Covent Garden'. But from 1673 we get a glimpse of him as the owner or leaseholder of a house in the then still rural Highgate, five miles from Westminster, and, therefore, too far for him to spend the night there after a day in the House of Commons; but when idle he withdrew there: in one letter he explains that he wants 'to injoy the spring and [his] privacy'. 'Marvell's cottage', which was pulled down in 1869, stood in a garden. Was he quite alone there, with only a servant-boy? Here we come up against the problem of 'Mary Marvell', the poet's 'wife'; that she was a fraud, and a posthumous one, has been argued with a high degree of probability, rather to the relief of his admirers; and Mary Palmer, who assumed the poet's surname for a time after his death, has been reduced from the status of a spouse to that of a (London) landlady, by 1667 (the year she gave as that of her marriage with Marvell) the widow of a tennis-court keeper who had died in poverty and the mother of several children. Yet she has achieved immortality by signing the brief and modest 'To the Reader' of the first edition of the *Poems*, certifying them to be 'Printed according to the exact copies of [her] late dear Husband'. This publication may have been at the time no more than a move in a cheating game played by people none of whom was too honest or at least scrupulous;[1] but without it the poems ran the risk of never being printed at all, or of the text's being tampered with by an editor of more pretensions to scholarship than Mary Palmer.

In default of a wife Marvell had friends, a small group above whom towers Milton. The Member for Hull no doubt frequented the house in Jewin Street to which the blind poet had returned when he came out of prison. There in 1662 or 1663 Marvell met a young man named Samuel Parker who had been bred a very precise Puritan but was soon to take Anglican orders and become the most intransigent

[1] See Charles E. Ward, 'Andrew Marvell's Widow', in *T.L.S.*, 14 May 1938; F. S. Tupper, 'Mary Palmer, alias Mrs. Andrew Marvell', in *P.M.L.A.*, June 1938, pp. 367–92 (a most important article) and p. 149, n. 1 *infra*.

of Conformists. This led to his being made a dignitary of
the Church but also to his becoming Marvell's victim in a
controversy. Answering a first attack Parker imprudently
recalled their meetings at Milton's house, in order to accuse
Marvell of betraying an ancient friendship, while other
Anglican controversialists hinted that Milton had a share in
The Rehearsal Transpros'd. In the *Second Part* of this pamphlet
Marvell claimed the whole responsibility for himself and
devoted one of his best-known pages in prose to a vindication of Milton. In the year 1673 such an apology required
much caution and tact:

> J. M. was, and is, a man of great learning and sharpness of wit
> as any man. It was his misfortune, living in a tumultuous time,
> to be toss'd on the wrong side, and he writ *flagrante bello* certain
> dangerous treatises . . . At his Majestie's happy return, J. M. did
> partake . . . of his regal clemency, and has ever since expiated
> himself in a retired silence.

Marvell then reminds Parker of the compromising remarks
he indulged in at the time, which Milton has 'too much
generosity to remember'. Therefore it is 'a shame . . . to
insult over his old age' by attributing to him Marvell's
'simple book' and, worse, 'to traduce him . . . as a school
master, who was born and hath lived much more in-
genuously and liberally then' his slanderer. Taking circumstances into account, Marvell's behaviour was no less
courageous than skilful; of course we know that Milton
never repented and we wonder that Marvell, among the
many charges made by Parker and his acolytes (some of
them ignominious, as sodomy) should have considered that
of having kept a school as the most stinging.

Less noticeable as an act of friendship and courage, Marvell's last tribute to Milton surpasses it in literary interest.
In 1674 there appeared the second edition of *Paradise Lost*,
preceded by a congratulatory poem of his. Marvell as a
critic accepts the proscription of rhyme, with which as a
poet he never dispensed; he mocks at himself for using it in
this poem, which compels him to substitute the rhyme-word
'commend' for the plainer and stronger 'praise'. But he
proves more independent when he appreciates the choice

of the subject, which he both sums up and questions in a
period of ten lines, worthy, by virtue of its majestic breadth,
of *Paradise Lost* itself. His original misgivings (he even
'misdoubts' Milton's 'Intent') that Milton

> would ruine (for I saw him strong)
> The sacred Truths to Fable and old Song,

have since found numerous echoes, fewer indeed among
believers than among infidels, which is paradoxical yet
human. But those critics who stop here when quoting mislead their readers unless they add that Marvell afterwards
apologizes for that insulting doubt: he owns himself now
convinced that Milton has treated of 'things divine . . . in
such state—As them preserves . . . inviolate'. Marvell's
initial recoil, sincere no doubt, also serves as a rhetorical
device to enhance the merit of the epic poet who has
triumphed over such difficulties. Thus, we may surmise,
Milton took it; if written just before publication this
commendatory piece must have given him one of his last
satisfactions on earth, for he died on 8 November of the
same year. Marvell promised Aubrey to write his life, a
promise that unfortunately was not kept.

After Milton, *longo sed proximus intervallo*, James Harrington, the author of *Oceana*, ranks highest among the literary
friends of Marvell's later life. Their acquaintance probably
began under the Protectorate and, according to Aubrey,
became close enough for our poet to write 'a good epitaph,
but it would have given offence', when Harrington died in
1677. As one of his enemies suggested (in 1673) Marvell
may well 'have made a speech once in the Rota', the short-
lived political club founded by Harrington in 1659, the
public meetings of which, presided over by Cyriak Skinner,
attracted the best wits in London; but the then Latin Secretary had his feet too firmly on the ground not to consider
those brilliant discussions as mere intellectual pastimes. Unluckily for poor Harrington the Royalists when again in
power took his Utopia more seriously; at the end of 1661 he
was arrested; he spent some time first in the Tower and
then in various provincial prisons; and when released he
suffered from an intermittent form of lunacy, which, however

inoffensive, must have saddened Marvell's intercourse with him.

If Marvell's epitaph on Harrington is lost we have two others composed by him for the sons of a Hampshire baronet and M.P., Sir John Trott, a close friend of his no doubt. Though couched in elegant Latin prose they would not detain us but for the covering letter of the second (1677), which contains, after commonplace attempts at comfort from biblical texts, this admission: ' 'Tis true, it is an hard task [for the bereaved] to learn and teach [resignation] at the same time. And, where yourself are the experiment, it is as if a man should dissect his own body and read the Anatomy lecture.'[1] The lurid metaphysical light still shone in Marvell.

His other letters to his friends and relatives are in a very different style. Among his correspondents figure Philip, fourth Lord Wharton, an old Parliamentarian who played, especially after 1675, an important part in the Opposition—Sir Edward Harley, a country gentleman of Herefordshire but with Presbyterian sympathies and destined to become a Whig (he is known to history as the father of Robert Harley, future Earl of Oxford, Swift's friend and Defoe's patron)—the two Thompson brothers, Sir Henry and Edward, wine merchants at York, closely linked in business with the Popples and in sympathy with Marvell politically—and above all his nephew William Popple from the time of his settling at Bordeaux, about Christmas 1669. More or less familiar in style, most of these letters have a common characteristic: they are written by a Londoner who keeps permanent or temporary provincials informed of political and social events. Such being their end they are generally written in the plainest manner, though not dully; the writer does not abstain from expressing now and then his own judgement on men and things; humour sometimes peeps out; occasional terse statements reveal the born stylist. Consequently we deplore the destruction of a large part of his correspondence by one William Skinner, who, at the end of the century, gave many 'valuable letters . . . to the pastry-

[1] Cf. Donne, *Devotions*, 9. Meditation: 'I have cut up mine *Anatomy*, dissected my selfe, and they [sc. my physicians] are gon to *read* upon me.'

maid to put under pie-bottoms'.[1] Yet it would be excessive
to raise the cry of sacrilege, for our author's letters cannot
on the whole compare for literary charm with those of the
contemporary French letter writers, especially the women.
His missives are too tightly packed with minute facts, art-
lessly placed side by side. And the interest of the matter
compensates for the bareness of the style only with the
professional historian, since this very interest is restricted
by the dryness of the allusions.

   A relative dryness, though: Marvell could do much better,
or worse, in what we now call telegraphese, as appears from
the 295 letters sent by him to the Hull Corporation that have
been preserved. The first bears date of 17 November 1660,
and the last of 6 July 1678, within six weeks of the writer's
death. But the series is far from continuous. During the
parliamentary sessions Marvell usually wrote as many as
three letters per week; but during the intervals between
sessions he very seldom wrote. Besides, part of the correspondence must have been destroyed by the addressees, as
incriminating; for instance no letter survives of the tenth
session (4 February 1672/3–29 March 1673), one of the
stormiest. And yet in what a cautious way Marvell informs
the Hull burgesses of parliamentary business! Very seldom
does he risk the least commentary on the debates, even
those few in which he has taken an active part; this commentary, when given, remains so impersonal that we cannot
tell, most of the time, which way he voted. Even measures
capable of raising his indignation are related with apparent
callousness, the stock instance being that of the reprisals
against the dead regicides, Cromwell, Bradshaw, Ireton, and
Pride: 'And tis ordered that the Carkasses and coffins of the
foure last named shall be drawn, with w^t expedition possible, upon an hurdle to Tyburn, there be hangd up for a

   [1] A few unprinted letters have been discovered in recent years. The most
interesting are the two to Sir Henry Thompson published by Caroline
Robbins in *T.L.S.*, 19 December 1958, and 20 March 1959. The latter, dated
14 November 1676, contains an allusion to Nathaniel Bacon's rebellion in
Virginia, a 'heady attempt' to which Marvell foresees 'an headlesse issue'—
whatever private feeling he may have entertained for Bacon's proclamation
of 'liberty to all servants and Negro's'. Here again, did Marvell speak his
mind? See also C. Robbins, 'Six letters [hitherto unpublished] by Andrew
Marvell', in *Études Anglaises*, 1964, pp. 47–54.

while and then buryed under the gallows. The Act for the
Militia. . . .' Marvell passes on to other subjects (4 December
1660). Even though 'Carkasses' then could mean 'corpses',
without any sneer, we should hardly have expected the
author of 'A Poem on the Death of O.C.' to write thus.
But it would be unfair to blame Marvell for the tone of this
correspondence; his electors, substantial Englishmen, expected from their representative facts, not ideas, news not
views, in return for the hard cash they paid out to him.
Religious, or rather ecclesiastical, questions interested them
deeply; next came public finance, and no detail of taxation
was too small for them. And naturally economic problems,
especially those affecting foreign trade, fired the souls of the
Hull shipowners and merchants.

A parallel correspondence deals solely with maritime
problems. It is addressed to the Hull Trinity House, in
which Edmund Popple several times served as warden;
hence the semi-private nature of these letters. Three-fourths
of them deal with one question: the building of a lighthouse
near Spurn Head at the mouth of the Humber; and, since
the first of them bears date of 18 May 1661, and no solution
had yet been reached when Marvell died, his zeal and patience
here deserve more praise than his efficiency as a business
agent. He found his reward less in occasional gifts of ale or
salmon, and once of 'tenne gynneys', than in the popularity
he earned—a bourgeois popularity, if we may be allowed
this oxymoron, for he does not hide his contempt for 'the
raffe of the meaner and most unexperienced mariners'. He
was thus paving the way, by his obligingness, for a re-
election that death alone prevented. He rendered similar
services to the London Trinity House and lived long enough
to be elected a Younger Warden of this powerful Corporation on 27 May 1678, after having been four years a member.
This honour, highly prized then as now, must have procured him one of his last gratifications in this world. If the
sea occupies far less space in his poetry than the countryside,
it figured more largely, it seems, in his daily concerns.

To the Hull Trinity Brethren and to the Mayor and Corporation alike Marvell occasionally underlined his own
devotion, the expression of it ranging from: 'if I wanted my

right hand yet I would scribble to you with my left rather than neglect your businesse' (1 June 1661), to the more convincing: 'I lose my dinner to make sure of this Letter' (14 November 1667). But we are only too familiar today with this anxiety to please and self-commendation of the *homo parliamentarius*. Therefore, the specifically historical interest of the correspondence with the Mayor and Corporation lies in the reports of the debates. The Press, still in its infancy and subject to censorship, did not rise above insignificance. Besides, both Houses wrapped their sittings in a veil of official mystery that was not removed until a century later. This accounts for the importance attached to their representative's letters by the Hull burgesses, and for the frequently repeated recommendations of secrecy he makes to the Mayor and Aldermen: blabbing would bring the House of Commons down upon him.

Was he at least protected by his membership of this House against the resentment of the Administration or high-placed persons? Theoretically yes, but only *sedente Parliamento*; and in fact several Members had to suffer for their independence, in legal or illegal ways. The greatest outrage, the cutting of Sir John Coventry's nose by some of the King's Guards (with the connivance, at least, of the Duke of Monmouth) as a revenge for a pointed question in the House, is told at length by Marvell in a letter to William Popple (*c.* 24 Jan. 1670/1), along with the Commons' vigorous and partly successful counteraction. Sir John was the nephew of two important men at Court; hence one can judge what dangers a less well-connected Member ran. During the polemics he took part in from 1672 onwards Marvell's opponents affected surprise at his ears' not having been cut off by the public executioner; he answered one of them, a clergyman, with witty unconcern: 'my ears . . . are yet in good plight, and apprehend no other danger . . . but to be of your auditory'. However, in a fragment of an undated private letter he seems to take the possibility of an attempt upon his life more seriously (which confirms Aubrey's report of his solitary drinking, out of caution, quoted in the preceding chapter): 'Magis occidere metuo quam occidi.' He probably means that his would-be assassin ran the greater risk: let us remember the fencing-lessons in Spain and the sword that every gentleman wore at his side even within the House of Commons. Marvell adds: 'non quod Vitam tanti aestimem, sed ne imparatus moriar'. Here speaks a brave man. When we judge his not always unimpeachable conduct as satirist and pamphleteer, we must not forget that, if he became a partisan, the party he chose was neither advantageous nor even safe; so that he has not usurped his reputation as a patriot.

After the dissolution of the Convention (29 December 1660) Marvell remained in London, while Ramsden returned to Hull in order to prepare their election to the new Parliament. Yet Ramsden came at the bottom of the poll, while Marvell was elected, though he had fewer votes than one Colonel Gilby, a staunch Cavalier.[1] Soon afterwards the two Members for Hull quarrelled, which Marvell attributed to 'some crudityes and undigested matter remaining upon the stomach ever since [their] Election'. This estrangement lasted less than a year, but it shows that Marvell's position had become far less comfortable since the wave of Royalist enthusiasm had brought in the Cavalier Parliament. Another incident more clearly proves that the majority of the new House of Commons looked askance at Oliver's sometime Latin Secretary. He had exchanged blows in the sacred precincts with Thomas Clifford, then a young private Member but later to become the C of the Cabal Administration. The only witness, probably an ardent Royalist like Clifford, seems to have given evidence against Marvell, and the Speaker too appears to have eagerly seized this opportunity to humble a former Cromwellian. Finally the House confirmed the Speaker's ruling and compelled Marvell to own himself guilty of having given the 'first Provocation of the Difference'. He and Clifford had to promise 'not to renew this Difference, but to have the same Correspondence they had before it did happen', a promise that our poet interpreted pretty freely since he gave at least two bobs to

[1] Mr. Wall informs me that Gilby had suffered imprisonment for the Royalist cause and was one of its most trusted secret agents in the period preceding the King's return.

Clifford in his satires, once comparing him, as Comptroller of the Household, to 'a tall Lowse brandish[ing] the white Staff'. But his resentment mainly turned, as well it might, upon the partial Speaker, Sir Edward Turnor, of whom he drew a portrait as wicked as it is amusing.[1]

Did this misadventure contribute to the decision he took soon after of going abroad? Anyhow, on 8 May 1662 he wrote to the Hull Trinity House to announce his absence. He excused it by saying he had to consider 'the interest of some persons too potent fot [him] to refuse and who [had] a great direction and influence upon [his] counsells and fortune'. Then, in order to reconcile them to his leaving them in the lurch he named 'my Lord of Carlile . . . a member of the Privy Counsell, and one of them to whom [their] businesse [was] referd', as a person he would 'make . . . absolutely' theirs by his going to Holland. It looks as if Marvell's 'own private affairs', as he calls them in the next letter, were really of a political, more or less clandestine, nature. We may well feel surprised at finding him again in touch with a Privy Councillor until we remember that the Earl of Carlisle, then plain Charles Howard, had served Oliver Cromwell faithfully and been wounded at Worcester fighting against his king; he had deserted Richard Cromwell only when Richard had deserted himself. Most likely Marvell and Howard had become acquainted under the Protectorate; and if Charles II had by 1662 heard of the former he bore him no more grudge than he did the latter; among the King's many faults spite did not figure.

But others, more Royalist than the King, kept an eye on the quondam Latin Secretary. John Lord Belasyse, a brave Cavalier during the Civil War, had been made, though a Roman Catholic, Governor of Hull at the Restoration. For all the courtesy he showed to the junior Member for Hull and the outward respect with which he was answered, there can have been no love lost between the two since Belasyse 'did take notice' to the Hull Corporation 'of the absence of . . . Mr. Andrew Marvell' and no doubt suggested that a writ for a new election should be applied for. The Corporation returned a deferential but dilatory answer, and at once

[1] Quoted in Chapter VI, *infra*.

warned their representative (27 February 1662/3). He obeyed the summons and on 2 April 1663 dated from Westminster a slightly ironical letter to announce that he had resumed his seat in the House.

Not for long, however. After throwing out some hints in letters he informed the Corporation, on 20 June, of 'the probability [that he might] very shortly have occasion again to go beyond sea'. Carlisle, having been 'chosen by his Majesty his Embassadour Extraordinary to Muscovy Sweden and Denmarke hath used his power which ought to be very great with [Marvell] to make [him] goe along with him Secretary in those Embassages'. Warned by experience, the Member for Hull invokes precedents to be temporarily relieved of his parliamentary duties and adds: '. . . you may be sure that I will not stirre without speciall leave of the House that so you may be free from any possibility of being importuned or tempted to make any other choice in my absence.' Politely, yet, we feel, as a matter of form, he also asks for the leave of his constituents, but he has obviously made up his mind to eat his cake as Ambassador's secretary and keep it as M.P. The Hull merchants on their part realized the commercial importance of the Embassy too well to raise objections. On 20 July Marvell sent farewell letters to the Hull Corporation and to the Trinity Brethren. In his exultation at going away he did not hesitate to declare that this voyage was a 'blessing of God' and a reward for his prompt return from Holland four months before: if, as is sometimes held, a dash of sanctimoniousness enters the composition of every good Puritan, this ingredient was not forgotten in the making of Marvell.

Unfortunately for us, our poet has left no account of his visit to Muscovy.[1] Under the Czar Alexis, Peter the Great's father, this mysterious country began to move towards Europe, and Western curiosity about it was awakening.

[1] Caroline Robbins, 'Carlisle and Marvell in Russia, Sweden, and Denmark, 1663–1664', in *The History of Ideas News Letter* (Columbia University, N.Y.), 1957, pp. 8–17, publishes from the State Papers at the Public Record Office five letters signed by Carlisle but written in Marvell's hand. Three of them are addressed to the King himself and two to 'Mr Secretary Bennet'. The style, at times humorous, may be partly Marvell's.

Milton had written before 1650 *A Brief History of Moscovia*, and Milton's friend probably knew it though it remained unpublished until 1682; but it was a mere compilation of the narratives of various English travellers, and Marvell's descriptions after his return may have stimulated the imagination of the great blind poet, then putting the last touch to his pictures of Eden and of Hell. As regards the Embassy, we must rest contented with a *Relation* composed (in not quite identical French and English versions, from either of which we shall quote as occasion offers) by a member of Carlisle's train, Guy Miège. However, this young Vaudois fresh from the Lausanne Académie proves an intelligent observer in the part of his book that is not filled by the *in extenso* report of vain negotiations and futile diplomatic chicanery. Carlisle's Embassy aimed at restoring to the English merchants at Archangel the privileges and immunities granted by a former Czar and withdrawn by Alexis on the occasion of the Regicide. It ended in complete failure: the ill will of the Czar's counsellors, the intrigues of the rival Dutch, Carlisle's haughty and abrupt manner contributed to this negative result, in proportions not easy to assess.

The Ambassador's 'family' numbered nearly eighty persons, among whom were a chaplain 'pour sa dévotion' and, 'pour sa récréation, un fort beau concert de musique'. Arriving at the bar of Archangel on 19 August, Carlisle sent 'Mr. Marvel his Secretary into the Town' to compliment the 'voyvod', who 'ordered him to be conducted by six Gentlemen to the Castle, through a Regiment of six hundred men'. After a first dispute concerning etiquette, the Embassy left for Vologda (12 September) where it arrived, by way of the Duina and Sucagna rivers, five weeks later. Carlisle had a boat for himself, his Countess, and his son; the train was distributed between six barges. They were towed by 300 Russians. Already feeling the cold they began to put on Eastern clothes. At Vologda they lost three months owing to Russian dilatoriness; they beguiled the time with Russian baths, hunting the white hare, and skating; the 'concert of music' also helped a lot, no doubt with the author of 'Musicks Empire' as an assiduous listener, if not a performer. He may well have taken part in the organizing of a 'pleasant farce of Mascarads' to commemorate Guy Fawkes' Day. But he reappears in Miège's narrative only after Christmas, and in his official capacity; he then unsuccessfully protested against the poor quality of the sledges prepared by the Russians for the last part of the journey; so that Carlisle had to hire better ones, with which it took the Embassy three weeks to reach Moscow. Each Englishman had his sledge, where he lay stretched at full length and slept most of the time: 'the solitude, the warmth of our furrs, and the agreeable motion of our sledges inviting us thereunto.' They also had each 'his bottle of strong water', which they used as 'an excellent preservative of heat', so that they found themselves at times as hot as if they had been by the fireside; which does not hinder Miège from denouncing the drunken habits of the natives.

The State Entry into Moscow was to have taken place on 5 February 1663/4, but the Embassy, after being kept waiting till twilight for the order to march, was halted outside the walls of the City and had to spend the night in the smoke and stink of 'wisbies' (sc. isbas). Marvell composed on the spot a Latin epistle of protest, addressed by the Ambassador to the Czar himself, of which this will serve as a sample:

Postquam, quod ignes fatui solent, per camporum et noctis errores me circumduxissent, pronuntiatur in ignobili hoc pago, ubi cum omnibus incommodis et (honor sit auribus) cum vilissimis insectis conflictor, pernoctandum.

His British Majesty would never have tolerated such neglect on the part of his servants, but 'reorum sanguine . . . tam barbarum et inhumanum facinus expurgasset'. Fancy the Merry Monarch hanging his Master of Ceremonies because the Envoy Extraordinary of some foreign prince had found fleas or even lice in temporary lodgings! The Secretary had adopted the Eastern style with great success.

In Moscow the Embassy occupied a stone mansion, comparatively fire-proof (which they appreciated). They were now pestered not by insects but by rats. Impartially Miège notes that the Ambassador's table was well furnished by their hosts and that Moscow offered many forms of entertainment. In the Court there was 'la plus grande splendeur et magnificence qui se puisse voir auprès d'aucun prince chrétien'. Besides, the English provided their own pastimes: 'Our Musique-master composed a handsome Comedie in prose, which was acted in our House.' There was horse-racing too, and at the end of Winter a football match, 'à la façon d'Angleterre', took place publicly in the presence of His Excellency.

The behaviour of the Russian officials wavered between barbaric courtesy and sly insolence, if we believe Miège who carps even at the banquet offered by the Czar to Carlisle and all his male followers (19 February 1663/4). This lasted nine hours, and 500 dishes were served. From a Russian official source we learn many additional details of its splendour. The Czar had donned his white furs—white hair inside, silver outside—to honour the foreign visitors; it was he no doubt, who, according to the Russian custom, sent to each one of his guests by name the portions of fish the list of which the *Dvortsovye Razriadi* (Palace Hierarchies) have piously preserved. 'Secretary of the Embassy Andrew Marvell' received the head of a sturgeon, considered a choice morsel.[1]

The negotiations had already begun; on 11 February Carlisle had been granted his first audience, arriving at the Palace in the Czar's own sledge, with the Secretary standing bareheaded before him. The Ambassador pronounced in English a long speech, perhaps composed and certainly turned into Latin by Marvell, the style of which here and there recalls to readers of Molière that in which Covielle was soon to translate to Monsieur Jourdain the compliments of His Turkish Highness. At this we might laugh, but we feel some discomfort when we read the imprecations against the English rebels, especially the surviving regicides, 'execrabiles illos fugitivos et parricidas', men fit to be hunted down everywhere and brought to condign punishment. These were not empty threats: George Downing, Carlisle's brother-in-law

---

[1] In 1928 we expressed regret not to have been able to consult an apparently still unpublished document, the *Poçolski Prikaz* (Order of Embassy) in which the negotiations are, it seems, related. We must reiterate this regret in 1964, having tried in vain what could be done by deputy: Russian records remain all but closed to Western scholars.

and Marvell's correspondent when they both served Richard
Cromwell, had captured at Delft and sent to London three
of the bravest regicides, who were ignominiously put to
death (19 April 1662) just before Marvell decided to go
and stay at The Hague with this devoted agent of every
English régime. Samuel Pepys seems to have reflected public opinion when he condemned Downing's conduct in his
secret diary. It is a pity Marvell had to suppress his true
feelings on this point.

Neither bombastic metaphors nor Royalist idolatry could
shock the Muscovite Court. But as the Ambassador at once
demanded reparation for the incident of the delayed entrance
into the capital the Russian commissioners retorted that
proper respect had not been shown to their master: he had
been addressed as 'Illustrissime' while he was entitled to
'Serenissime'. Marvell, touched to the quick, undertook in
his answer to give the Russians, no great Latinists, a lesson
out of the best classical authors. Then, possessed with the
spirit of controversy, he claimed for his own master the
title, omitted by the Russians, that the Merry Monarch held
dear above all others: 'Defensor Fidei'. Was Marvell laughing in his sleeve? We may hope so, we cannot be sure.

The negotiation, already doomed, dragged on till 14 June,
when Carlisle took his leave. The better to signify his discontent he refused the Czar's parting present of sables not
only for himself but also for his train, who thought it rather
over-scrupulous of him. On 24 June the English left Moscow, some on horseback, some in carriages, and proceeded
towards Riga by stages of forty or fifty versts a day. In spite
of mosquitoes and the too frequent presence of crayfish on
the menu this journey was not found too disagreeable,
thanks to the shade provided by the forests through which
they passed. At last, on 22 July, they reached the Livonian
frontier at Nihuysen with much relief. Miège concludes the
first part of his narrative with a most rational remark:
'Ainsi nous quittâmes la Moscovie et ses habitans après y
avoir demeuré près d'un an entier; ce qui étoit trop long-
temps sans contredit pour une ambassade inutile.'

But Carlisle's mission was not quite over: he embarked
at Riga for Stockholm. There Marvell must have given a

thought to Christina, now wandering abroad. The second successor of that whimsical queen, Charles XI, a child of nine, listened with admirable gravity to a compliment read in English by the Ambassador, then in Latin by Marvell. For the Queen mother, a German princess, Marvell translated the Ambassador's compliment into his best French the next day. A month later, without having achieved anything of importance, they took leave in the same forms, but with the Queen mother they surpassed themselves in ingenious flattery: 'about the middle of his speech, where he saith, *That the boldest eloquence would lose its Speech*, his Excellence made a long pause. . . . For my part at first I believed it was the sincerity of my Lord Ambassadors discourse that produced this effect, and that . . . his speech had failed him. . . . But when I saw the Secretary . . . stop in the same place when he interpreted the Complement in *French*, then I concluded the thing had been contrived.'

Leaving Stockholm on 13 October Carlisle went to Copenhagen for his third and last Embassy. Compliments were recited in the same way; Danish hospitality equalled Swedish, but negotiations came to no better end than at Stockholm. The British Government wanted Denmark to join in the war then preparing against the United Provinces. The Ambassador did his best, and there is no reason to think that Marvell did not exert himself in the same cause; but the jealousy between the two northern monarchies prevented them from intervening either jointly or separately.

On 15 December Carlisle left Copenhagen to embark at Elsinore; but, adverse winds having driven him back to this port, he landed again and set off to travel overland to Calais, via Hamburg. At Bockstoudt, between this town and Bremen,

the secretary's waggoner would not stir, unless there might go along with him another waggoner his comrade, who would have been as useless to us as his waggon. The secretary not able to bring them to reason by fair means, tried what he could by foul, and by clapping a pistol to his head would have forced him along with him. But immediately his pistol was wrested from him, and as they were putting themselves into a posture to abuse him, we interposed so effectually that he was rescued out of their hands.

Miège calls these Germans 'a barbarous rout of peasants and Mechanicks'.

This incident, in which our poet once more showed the quickness of his temper, was the last. The Ambassador and his secretary reached London on 30 January (a memorable anniversary) 1664/5. But Marvell had not yet done with his diplomatic duties: Charles II asked Carlisle to put down in writing a compendious narrative of the chief things that had happened in Russia, in order to confound the Czar's Ambassadors already arrived with a complaint against the insolence of the English. This narrative, given in full by Miège, satisfied the King, who fully approved his Ambassador.

Marvell returned in time for the tail-end of the fourth parliamentary session. He attended the short fifth session, held at Oxford on account of the Plague, in October 1665. He even arrived a few days early, 'for the sake of the public *Library*' Wood assures us. Perhaps he found the more comfort in reading old books because the present persecution of the Nonconformists afflicted him. It was the price paid by the Government to the majority of the House of Commons for the 'supplyes in reference to the Dutch warre', begun *de facto* in December 1664 with an attack on Dutch colonies and officially declared in the following March. Though Marvell must have felt sad at its internal religious consequences, the war itself could not have surprised him, nor is it likely that it displeased him at that time. The failure of the Embassy to Moscow must have left some rancour against the Dutch in the mind of Carlisle's former secretary. His 'Character of Holland', written twelve years earlier, was printed, for the first time so far as we know, with suitable omissions and additions (not his it seems) and without his name. It does not appear that he resented this publication.

One more gap in his correspondence prevents us from knowing his impressions of the Fire of London, if he saw it. But we do know from letters written later that he shared the general discontent against the Government, held responsible for this calamity, and the popular suspicion of the Papists: these were believed to have set the City on fire in

the interest of the French King, who was indeed allied with
the Dutch but helped them as little as he could. Marvell even
seems to have sympathized with the campaign against the
Clarendon administration as regarded another grievance:
the importation of Irish cattle, lately allowed, which angered
the landed interest worse than the former two. A heterogeneous Opposition, the first form of the Country Party,
thus assembled itself around the Duke of Buckingham, the
husband (from 1657) of Marvell's sometime pupil, Mary
Fairfax. Whether or no there existed personal relations between the libertine nobleman and the more or less Puritan
M.P., the latter certainly supported the former in his attempt
to overthrow Clarendon; Marvell's deepest motive was
probably religious but, feeling that the Commons would
not follow him on this ground, he attacked the Lord Chancellor on that of national honour. The bold incursion of the
Dutch fleet, under Ruyter, into the Medway (10–15 June
1667) sealed Clarendon's fate, though in fact he had no direct
responsibility for this wound to English pride. Marvell's
satires against him, though probably begun before it, were
not completed and circulated until after this shameful
episode. 'Clarindon's House-Warming' certainly, 'The last
Instructions to a Painter' possibly[1] found their way into
print that very year of the Lord Chancellor's downfall (the
Great Seal was taken from him on 30 August). The two
satires, with their adjuncts, the epigrams 'Upon his House'
and 'Upon his Grand-Children' (this one particularly fero-
cious), make up an indictment against the unfortunate
statesman. Marvell could not be impartial; in fact, as a
Member of the House of Commons, the very Constitution
of England made him a fraction of the public prosecutor.
And he did take an active part in the proceedings that led
up to the impeachment. We have reports of four speeches

---

[1] I owe to Professor Robbins information concerning a lately noticed
tract that contains 'The last Instructions to a Painter' and 'The Loyall Scot'
(*v. infra*, p. 141). There is no title-page and the dating must remain conjectural until another copy turns up, but it may be as early as 1669. This tract
was bound up by an eighteenth-century collector with others in a volume
that was bought by Benjamin Franklin in 1771 and has been since 1801 in
the possession of the Library Company of Philadelphia (press-mark 935 Q).
I think there may well have been an even earlier printing of 'The last Instructions', of the same perishable nature.

made by him between 14 October and 6 November,[1] and on account of their hopeless obscurity we cannot affirm that he tried to load Clarendon as much as possible. His last speech indeed seems to show this bias almost ludicrously; he wanted the charge to include an article to the effect that Clarendon had called 'the King an inactive person, and undisposed for government'. The most idolatrous Royalist could hardly deny the truth of this judgement in his heart of hearts, but Marvell may have seen there an opportunity to ruin the fallen minister irretrievably in the opinion of the King (who in fact laughed it away)—or else he wanted to expose, deviously, some of Clarendon's accusers whose motives he had already found out.

The apparent unanimity of the House of Commons indeed came to an end as soon as the Act of banishment against Clarendon received the royal assent (16 December). The same day Parliament was adjourned. When it met again (6 February 1667/8) dissensions appeared among the conquerors. In 'The last Instructions' Marvell had already advised the King to beware of Arlington, Buckingham's rival in the royal favour. On 15 February, when the House debated the inadequacy of the intelligence during the recent Dutch war he again attacked the same statesman, comparing 'somewhat transportedly' the great times of English espionage under Elizabeth, or even James I (he might have added Oliver even more pertinently and from personal knowledge, but abstained), with the pitiful present. This shows in Marvell as a parliamentary orator an impetuosity generally held back in prudent silence. He spoke seldom, but when he spoke he did not quite control himself; either trait no doubt accounts for the other as both cause and effect. Anyhow, his speech made some stir in official circles, since Pepys alluded to it in his diary, without, however, naming Marvell (he never does); and Arlington himself mentioned it in a letter to Sir William Temple, the then British representative at The Hague; the Secretary of State singled the incident out of the debate: 'Mr. Marvell hath

---

[1] See Caroline Robbins's edition of *The Diary of John Milward*, 1938; also her 'Note on a hitherto unprinted speech by Andrew Marvell', in *M.L.R.*, 1936, pp. 549–50.

struck hard at me', adding however: 'This day [17 February] he hath given me cause to forgive him, by being the first man that, in the midst of this enquiry, moved the taking into Consideration of His Majesty's Speech', to good effect. It hardly needs saying that this speech asked for money. The Commons mostly turned a deaf ear on such begging and took up any other subject in preference. Therefore, the Member who recalled them to it deserved the gratitude of the Government. Perhaps Marvell had thus tried to retrieve his rash words of two days before. But a more honourable motive for this move can be found: the Speech from the Throne recommended toleration.

From 1668 to 1672 Marvell's life includes no event of major importance and his literary output weighs little. National life during these four years appears to us as barren as it is confused. However, this lull assumes some interest for the biographer as well as the historian once they see in these years the preparation for the great struggle of 1672 and 1673, a struggle that was to stimulate the writer in Marvell to an activity beyond expectation.

After the treaty of Aix-la-Chapelle (May 1668) peace reigned in Europe, but Louis XIV was, with the utmost secrecy, preparing war against the United Provinces. The Duchess of Orléans, Charles II's sister and Louis XIV's sister-in-law, negotiated between the two sovereigns the secret Treaty of Dover (22 May 1670) by which they divided the Dutch territories and possessions. Yet His Britannic Majesty was still a party to the Triple Alliance with the Netherlands and Sweden in order to check French progress in the Low Countries. The English Parliament still voted money for the Fleet against France, which Charles had already promised France to use against Holland. English opinion already entertained some suspicions. Marvell for one had announced to his nephew, as early as April 1670, 'Family Counsels' that clearly boded no good. Therefore, we feel something stronger than surprise at Marvell's writing in the same year,[1] presumably in the latter half of it, six

---

[1] As was revealed by E. E. Duncan-Jones, in her letter to *T.L.S.*, 26 April 1957, p. 257, which radically altered the dating and the circumstances. See also, ibid., 17 May, p. 305 and 4 October, p. 593.

Latin elegiac distichs, 'Inscribenda Luparae', to the praise
not only of the palace of the Kings of France, but of Louis
himself, culminating in:

> Sunt geminae *Jani* portae, sunt Tecta *Tonantis*;
> Nec deerit *Numen* dum Ludovicus adest.

Not even Boileau ever went so far in idolatry. The mystery
only partially clears up when we learn that Colbert had
instituted a competition with a prize (1,000 pistoles, which
sounds extravagant) for the best inscription to be set up on
the pediment, facing Saint-Germain l'Auxerrois, above the
great colonnade then nearly completed. 'The best wits of
France and Italy' were competing, along with some Englishmen, but Marvell of all people! The most honourable explanation is that he combined admiration for *le Roy Soleil*,
then at his brightest, with fear of French policy for his own
country and patriotic determination to counter it. More
recent history might provide instances of such a combination of feelings.

Yet foreign policy, for Marvell as for the mass of his fellow
countrymen, proved less absorbing than home politics,
dominated by religious problems. Since the House of Commons remained faithful in this field to the spirit of persecution for which Clarendon had borne the blame, Marvell
turned to the King, or at times to the Upper House. On
21 March 1669/70 for instance he writes to his nephew:

> The terrible bill against Conventicles is sent up to the Lords. . . .
> They are making mighty Alterations in [it] (which, as we sent up,
> is the Quintessence of arbitrary Malice,) and sit whole days, and
> yet proceed by Inches. . . . So the Fate of the Bill is uncertain, but
> must probably pass, being the Price of Money.

If he abhors the sincere intolerance of the Commons Marvell
rightly despises the King who, naturally tolerant himself,
sells them the power to satisfy their hatred. This same House
truckles to the Court on every other subject. Thus are explained some disheartened remarks in the Member for Hull's
private letters. The above-quoted one concludes: 'In such
a conjecture, dear *Will*, what Probability is there of my doing
any Thing to the Purpose?' Some weeks later, to the same

correspondent, Marvell thus refers to Parliament: 'We are all venal Cowards, except some few.' Over a year later, to 'a friend in Persia',[1] he writes this summary of the financial debates in the House:

Nevertheless such was the Number of the constant Courtiers, increased by the Apostate Patriots, who were bought off, for that Turn, some at six, others ten, one at fifteen, thousand Pounds in Mony, besides what offices, Lands, and Reversions, to others, that it is a Mercy they gave not away the whole Land, and Liberty, of *England*.

These renegades are those he praised in 'The last Instructions to a Painter'; they are now branded for their desertion of the Country Party in another verse satire, 'Further Advice to a Painter' (*c*. January 1670/1), which may be his.

Yet one should not take his fits of dejection quite seriously, nor miss the occasional seasoning of humour. And he had his more hopeful moods, for instance when he wrote 'The Loyall Scot' (1669 or 1670?). Here he agrees entirely with the King's policy, aiming at the transformation of the personal union between England and Scotland into a parliamentary one; of course he blames, by means of a conceit, the persistence of the division on the Anglican clergy: ''Tis Holy Island parts us not the Tweed.' Near the end of this piece, where satire figures largely but whose purpose is persuasion by praise, a paragraph exalts the King's wisdom: 'Charles our great soul . . .—Knowes the last secret how to make them one.' And even though the 'secret' is revealed to us only through a poetical but far from lucid comparison with a beehive, Marvell's intent appears clearly. Great must have been his disappointment when the negotiations between the two Parliaments fell into a lethargy.

Indecision indeed is the characteristic of these years. It results mostly from the intrigues within that early version of the modern Cabinet, which bears in historical handbooks the more or less accurate name of 'the Cabal'. As one of Marvell's letters to his nephew (14 April 1670) shows, its composition varied from time to time, and the number of

---

[1] E. E. Duncan-Jones, in *N.Q.*, June 1957, pp. 466–7, identifies him as Thomas Rolt, of the East India Company.

its members was not limited to the five whose initials made
up the word: 'The governing Cabal . . . are *Buckingham*,
Lauderdale, Ashley, Orrery, and *Trevor*. Not but the other
Cabal'—presumably the Duke of York and his friends—
'too have seemingly sometimes their Turn.' Now Marvell,
who here seems disgusted with both Cabals, at times shows
sympathy for members of the former, e.g. the Earl of Orrery.
This Irish nobleman, Lady Ranelagh and Robert Boyle's
brother, had, when still only Baron Broghill, done brilliant
service under Oliver Cromwell; in 1669 the old Cavaliers
tried to have him impeached by the House of Commons in
which he sat, but the motion was defeated by three votes.
At this narrow escape the Member for Hull expressed his
satisfaction in a letter to the Corporation, with unusual
openness.

As regards Buckingham, if Marvell ever had illusions on
his morals, they must have vanished soon: the Duke's
scandalous adultery with the Countess of Shrewsbury, the
Earl killed in a duel with his wife's lover, the Duchess
expelled from home in order to make room for the titled
concubine, all these incidents (belonging to 1667/8) must
have shocked Mary Fairfax's former tutor even more than
other honest Englishmen. Yet when in a private letter
(9 August 1671) Marvell relates further instances of the
Duke's extravagance, profligacy, and folly, his tone sounds
more sorrowful than indignant. Other indications, vague
indeed, lead us to think that the Member for Hull still hoped
for Buckingham's conversion, a conversion he was to hail
as achieved some years later, and that meanwhile he relied
upon the Duke to defend the Nonconformists' cause before
the King. An odd defender of the austere and often sour
Puritans, this elegant and witty libertine, atheistical yet
superstitiously addicted to alchemy and astrology! But Marvell did not stand alone in seeing Buckingham as an apostle
of tolerance and a champion of the Protestant cause: though
the Duke inflicted many an humiliation on his virtuous wife
he made up for it by advising the King to repudiate his
Queen, as blameless as the Duchess, but also barren, and
moreover a Papist. If only Charles took Buckingham's advice
and remarried, this time with 'a good virtuous Protestant

here at Home' (letter to Wm Popple, 14 April 1670)! Then he might beget a legitimate heir, and thus bar the Duke of York from the succession. On the other hand, Buckingham's vindictiveness kept on persecuting Clarendon's friends, especially the most eminent and honourable of them, the Duke of Ormond, until lately Lord Lieutenant of Ireland. On 6 December 1670 Ormond barely escaped with his life from an attempt upon it by one Colonel Thomas Blood, also an Irishman; and Buckingham was suspected of having abetted this bold villain. Some months later, on 9 May 1671, the same Blood almost succeeded in stealing the Crown Jewels out of the Tower. Marvell not only related this daring feat to his 'friend in Persia' with admiration, but also composed a double epigram, Latin and English, in which he almost approved Blood for having, so as to recoup himself for confiscations, 'Upon the English Diadem distrain'd'. Indeed the point of the epigram is in the contrast between the disguise adopted by Blood, a parson's gown, and 'his Lay Pitty', which prevented him from killing the keeper and thus getting away with the Jewels:

> With the preists vestments had hee but put on
> A Bishops Cruelty, the Crown had gone.

The satirist of the Anglican clergy could not miss so good an opportunity of railing. More surprisingly, there may have arisen out of this a conjunction of Marvell and Blood. A document, enigmatic indeed, links their names in a suspicious manner; it is an informer's report to Joseph Williamson,[1] secretary to Arlington, Secretary of State, dated 21 September 1671. It says that Buckingham, during his Embassy to France (in the summer of 1670) had tried to dispel English fears caused by Charles II's rapprochement with Louis XIV, but 'finding by the fanatics that it was disgusted', he now crosses it. Then follows this condensed piece of information: 'Marvell with Bl[ood] from Bucks.' Such evidence cannot,

---

[1] E. E. Duncan-Jones, 'New Allusions to Marvell', in *T.L.S.*, 20 June 1958, has shown that Williamson was at Saumur in 1656 and apparently on good terms with Marvell.—He is called 'Latin Secretary' by Pepys (6 February 1663). He was also 'a genuine son of Jubal'. So that Marvell and he had much in common, but politics eventually made them enemies.

of itself, carry conviction; yet there is no inherent impossibility in this queer association of duke, satirist, and robber.[1]

Is there any connexion between Marvell's interest in the Irishman Blood and a design known to us only by a letter to William Popple written in late April 1671? 'I think it will be my Lot to go on an honest fair Employment into *Ireland*. Some have smelt the Court of *Rome* at that Distance.' He probably expected the then Lord Lieutenant, Lord Berkeley of Stratton, to be replaced by a better Protestant, who would take him in his train. But Berkeley, after spending some uncertain months in England, went back to Dublin Castle. If Marvell had gone to Ireland he would no doubt have felt there much like Edmund Spenser; his political reputation with posterity is the better for his not having gone. But even this abortive scheme shows that in 1671 Carlisle's former secretary remained in touch with people very near the King. This will help us to understand his action in the next year.

On 15 March 1671/2 Charles II issued his *Declaration of Indulgence*; and two days later he declared war on the United Provinces. Taken by surprise, the English found themselves before difficult cases of conscience. Between the still unpopular Dutch and the increasingly suspected French, between religious and political freedom, between fact and law, choice had to be made. While the large majority of the nation protested against the royal encroachment on the rights of Parliament, Marvell sided with the King and the Cabal. In the autumn of 1672 he published *The Rehearsal Transpros'd*, a voluminous pamphlet that will be examined in a later chapter. Suffice it here to note that this apology for the *Declaration of Indulgence* achieved a great success thanks to its lively style, in spite of the unpopularity of the cause it supported. Within a few weeks his pamphlet made Marvell more famous than his lyrical poetry, his public

---

[1] A literary connexion has been traced by William R. Orwen between 'Marvell and Buckingham', in *N.Q.*, 6 January 1951, pp. 10–11: the Duke may have had the 'Horatian Ode' in mind when he wrote 'An Epitaph on Thomas third Lord Fairfax' (1671 or 1672?). If so, Marvell returned the compliment by calling his first pamphlet *The Rehearsal Transpros'd*. See *The Rehearsal*, Act 1, scene 1: 'putting Verse into Prose should be called Transprosing'.

services, and even his satires had done in twenty-five years. The King, 'not a great reader of books', read this one, which 'had done him right', liked its wit, and protected the author against the reprisals of the Church.

Marvell trusted that the policy of toleration would succeed. But some three months after the publication of *The Rehearsal Transpros'd* his hopes and the King's vanished in smoke. Parliament, which had not sat for nearly two years, met on 4 February 1672/3, and as early as the 18th decided by 168 votes against 116 that penal laws could be suspended only by an Act of Parliament. The King at first indignantly refused to withdraw his declaration, but soon yielded. This concession did not satisfy the Commons and they forced the Test Bill against Roman Catholics upon the King. The majority was such that the House did not divide. Marvell, even if he did not join in 'remonstrating to the Declaration', as his arch-enemy was soon to accuse him of having done, no doubt welcomed the Test Bill. He may have been taken in by a clever but unscrupulous move of its Anglican promoters, who allured the friends of the Protestant Nonconformists with the hope of relief for these by legislation. But they proceeded so slowly about it that they managed to reach the prorogation of 29 March 1673, *infectā re*. Duped or not, Marvell at once set to write the *Second Part* of *The Rehearsal Transpros'd*, in which he put a brave face on unpleasant happenings and pursued his plea for toleration. He was actuated by high conviction and even more by author's pride, rather than by any expectation of success for that cause in the foreseeable future. For the Test had put an end to the Cabal Administration, and, in the Roman Catholic Clifford's place, Sir Thomas Osborne, to be created Earl of Danby the next year, had become High Treasurer and virtually Prime Minister. He was to remain in office until after Marvell's death, and from this bigoted Anglican the Nonconformists had nothing to expect but more persecution. Besides, the problem that now engrossed the minds of Englishmen, and Marvell's as much as anyone's, was that of the succession to the Throne; the Duke of York had declared himself a Papist by refusing to take the Test, and the likelihood of the King's begetting lawful issue dwindled every year, while the Duke's second marriage, this time to a Roman Catholic princess, lessened the likelihood of the Crown's passing to his Protestant daughters, Mary and Anne. In these circumstances we need not wonder at Marvell's change of mind. He withdrew from Charles II a support that had never been rooted in sentimental loyalty. Since the sovereign had proved unable to carry out that part of his personal policy of which Marvell approved, the Member for Hull began to entertain seditious notions; he called in question the dynasty and even, it seems, the hereditary monarchy.

While there is little doubt of this evolution, its date and mode are not easy to determine. Not because of the absence of documents; on the contrary uncertainty arises from their conflict. Moreover they lack unassailable authenticity when they are sincere, and unquestionable sincerity when they are undoubtedly authentic. Among those of the latter sort we must place both the *Second Part* of *The Rehearsal Transpros'd*, which came out, with the author's name on the title-page, in the winter of 1673-4, and the letters to the Hull Corporation. The private letters, too rare and very cautious, deserve more credit, but the best evidence would be found in the anonymous verse satires if we could tell with assurance which of those traditionally ascribed to him really came from his pen. It would be highly imprudent to date the stages of Marvell's third (and last) major political conversion by means of writings that probably do not all belong to him and not one of which belongs to him certainly. But if we accept 'A Dialogue between the Two Horses' as his, by comparing its tone with that of 'The last Instructions to a Painter' we can measure the distance Marvell had travelled from the summer of 1667 to the winter of 1675-6. The earlier satire ends with an appeal to the King in which the poet inveighs against those who

> The *Kingdom* from the *Crown* distinct would see, . . .
> (But *Ceres* Corn, and *Flora* is the Spring,
> *Bacchus* is Wine, the Country is the *King*.)

Even if we discount the tactical element in this we are hardly prepared to find in the later satire such an exchange of speeches as this:

De Witt and Cromwell had each a brave soul.—
I freely declare it, I am for old Noll.
Tho' his Government did a Tyrants resemble,
Hee made England great and it's enemies tremble.

And after a wistful recollection of the Tudors, of 'old Besse
in the Ruffe', the dialogue ends with these speeches:

But canst thou Divine when things shall be mended?—
When the Reign of the Line of the Stuarts is ended.—
Then, England, Rejoyce, thy Redemption draws nigh;
Thy oppression togeather with Kingship shall dye.—
A Commonwealth a Common-wealth we proclaim to the
    Nation;
The Gods have repented the Kings Restoration.

As a piece of political thinking this satire does not achieve
perfect consistency, and we need not infer that Marvell, even
if he wrote it, had become a doctrinaire upholder of the
Commonwealth (of which the Protectorate retrospectively
seemed a part). Rather, he was as always ready to welcome
any régime, whether authority resided in 'a single person'
or in 'a representative' (assembly), provided all Protestants
were safe and the greatness of England assured.[1]
    To those verse satires may be added an amusing piece of
prose, not so passionate but biting enough: a parody, possibly written in advance, of the King's Speech at the opening
of the thirteenth session of the Cavalier (by this time the
Pensionary) Parliament on 13 April 1675. Charles's usual
protestations of future thrift if his loyal Commons would
only relieve his too obvious present necessities provide the
main matter of this lively skit; the Court and Administration
are also glanced at; but the most significant sentences concern the members of the House of Commons: 'The nation
hates you already for giving so much, and I'll hate you too,
if you do not give me more. So that if you stick not to me,
you must not have a friend in England.' Marvell here reveals

---

[1] L. N. Wall, 'Marvell's Friends in the City', in *N.Q.*, June 1959, p. 206,
shows that as late at least as February 1675/6 'the nonconformist party there
were keeping a foot in both camps', and still had backstairs access to the
King at Whitehall. Wall, therefore, revives Thomas Cooke's assertion (1726)
that Charles II 'had often been delighted in [Marvell's] company', without
limiting it in time.

his wish to see a quarrel between King and Commons, which would result in a dissolution and new elections; then the revolutionary spirit of 1640 might arise again. In the House of Lords Shaftesbury, now in opposition, had the same object in view. But the pension paid in secret by Louis XIV enabled Charles II to do without his Parliament until 15 February 1676/7, and the Member for Hull had to content himself with writing another pamphlet in favour of the Nonconformists, or rather against their Anglican persecutors, *Mr. Smirke: Or, The Divine in Mode*. This tells us nothing of Marvell's properly political opinions since it carefully avoids any attack on the civil authorities, so as not to tighten the bonds between them and the ecclesiastical.

In this same year 1676 Marvell began to have some worries, which were later to involve him rather dangerously, on account of his connexion with certain men of business in the City. We have seen that two of the Thompson brothers corresponded with him from Yorkshire. They appear to have been distant relations of his by marriage and through his mother. A 'cousin' of theirs, Richard Thompson, and his own cousin Edward Nelthorpe, also a relation of Marvell's, had entered in 1671 into a partnership with two other citizens, John Farrington and Edmund Page, as merchant bankers in London. They were engaged in a wide range of trade: 'That of Wine, that of Silk, that to Russia, &c.' By 10 March 1675/6, being in financial difficulties, 'they had sumon'd their Creditors', as we learn from a jubilant letter addressed by the Lieutenant of the Tower to Williamson, now Sir Joseph and a Secretary of State. It appears that they led the opposition to the Government in the Common Council and had at least Nonconformist sympathies. The Lord Mayor seized upon the opportunity of eliminating them, as disqualified, from the next election (in December 1676). On 12 February 1676/7 their bankruptcy was referred to by Marvell in a letter to the Mayor of Hull, without comment. He must have considered, however, that they had been unfairly treated on account of their stand for the liberties of the City; so that we need not be shocked at his sheltering them from the harsh bankruptcy laws of the time. For this purpose he seems to have caused his landlady, or housekeeper, Mary Palmer, to take a house in Great Russell Street 'about the Month of June'; here he harboured Nelthorpe and Richard Thompson. He may even have connived at the concealment of some part of their personal assets, which would not be so easy to excuse, especially if he were himself a creditor and thus enjoyed an illegal preference. But since all other evidence points to his having been poor rather than well off one may credit him with disinterested motives. He probably forwarded a Bill in the House of Commons that gave the two insolvents temporary protection till Easter 1678, after which Richard Thompson took refuge at Chichester with an old agitator of the Parliamentary army, Major Braman, and Nelthorpe seems to have played a game of hide-and-seek with his creditors. After Marvell's death there was more manœuvring on the part of the bankrupts; Mary Palmer seems to have acted in agreement with them at first when she obtained the administration of Marvell's estate, but eventually she quarrelled with Farrington and a lawsuit resulted, which was not settled by the Court of Chancery before June 1683: Farrington won his point, so far, but litigation continued on this pitiful business.[1]

With the opening of the fifteenth session we enter the last phase of Marvell's life, short but well filled. Not however with poetry: one brief piece in Latin elegiacs, 'Scaevola Scoto-Britannus', proves, if it needed it, the poet's persistent hostility to prelates, since it praises almost unreservedly the fortitude of James Mitchell under the torture of the boot after his attempt on the life of Archbishop Sharp. To the end Marvell was to continue his sympathy to the Scottish Covenanters, witness his letter to his nephew of 10 June 1678.

But the internal situation in England and continental politics were his habitual concern. He went on hoping for the dissolution, for which a specious legal case, grounded on two Statutes of Edward III, was made after an adjournment of over a year. The Commons 'handled it so tenderly as if

[1] On the whole very complicated business see F. S. Tupper, *ut supra*; Caroline Robbins, letter to *T.L.S.*, December 1958, p. 737; L. N. Wall, *ut supra*, pp. 204–7.

they were afraid to touch it', but the Lords, less partial in this matter, debated it 'with more earnestnesse much'. Four peers went so far in their opposition that Danby managed to have them sent to the Tower by a vote of their House. Among them, besides Shaftesbury, by now the acknowledged leader of the Country Party, there were Wharton, Marvell's correspondent and host in the country, and Buckingham, lately reconciled with his wife, repentant and a patriot again. Marvell had forgiven the Duke his former vagaries as early as July 1675, because of his 'exposing and abusing' the Bishops' Bench, 'never the like, nor so infinitely pleasant'. So that the pamphleteer was soon to praise the four peers unreservedly and moralize over the incident: 'Thus a prorogation without precedent was to be warranted by an imprisonment without example . . . whereby the dignity of Parliaments . . . did at present much suffer, and may probably more for the future; for nothing but Parliament can destroy Parliament!'

With less reason Marvell's fears were aroused by Danby's next move: a Bill intended to make penalties against Roman Catholics less Draconic (which, to Danby's mind, would have made them more effective). Marvell in his letters to his constituents, expressed, or feigned, grave anxiety and, when the House of Commons rejected the Bill ignominiously, he exulted so highly that he wrote to them this good news at 'almost nine at night, . . . fasting'. Of more consequence was another Bill Marvell also abhorred, to such a point that he spoke against it in the House on 27 March 1677. 'An Act for further securing the Protestant Religion, by educating the Children of the Royal Family therein; and for the providing for the continuance of a Protestant Clergy' embodied Danby's sincere concern to limit the powers of the Duke of York if he succeeded his brother; and the Duke had quite logically protested against it in the House of Lords. The Opposition in the Commons, which could give no logical reason openly, fought this half-way solution because they secretly aimed at the total exclusion of the Duke from the succession. Marvell's arguments against the principle of the Bill are, therefore, feeble and even disingenuous. He had stronger and more honourable objections to the exorbitant

powers Danby proposed to give the episcopate, contrary to
the Elizabethan settlement of the Church. Marvell considered the bishops, with few exceptions, as *ex officio* persecutors of the Nonconformists, and once more he used
ridicule to defeat ecclesiastical claims. In the middle of his
speech he supposed that the same powers were entrusted
to another sort of men, e.g. physicians:

The College of Physicians have a Charter from the King, and
are his sworn servants; let these come to the King to administer
the Oath. 'Tis a pretty experiment. Just a tryal, whether the
Loadstone will attract the Iron, or the Iron the Loadstone. Who
can think that any body of men, that must depend upon the
King etc.? Which way, think you, it draws? We have seen (and
he hopes we shall never see it again) in *Henry* VIII's, *Edward* VI's,
Queen *Mary*'s, and Queen *Elizabeth*'s time, all sorts ready to turn
one, one way, another, another. 'Tis appointed by the Bill, 'that
the Bishops should wait upon the King at *Whitehall*, etc'. He
thinks not but Physicians, may be thought by a Popish King, as
proper a cure for his soul, as Bishops. The Chevalier de *Menevi-
cette*, Physician to the Great *Turk*, was by him made Patriarch of
Antioch [. . .] Whatever Prince God gives us we must trust him.
Let us not in prevention of future things so remote, take that
immoderate care in this Bill. *Sufficient to the day is the evil thereof.*
Here is pricking of Bishops, as if pricking Sheriffs. If the King
does not, they must.

After some high-sounding considerations Marvell returned
to the familiar style:

So great a power assembled upon such a body of men! The
Bill he spoke of, pretended, that the Dean and Chapter of *Durham*
would have benefit by a ballast shore to be erected at *Yarrow
Sleake*, on *Newcastle* side. Says one, 'it will narrow the river'.
Says another, 'it will widen it'. 'Twas then said, 'that Gentlemen
love not to play tricks with Navigation', much less should the
Nation play tricks with Religion. But whether this Bill will prevent Popery or not, this will secure the promotions of the Bishops;
'twill make them certain. He is not used to speak here, therefore
speaks with abruptness.

Even if we make allowances for the very imperfect report of
this speech in *Grey's Debates*, we must pronounce it to have
been a rather rambling performance, which will not surprise

him who has read *The Rehearsal Transpros'd.* This very fault makes it all the more interesting for Marvell's biographer; we see gathered in it all the aspects of his personality and style: besides his Puritan inheritance his own temperament appears; quotations from the Bible alternate with amusing anecdotes, the fruit of wide reading and conversation with polite people; the burlesque at the expense of physicians is succeeded by the metaphysical image of the magnet; lastly the indefatigable agent of the Hull burgesses and Brother of the London Trinity House stands revealed in the nautical comparison that opportunely teaches politicians to disturb the course of events no more than that of rivers.

This speech failed to prevent the House from committing the Bill, but it contributed no doubt to the later silent dropping of Danby's scheme. The consequent resentment of the Court Party came near to procuring for Marvell the same fate as had lately befallen the four Lords. Already on the 28th the Speaker, Sir Edward Seymour (once praised by Marvell for his opposition to Clarendon but since considered by him as a 'recanter'), speaking not from the Chair but from his place in the House on a totally different subject, glanced at the irreverent comparison of physicians with bishops, in its author's absence. The next day Marvell, going to his seat, 'stumbling at Sir *Philip Harcourt*'s foot, and in recovering himself, seemed to give Sir *Philip* a box on the ear'. Seymour, now in the Chair, immediately thought it 'his duty to inform the House of it'. Since Marvell was Sir Philip's friend he could easily explain that the thing was done in jest. But he rashly added to his vindication a retort to Seymour, inviting him to 'keep himself in Order for the future'. After private members had commented variously on the incident (one roundly moving 'to have *Marvell* sent to the *Tower*') Mr. Secretary Williamson, an old acquaintance though now a friend no longer, 'would have *Marvell* withdraw', so that the House should 'consider of' his insolence to the Speaker. At that stage the Member for Hull saw that matters were going badly for him, so he spoke again, in a much more subdued style, concluding that, if they thought fit, he would 'withdraw, and sacrifice himself to the censure of the House'. This apology eventually proved sufficient, and Williamson, seeing it was no use to insist any longer, declared himself 'satisfied'. A private member, Sir Thomas Meres, then drew the lesson of the incident: 'By our long sitting together, we lose, by our familiarity and acquaintance, the decencies of the House.' The point of the story lies in Marvell's taking up of Sir Thomas's remark almost verbatim in his next pamphlet (an anonymous one) in order to tax his colleagues in general with indecorous behaviour: 'By this long haunting so together, they are grown too so familiar among themselves, that all reverence of their own Assembly is lost'; and then he added his own note: 'that they live together not like Parliament men, but like so many good fellows met together in a publick house to make merry.' Marvell, who had not mentioned the incident to the Hull Corporation, once more showed himself dextrous, if not ambidextrous. He had the Puritan's disposition to confess his neighbour's sins in preference to his own.

This worn-out and corrupt House of Commons somewhat redeemed itself in Marvell's eye by its growing hostility to France, though he knew well enough that the motives of the majority were not purely patriotic. But neither was the Opposition over-scrupulous. Marvell's own sympathies had been with the Dutch from the beginning of this war, and as early as June 1672 he was writing to his nephew (at Bordeaux!) 'Affairs begin to alter, and Men talk of a Peace with *Holland*, and taking them into our Protection; and it is my Opinion it will be before *Michaelmas*, for some Reasons not fit to write. We cannot have a Peace with *France* and *Holland* both.' Though disappointed at the time, he did his best to turn his hopes into realities. Evidence, disturbing though not conclusive, has lately turned up of his association with a group of Englishmen who, even before their country made a separate peace (9 February 1673/4) acted in the Dutch interest. His name, however, does not appear in any document before May 1674, so that no charge of treason can be proved against him, even if others (including Peter du Moulin) be found guilty of it. He was suspected by a Government spy of visiting Holland secretly earlier in the year and spending one night at The Hague to speak with the Prince of Orange. So vague an information would deserve

little credit, did not another document (of 22 June 1674)
reveal that among the conspirators Marvell, the only M.P.
there mentioned, went by the code name of 'Mr. Thomas';
and a third document, of 30 June, says that the same 'Mr
Thomas', then in the country and not intending to return to
Town 'for some time' (Parliament was not sitting), had a
'difference' with at least one other member of the group,
who 'believed it [?] was Mr Thomas's fault'.[1]

At a higher level the same tortuous and complex methods
prevailed. Today we know that Louis XIV, the chief author
of the war in 1672, began to desire peace by 1674. From England he expected nothing better than neutrality, and to this
end he bribed the King and some leaders of the Opposition
impartially. The Prince of Orange breathed nothing but war.
Danby no less than Marvell wanted Charles to support his
nephew and the Protestant cause against Louis, who played
off the Opposition against the Prime Minister. The Commons, vociferous against France, yet refused to vote the
subsidies without which England could not join in the war.
Indeed their mistrust was but natural; they remembered
Charles's duplicity in 1670–2: once bitten, twice shy. Marvell wrote to his constituents, as late as 22 May 1677, voicing
their feelings as well as his: 'As farre as a man may guesse
there will be no mony given this sitting but upon very
visible and effectual termes.' The King, refusing to declare
war on France before he had the money, stood on his Pre-

---

[1] The discovery of this 'Dutch Fifth Column' in England was made by
K. H. D. Haley, *William of Orange and the English Opposition 1672–4*, 1953.
L. N. Wall, 'Marvell and the Third Dutch War', in *N.Q.*, July 1957, pp.
296–7, and Sir Gyles Isham, 'Abram van den Bempde', ibid., November
1957, pp. 461–3, have provided information on one of those Dutch agents
who was bound to Marvell by an 'inviolable Friendship', according to
Thomas Cooke (1726). To what lengths Marvell's party spirit, prompted by
his developing gallophobia and newly born concern for the safety of Holland,
could carry him is best seen in a hitherto unpublished letter of his (see *supra*,
p. 125, n. 1) of 24 October 1674. He tells Edward Thompson of the complaints
made by the English regiments still serving with the French army, as volun-
teers, and adds: 'The best is the complainants will daily diminish: most of
the Officers of Churchils Regiment hauing been killd, and Soldiers pro-
portionably: and of Littletons Regiment of Horse himselfe slain and but
forty men escaped & the other English had their part.' Of course 'Churchil'
is the future Duke of Marlborough; probably Marvell would have rejoiced
to hear that he too had been killed. Even if Marvell is jesting, his is a bitter
jest.

rogative, so that English policy found itself in a deadlock.
Parliament was adjourned on 28 May and again on 16 July.
No member resented it more than Marvell, and he used his
enforced leisure of the summer and autumn to write *An
Account of the Growth of Popery, and Arbitrary Government in
England. More Particularly from the Long Prorogation, of November, 1675. Ending the 15th of February 1676* [1677], *till the
Last Meeting of Parliament, the 16th of July, 1677*. In fact
Marvell brought his narrative up to a later adjournment
(3 December). With this reservation the long title of the
work gives a good idea of its plan: it is a history of the
Restoration from the war with Holland begun in 1665, very
compendious at first but growing more and more detailed,
and subordinating all the facts to a rigid, simple, indeed
over-simplified, theory: all the internal grievances, all the
external humiliations suffered by England for the last ten
years are caused by a small group of mysterious characters
whom Marvell calls 'the popish conspirators' (the only two
he names have dropped out of the highways of history). So
that we now incline to dismiss this indictment as out of all
proportion to the real importance of those indicted. But we
must not forget that the pamphleteer, even though anonymous, could not implicate the real culprit, viz. Charles II.
He even exonerates the Duke of York; nay, he praises him,
and Clifford, for honestly resigning their offices rather than
take the Test. If one objects that such a conspiracy of
nobodies does not greatly endanger either the political rights
or the Protestant faith of England, Marvell answers that the
conspirators have the support of the Papacy, the Jesuits, and
above all the French King. So that this pamphlet, lucid and
moderate in its wording, which included official documents
not before divulged and contained enough verifiable truths
to endow its most hazardous conjectures with plausibility,
attacks Louis XIV rather than Charles II. After having
written first against Holland, next against Spain, Marvell
now concentrates all his animosity against France, an evolution that makes him a good representative of English public
opinion between 1650 and 1678. The mean persecution of
the Huguenots, including those arch-Royalists he had con-
versed with at Saumur, came to his knowledge the more

movingly since his nephew witnessed at Bordeaux all those petty steps towards the Revocation of the Edict of Nantes. Yet the feeling to which the pamphleteer appeals is rather the jealousy aroused by the power of the *Grand Roy* and even more the French commercial and maritime expansion. While Louvois, the arch-persecutor, is not named, Colbert, beside an allusion in the *Account* itself to his unfairness, bears the brunt of a whole appendix against the privateers he is accused of encouraging. Thanks to a brutally protectionist customs tariff France exports ever more and imports ever less. Here Marvell voices the grievances of those moneyed men with whom he has private dealings. Elsewhere he sums up, with obvious approval, political (not to say—again—Machiavellian) arguments used by others in the House of Commons, e.g.: 'That enmity against the French was the thing wherein this divided nation did unite, and this occasion was to be laid hold on, as an opportunity of moment amongst ourselves.'

And speaking for himself he is not above preferring rather frivolous accusations, as when he sneers at the 'conspirators' for calling Louis XIV 'the king of France', while a good Englishman should only grant him the title of 'the French king'; but here again the Puritan proves more precise for others than for himself, since he uses the disloyal style in a verse satire and in a private letter. And, in another private letter (17 December 1677) he allows admiration to appear, by the side of fear and envy, when he quotes with explicit agreement a political friend's reluctant praise of the French: 'they fight when others are gone to bed, and before they be up'. Marvell feels all the more that the too wide-awake People should be weakened. In the former private letter he had recalled with scorn the charge made against him some years before (by a Nonconformist divine) that he was 'an Intelligencer to the King of France'; so that we cannot imagine that he would have approved the transactions between the leaders of the Opposition and the French Ambassador in London, had he been acquainted with them. We should see in the author of the *Account* the supporter, possibly the agent, but also the dupe of Shaftesbury, to whose glorification the whole pamphlet tends. Alone of the four

Lords sent to the Tower the Earl still lies there because he has refused to make his submission; therefore, his three associates are only 'confessors', while he is almost 'a martyr for the English liberties and the Protestant religion'. Marvell could well admire him all the more because he himself had not chosen the straight and narrow way (to the Tower) in somewhat similar circumstances. But, if we had any doubt of the sincerity of the pamphleteer on this point, a private letter of 7 August 1677 shows the same exaltation of Shaftesbury, more explicitly depressing Buckingham in comparison. The Duke had first desired 'a moneths aire' for his health and 'procured' it 'easily' through 'Nelly [Gwyn], Middlesex [later Dorset], Rochester, and the merry gang'; whereupon 'he layd constantly in Whitehall at my L: Rochester's logings leading the usuall life'. The Duke of York and Danby 'remonstrated to the King that this was to leap over all rules of decency'. Marvell here seems to incline rather to 'the Ministers of State' than to 'the Ministers of Pleasure'. The former finally prevailed, and Buckingham eventually 'presented a more acknowledging Petition than either Salisburyes or Wharton's' with equal success. 'People were full of vaine imaginations what changes he would make in Court but he loves Pleasure better than Revenge and yet this last is not the meanest luxury.' The satirist does not try here to conceal his own revengefulness, nor his disappointment with Fairfax's son-in-law. Only in Shaftesbury's Roman fortitude does he find comfort; and to exemplify this virtue he relates 'an incredible story', which yet he does not doubt, of the prisoner's scornfully rejecting overtures made by the Duke of York and threatening him to 'come betwixt him and his great hopes'. The story with its pompous conclusion has the same tone as that of Marvell's rejection of the bribe.

To promote his ambitious plan of altering the succession Shaftesbury must produce a claimant to the Crown. He was later to find him in Monmouth, Charles II's best-beloved bastard. Would Marvell have approved of the choice, had he lived a year or two longer? In 1670 Monmouth had shared the moral responsibility for the assault on Sir John Coventry, and the next year had actually taken part in the cowardly murder of a poor beadle. In his private

correspondence Marvell had judged severely both these two
crimes and the pardon granted by the King. But by 1674
we find the Member for Hull and the Duke communicating,
formally indeed but courteously. Marvell's visits to Monmouth became more frequent at the time of the publication
of the *Account*. Their ostensible object was purely local, the
Duke being High Steward of Hull. Marvell told his constituents of His Grace's 'great civility' to them. He seems
to have allowed himself to be captivated by the affable
manners and the fine presence of this vain, selfish, shallow,
and libertine man, so that, forgiving all youthful peccadillos
in consideration of an ostensible Protestantism, he may
have adhered *in petto* to a future Pretender whose success
would have eliminated the odious Duke of York. This is
mere conjecture, and if he did incline that way Marvell's
caution and reserve no doubt made him keep to himself an
opinion that could not be expressed at all safely in his lifetime.
However, another possible claimant presented nobler qualities (beside a less spurious hereditary right): William of
Orange, Charles I's grandson by his mother, had lately
strengthened his position by marrying his first cousin, Mary,
the Duke of York's elder daughter, on 24 October 1677.
But Danby's devoted support caused the Prince to be looked
at askance by the Opposition, and especially by Shaftesbury.
So that in the rivalry soon to oppose Monmouth and William
of Orange we may infer (but again as a mere conjecture)
that Marvell might have preferred the less able and worthy
of the two.

Can we indeed, from the *Account* (our author's last work,
save for a purely theological pamphlet) not only determine
his politics at the end of his life but imagine how he would
have behaved during the period of the so-called Popish
Plot? Certainly he had formulated the programme of the
party that would then be nicknamed Whig: reduce the King
to political impotence while continuing to him marks of
respect. From the satirist to the Merry Monarch this respect
could be no other than feigned, but, as we have repeatedly
noted, Marvell had nothing in him of the doctrinaire and
minded outward forms little if he could secure realities. He
here places his pen at Shaftesbury's service and gives the

Earl's ideas their most persuasive, least revolutionary expression because this now seems to him the readiest way of
promoting England's greatness, Protestant ascendancy, and
toleration for Dissenters. He implicitly condemns his own
former tactics, as can be seen in his censure of the *Declaration of Indulgence*, so highly praised by him at the time. Of
course anonymity prevents him from making a candid re-
cantation; but, had it been possible for him to speak out,
would he have pleaded guilty for his earlier pamphlets? We
wonder.

   Though Marvell briefed the Whigs of 1680, yet one must
not look into the *Account* for the theory of the parliamentary
régime as the eighteenth-century Whigs were to practise it
in a wholly empirical manner. No more than his contemporaries, including Locke, did he see that the executive
power could best be transferred from King to Parliament
through an homogeneous Administration, recruited from
the two Houses and politically responsible to them. He
shared the aversion of his age for 'cabals' and 'cabinet councils'; he did not distinguish between Ministers of State and
permanent Civil Servants; for both alike he understood
responsibility in the old sense of the word: he dreamt of
frequent impeachments, of penalties, no doubt reaching to
the scaffold or the gallows, inflicted by the Courts of Law
or by Parliament in its legal capacity upon the peculators
and traitors he saw almost everywhere. He did not explicitly
question the King's right to choose his counsellors but laid
down one limitation to the exercise of this right: the inter-
diction to take them from among the Members of the House
of Commons. In order to preserve this assembly from corruption a seat in it should be made incompatible with office,
e.g. the management of the Exchequer, the Navy, the Army,
the Colonies, or Trade. One of the most amusing pages in
the *Account* exposes the incapacity of a Member of Parliament to check the actions of a monarch whose pay he takes
at the same time. Over two years before, Marvell had acted
as teller for the ayes in a division on a Bill 'that any Member
of P^t who shall hereafter accept any Office after his Election
there shall be a new writ to elect in his place'. Did he
remember on that day his own amphibious position under

Richard Cromwell? Anyhow, he could not imagine that this separation of powers would be adopted a century later in America though rejected by his own country.

So far as Marvell foresaw the party system he condemned it. He says of his colleagues: 'it is as well-known among them, to what Lord each of them retain, as when formerly they wore coats and badges.' This is no bad definition of the eighteenth-century Whig Connexions; but what follows applies to every parliament with strongly organized parties: 'there is no place for deliberation, no perswading by reason, but they can see one another's votes through both throats and cravats before they hear them.' Yet the question arises once more: did Marvell conform his practice to his theory? Did he not on the contrary share in the organization of the still unnamed Whig party? Hostile assertions, worthy of little trust, make him the 'Record-keeper' of the faction, the secretary of one of the seditious clubs founded as early as 1673. Let us beware of affirming but also of denying it. Such a contradiction would not be the first he must be credited with.

The *Account* caused enough of a stir for the Government to take notice of it. The *London Gazette* for 21–25 March 1677/8 offered a 'considerable' reward 'to any who could inform of the Author or Printer'. An anonymous pamphlet dated 18 April 1678 and entitled *A letter from Amsterdam, to a Friend in England*, written covertly in the interest of the Administration, alluded very clearly to Marvell, though it gave only his Christian name, followed by the description: 'a shrewd man against Popery'. And Marvell himself, in his last private (and probably unsigned) letter, dated 10 June 1678, tells his nephew of the *Account*, adding: 'Three or four printed Books . . . have described, as near as it was proper to go, the Man being a Member of Parliament, Mr. *Marvell* to have been the Author; but if he had, surely he should not have escaped being questioned in Parliament, or some other Place.' This badinage shows that he did not feel in much danger. In fact the Secretary of State, still Sir Joseph Williamson, seems to have been in no hurry to discover the author, though he had early imprisoned the printer. When an informer sent the Secretary a report fathering the *Account* on Marvell, Marvell had been dead for six days.

Possibly the King again intervened to slow down the proceedings. From January to the end of May Charles tried to conciliate the Commons, since he had become very earnest about the war, especially after the taking of Ghent by Louis XIV on March 2/12. But the Commons preferred to tackle the subject of severer persecution of the Papists. The sixteenth session opened on 23 May with excitement at its highest. Marvell notes in letters to Hull that the House is unusually full. It was almost equally divided but mistrust prevailed. On the 31st a Committee of the whole House indeed voted 'That a supply should be given to his Majesty' but only 'toward the paying and disbanding of all the Forces raised since the 29th of September'. The game was up. On 22 June Marvell wrote: 'many Members go daily away and all here are weary.' On 6 July he relates that the voting in a division was 78 against 68, 'so thin is the House'. This is the last letter of his that has been preserved. Nine days later Parliament was prorogued. On the 31st peace was signed at Nimeguen between Louis XIV and the States General of the United Provinces to which Charles had been prevented from giving sufficient assistance to continue the war. Three days later the Prince of Orange, pretending not to have been informed, tried to surprise Marshal Luxembourg; at the bloody and aimless battle of Saint-Denis (or Mons) the English auxiliary forces (in the pay of the States) under the Earl of Ossory (Ormond's son and a Tory, without the name as yet) prevented the French from completing their defeat of the Dutch and Spanish. If Marvell heard of it, it was the last piece of public news he learnt in this world.

On 29 July he was visiting Hull, for the first time it seems in many years. On 16 August he died in London at the house in Great Russell Street he had caused Mary Palmer to rent the year before.[1] In the seventeenth century such sudden death always roused a suspicion of poison. A contemporary poem asks 'whether Fate or Art untwined his thread' and leaves it in doubt. Others freely ascribed the poisoning to the Jesuits. In fact Marvell was killed, strictly in accordance with the rules of medicine, by an old-fashioned physician

[1] L. N. Wall, 'Marvell's Friends in the City', N.Q., June 1959, p. 204.

who, finding him laid up with a tertian ague, bled and sweated his patient into a profound sleep, during which he died 'apoplectice', i.e. comatose. The grim joke is that the 'conceited doctor', who used to rave against the 'cortex peruvianus', might have saved Marvell by administering a single ounce of that bark introduced into Europe by the Jesuits and known as the Jesuits' powder. So much is revealed by a medical treatise published in 1692 by Richard Morton; its unimpeachable testimony disposes of the rumour accusing the enemies of English freedom of having poisoned its most steadfast champion.[1] But the rumour at least shows the part Marvell was beginning to play in the estimation of the public. From his satirical Nebo he had glimpsed the Promised Land. England was soon to hear his call and awaken to her perils. But since this awakening took the ugly form we know of, it was better for him that he did not run the risk of staining his reputation as a champion of religious tolerance by joining in the cruelties exercised on the Roman Catholics as a consequence of the spurious revelations of Titus Oates, who was to borrow from the *Account* the most specious features of his Popish Plot.

[1] F. S. Tupper, *ut supra*, discusses the circumstances of Marvell's death in an appendix; after reviving the suspicion of poisoning, but this time against some of Marvell's political and business associates, he finally comes back to Morton's version, plausibly adding that the fits of the ague seized Marvell on his way from Hull to London.

VI

THE SATIRIST IN VERSE

THE critic who undertakes to write on Marvell's satires
ventures on quicksands. Apart from the three early
pieces, 'Fleckno', 'Tom May's Death', and 'The Character of Holland', the canon of his work as a satirist consists
of a series of decreasing probabilities, beginning on the
hither side of certainty and ending just short of utter in-
credibility. One thing can be affirmed: from 1667 onwards
Marvell wrote against the Court verse that was circulated
at least in manuscript, sometimes perhaps in broadsheets or
booklets. His enemies, answering his long prose pamphlet
The Rehearsal Transpros'd in 1673, make scornful references
to those writings of his, e.g.: 'If you must be scribbling,
betake yourself to your own proper trade of lampoons and
ballads.' But Marvell took good care not to provide the
authorities with any incriminating evidence. His name appeared on a printed satire only in 1689, after the Revolution
had rid England of his old enemy, James II. But thenceforth,
during some fifteen years, unscrupulous booksellers freely
used his name to vend their goods. Eighteenth-century
additions to the canon, made from documents now lost,[1]
inextricably mix the likely and the absurd. In the nineteenth and twentieth centuries criticism has aimed chiefly at
eliminating the spurious, with some measure of success.
For the present the satires fathered on Marvell at one time
or another fall, roughly, into two groups, the probable and
the improbable. The former group includes: 'Clarindon's
House-Warming' (July 1667) with perhaps its two adjuncts,
'Upon his House' and 'Upon his Grand-Children'; 'The last
Instructions to a Painter' (autumn of 1667); 'Further Advice
to a Painter' (1670–1); 'The Loyall Scot', at least most of

---

[1] One volume, acquired by the Bodleian in 1945 (MS. Eng. poet. d. 49)
and described and discussed by Hugh Macdonald in *T.L.S.*, 13 July 1951,
may well be one of the documents referred to above. See Margoliouth's
additional note on this point, in his revised edition, 1952, pp. xiv–xv.

it (between 1669 and 1673); 'The Statue in Stocks-Market' (1672?); 'The Statue at Charing Cross' (July 1675); 'A Dialogue between the Two Horses' (end of 1675); to which may be added two pieces in Latin verse, 'Bludius et Corona' (1671) and 'Scaevola Scoto-Brittannus' (1677). The latter group includes: 'The Kings Vowes', also called 'Royal Resolutions' (May 1670); 'Nostradamus's Prophecy' (1671–2?); 'Britannia and Rawleigh' (beginning of 1674?); 'Upon his Majesties being made free of the Citty' (December 1674); and 'The Chequer Inn' (1675). We shall ground our conclusions on the satires of the former group only, though we may occasionally refer to, or even quote from, those of the latter group. This survey thus runs the risk of precariousness but it would do so anyhow, and the risk is the smaller because in the matter of authorship negative proof is almost as difficult to supply as positive proof.[1]

Besides, we derive some comfort from this observation: all the additions to and subtractions from the canon proposed for over two hundred years do not appreciably alter Marvell's characteristics as a satirist.

Political satire in verse is as old in England as Magna Carta and derives from the same instinct. But we shall look for Marvell's predecessors no further back than the Civil War,[2] and even confine ourselves to one of them. No doubt

---

[1] Thus I wrote in 1928. Since then little has been done to alter the canon of Marvell's satires. However, G. de F. Lord, 'Two New Poems by Marvell', in *Bulletin of the New York Public Library*, November 1958 and July 1959 (contradicted by E. G. Fogel, ibid., May 1959) makes a gallant, but to me unconvincing, attempt to establish Marvell's authorship of the 'Second' and 'Third' 'Advices to a Painter' (see *infra*); he does not answer Margoliouth's main argument for rejecting it: whoever wrote these also wrote the 'Fourth' and 'Fifth' 'Advices', which Marvell certainly did not.—As regards 'Britannia and Rawleigh', the case for its rejection has been strengthened by H. F. Brooks; see Margoliouth's additional note, *ut supra*, p. xiv. Godfrey Davies, in *H.L.Q.*, 1945–6, ix. 311–18, dates this satire earlier than Margoliouth and I did, by at least a year; his dating I accept; but he leaves the authorship unsettled. So does E. S. de Beer for 'Nostradamus's Prophecy', the 'Second Part' of which he, in *N.Q.*, 20 August 1949, pp. 360–2, separates from the first as regards the date of its composition: not earlier than April 1673. Margoliouth ignored this correction, plausible if not decisive.

[2] A recent well-informed and very readable book, *Poetry and Politics under the Stuarts*, 1960, by an historian of high repute, C. V. Wedgwood, does not materially affect Marvell's position in the general perspective.

Marvell had read or heard many of the minor *Rump Songs* and their less numerous counterparts against the Cavaliers, but we cannot assess his indebtedness to them; we know, however, how much he owed to John Cleveland. This poet, in the eight satires that can safely be ascribed to him, proves himself a hard fighter, assured in his political principles, incapable of nuances. Each of his couplets deals a straight blow. No feints are used, no preparations; no gradation even, no combination, nor order. He has been ingeniously compared to one of his heroes, Prince Rupert, a brilliant cavalry officer but an indifferent general, irresistible in a charge but worthless for the defence of a town. Accordingly he aims at rivalling Archilochus' 'keen iambics' and invites his own decasyllabics 'badger-like [to] bite till [their] teeth do meet'. His imagery derives from that of the metaphysicals, whom he tries to outdo in hyperbolical conceits, verging on burlesque even in his lyrical verse. But this outré style could not scare away Marvell, and for the influence of the older man (Cleveland had been born in 1613) on the younger one we have stronger evidence than a general likeness. They may have known each other at Cambridge since, while Marvell was an undergraduate and then B.A. at Trinity, Cleveland was a fellow of St. John's and there wrote his first satire against the Puritans in 1640. At any rate Marvell knew of Cleveland even before the unprecedented success of the printed collections of the Royalist poet's verse: there were some twenty editions, it is said, between 1647 and 1687.

Cleveland's most famous satire, 'The Rebel Scot', was written in 1643 or 1644, when the Covenanters crossed the Tweed to assist the English Parliament. A quarter of a century later, in the national humiliation caused by Ruyter's incursion in the Medway, a Scotsman preserved British honour: young Captain Douglas refused to leave, when it was set on fire, the *Royal Oak* with whose defence his company had been entrusted; he was burnt to death. This tragic end, first related by Marvell in 'The last Instructions to a Painter', later became the subject of a separate poem, which he entitled 'The Loyall Scot' so as to make it a counterpart to Cleveland's satire. In order to proclaim his intention he describes, in a sort of Prologue in the Elysian Fields, Douglas's arrival among the heroes of former days: to welcome him these elect Cleveland, who will thus make amends to the nation he has slandered. The satirist readily complies. There follow Douglas's portrait and the account of his death; but, as if the heroic episode were a mere excuse, Marvell then makes Cleveland plead eloquently for the parliamentary union of England and Scotland; and imitation as well as his own temperament turn praise and argument to railing against the supposed obstacle to the Union, viz. the Anglican clergy and above all the bishops; and in one passage (ll. 106–16) three or four taunts against the Scots are turned into sneers at the English prelates. True, Marvell's authorship of this part of the satire has been questioned;[1] but, even if we confine ourselves to evidence gathered from poems or even prose works undoubtedly his, we can list over half-a-dozen patent borrowings or echoes from Cleveland.

One might ask whether another Royalist satirist, far greater and better known today, the author of *Hudibras*, did not give lessons in the art to Marvell. But in spite of his seniority it seems that Samuel Butler rather borrowed from 'The Character of Holland' than Marvell from Butler's lines on the same country. What traits they have in common may well proceed from Cleveland's influence on both. Anyhow, Marvell, who preferred the octosyllabic couplet, as we have seen, for his lyrical poetry, never used it for satire, which divides him radically from Butler, whose talent he yet praises in the two parts of *The Rehearsal Transpros'd*. And it is in this prose pamphlet, if at all, that he reveals the influence of Hudibrastic burlesque.

If Cleveland alone deserves to be called Marvell's master in political satire, we must not forget that this, however peculiar as regards its matter and purpose, is only a species of the satiric genre. And in this broader sense we may say that Marvell had many models, some ancient, others modern,

---

[1] The probability of its being Marvell's has increased with the discovery of the tract in the possession of the Library Company of Philadelphia (see p. 137, n. 1). The major part of the passages hitherto known through manuscripts only are found in this printed text, which may well be contemporary and at any rate does not derive from any other one collated so far.

as for his lyrical verse. We need only repeat here the names
of Horace among the former and Donne among the latter.
Of course this double line of descent appears chiefly in
'Fleckno', a youthful, almost a tiro's work and Marvell's
only non-political satire, which treats the traditional theme
of the poetaster-bore, adding to it a few traits borrowed
from that of the ridiculous feast.

While not a single one of the Greek satirists, not even
Aristophanes, seems to have been drawn upon, one can
assert that Marvell knew all their Latin rivals. Martial, more
or less directly, has prompted our poet's epigrams, English
as well as Latin. As for Juvenal, he remained, from Marston
and Hall through the young Henry Vaughan to Dryden
himself, a favourite with the English satirists, who did not
mind his excesses.

It is possible that Marvell had read satires in all the four
foreign living languages credited to him by Milton. In Rome
he must have enjoyed the Pasquins, and some thirty years
later have taken the hint from them when he wrote his
pieces on the statues in London. In France his preference for
the free humour of the sixteenth century and those who
maintained it in the seventeenth makes it probable that he
had read the *Satire Ménippée*, Agrippa d'Aubigné's *Les
Tragiques*, and Mathurin Regnier's *Satires*; from these last
one or two sallies may have passed into 'Fleckno'. Compare
the French pedant's garb:

> Pour sa robbe elle fut autre qu'elle n'estoit
> Alors qu'Albert le Grand aux festes la portoit

with the English priest's:

> And above that [= his 'Sotana'] yet casts an antick Cloak,
> Worn at the first Counsel of Antioch;

As to Boileau, his junior by fifteen years, Marvell probably
knew his work only when his own very different manner
had been established.

To say that a satire is political defines its content in a very
summary way. It may relate political events ironically, or
caricature political characters, or present political manners

in an unflattering light, or again attempt to discredit political theories by mocking them. Marvell's satire does all these but in very unequal proportions.

The share of the event, the actual happening, largely outweighs the others. Here the author's mind appears intent on the facts, the concrete. Just as in his letters he shows himself a gazette-writer in prose, here he reveals himself a political journalist in verse. The term 'rimed chronicle', too limited to cover all his satires, perfectly fits the longest and best known of them, 'The last Instructions to a Painter'. In it Marvell tells nine or ten months of the history of England, diplomatic negotiations, parliamentary debates, naval operations, intrigues of the bed-chamber or the lobby, and his narrative seems to be written day by day, as the events impress him immediately. The poet follows the chronological order even more docilely than he had done in 'The First Anniversary of the Government under O.C.'. For the two poems have a fairly similar structure, which the difference in the tone cannot conceal: what substitutes raillery for praise is less the choice of the poet than the decline of England, glorious in 1654, humiliated in 1667.

The only satires in which an attempt is made to rise above current affairs belong to the group more doubtfully Marvell's. There only the satirist sometimes tries to see things from a higher point of view. And anyhow such attempts remain exceptions; most commonly a single piece of news provides him with the matter of a piece of verse. The Lord Chancellor builds himself a palace out of the money he has (according to our poet) dishonestly accumulated: we have 'Clarindon's House-Warming' and 'Upon his House'. Colonel Blood has tried to steal the Crown in the Tower: Marvell seizes upon the opportunity to write two epigrams. A wealthy banker, Sir Robert Viner, sets up an equestrian statue of Charles II on an open space in the City, but before the last touch has been put to the work bankruptcy surprises the loyal subject, and that through the King's financial dishonesty: here is the whole substance of 'The Statue in Stocks-Market'. The Earl of Danby, emulous (Marvell suggests) of the reputation Sir Robert has acquired through his artistic munificence, or wanting 'to comfort the hearts of the poor Cavaleer', ruined by the Civil War and allowed to starve by the Restoration, offers the public a statue, also equestrian, of the Royal Martyr. But the High Treasurer does not prove more expeditious than the City goldsmith: an excellent occasion to ask, concerning this still veiled monument, and the 'prorogation' that the despotic Danby inflicts on the late King as he has done on Parliament, a series of bantering questions—in 'The Statue at Charing Cross'. Among the less doubtful satires, only 'A Dialogue between the Two Horses' submits the régime to a more general and abstract survey. Everywhere else all the other motifs are subordinated to the event, related, described, commented upon, or just recalled in a brief allusion.

But this subordination obtains only in the literary field, not in the philosophical one. Men, for Marvell, direct events, or if they allow themselves to be driven by events, that is indolence or cowardice on their part. A Clarendon, a Duke of York are responsible for the calamities that overtake England, for these are caused by their malignant activity; hardly less guilty than those melodramatic villains is the log of a King who if he chose could put everything in order again but does not take the trouble to do it. This conception of history (or maybe we should rather say 'this hypothesis convenient for the satirist') seems logically to entail an elaborate study of the recesses of the characters' minds in order to find there the springs of the fate of the nation. But patient and detailed moral analysis is not in our poet's line. By way of compensation he who never wrote for the stage yet possesses a certain dramatic sense; he nearly always presents his victims in motion. If we consider that two of his satires are addressed to an imaginary painter whose pencil they pretend to direct we shall wonder at the small number of full-length portraits. When we think that Marvell is going to make a character sit for him he passes on at once to the story of his life, of his deeds. The physical description is often picturesque but the moral one remains summary.

Besides, Marvell scatters his shots too widely: in 'The last Instructions to a Painter' there appear 84 contemporaries in 990 lines; in Dryden's *Absalom and Achitophel* there were to be 27 in 1,030 lines. Sometimes names, now forgotten,

follow one another in a dry enumeration, without even the
alms of an opprobrious epithet. It matters little whether the
modern editor succeeds or not in identifying these mutes:
they march past with a gesture, we see the gesture and ask
for no circumstances. Sometimes an obscure nobody is
honoured with a paragraph or a stanza, and yet we do not
trouble about the likeness; if we are amused our sense of
justice lies asleep, even our sense of human complexity.

Not so with Marvell's highest-placed victims, Charles II,
the Duke of York, and Clarendon. The modern reader ex-
pects here more nuances, if not greater impartiality; he
wants to see composed portraits in which the painter's art
enhances the shadows by means of the lights. Will he find
them?

For Clarendon, obviously not. Whether in the long narrative of 'The last Instructions' or in the pleasant figment of
'Clarindon's House-Warming', Marvell merely aims a number of burlesque shafts at his arch-enemy-for-the-moment,
without taking the trouble to work out the general effect.
The 'Chanc'lor's Belly', the 'tallow' worthy of a prize ox,
the gouty decrepitude that a prorogation of Parliament cures
miraculously, those features culled here and there will do
for the body. As for the soul, the ostentatious pride that
makes Clarendon sit 'in State Divine like *Jove* the *fulminant*';
his self-assurance, all the more laughable that this would-be
statesman, hoary with years of service, remains a mere
pedant; his uncontrolled anger after the issue has proved
that pretended wisdom a fraud; in the time of his power
rancour and greed:

> Gain and Revenge, Revenge and Gain are sweet:
> United most, else when by turns they meet.

Arbitrarily Marvell makes avarice the ruling passion of the
Chancellor, whose merits all disappear. His political stead-
fastness, loyalty to the King during the long exile, wide
learning, admiration for and friendship with so many contemporary scholars and poets, all these count for nothing
with Marvell. Of course the great *History of the Rebellion*, as
yet unfinished, was unknown to the satirist, but he knew the
ample and yet easy prose, majestic without being pompous,

precise without vulgarity, of so many papers written by
Edward Hyde for his King; he knew it and he called it
'flippant', which strikes us as not only unfair but inept. Of
all the stings in the satires this one probably rankled worst
with Clarendon, if he read them; if he did read them the
statesman and historian's complete silence on his accuser
amounts to a crushingly scornful rebuke.

On the Duke of York there is surprisingly little anyhow,
and next to nothing remains if we leave out the more doubtful satires. At any rate Marvell shows himself less unfair to
him than to Clarendon and at least respects the bounds
beyond which plausibility itself vanishes.

Of Charles II a portrait far more interesting, because of
its finely graded tints, can be extracted from the satires. Successive sketches here bear witness to the author's political
evolution, and even more to the figure's complexity; they
do not contradict, they rather correct, by complementing,
one another. Now, of Marvell's great victims Charles most
deserves the reprobation of the Puritan moralist, and even
of the moralist *tout court*. But beside the tactical reasons our
poet had for dealing gently with the King, we discern a
sympathy between two dispositions curiously similar at
bottom, though diverted by education and the circumstances
of life in almost opposite directions. This accounts for the
surprising moderation of the first charges levelled at the
King and, mixed with the violence of the later ones, surprising reappearances of hope and trust.

Unfortunately we come up against the same difficulty as
for the Duke of York: the most telling passages occur in
satires of very uncertain authorship. The chances that Marvell wrote the justly famous opening of 'An Historicall
Poem' are so small that we dare not base our appreciation
on these lines. But since the evidence against his penning
'Upon his Majesties being made free of the Citty' is nil and
though the evidence for it is very slight we can at least say
it is Marvellian in its humour and gives such a character of
Charles as the Member for Hull would have agreed with.
The author is addressing citizens, strict on diligence in one's
vocation and on commercial honesty; therefore, wanting to
set forth the sovereign's laziness and costly lustfulness, he

presents him as a naughty apprentice. In a dozen stanzas we
have a portrait in action: no subtle analysis but alert observation and lively staging. The originality here consists in the
allegorical use of incidents familiar to popular literature
with a moral purpose; we only miss the inevitable end, viz.
the hanging of the ne'er-do-well, the haunter of taverns and
playhouses, the gull of actresses and other courtesans, the
father of foundlings reluctantly taken in charge by the
parish, a dishonest borrower, a braggart and a coward, and
one who would 'burglar' his own master did not his heart
fail him at the last minute. But, doing this, the writer of the
song (a parody of those sung at the Lord Mayor's table the
two preceding years) has shown Charles II to be no monster,
only a selfish and sensual man of a very common variety
whom his crown alone places outside ordinary humanity:
not a comforting conclusion, yet a refreshing one after so
many contemporary declamations against 'Sardanapalus'.
On this occasion Marvell, if it be he, has exceeded the realm
of merely political satire and, via the satire of manners,
attained to the satire of character.

Alas! this breadth of treatment remains quite exceptional
with him. He avails himself but little of the opportunities
that offer of discovering the general in the individual. When
he attacks the Countess of Castlemaine he does not see in
her the royal favourite *par excellence*, he just tells a scandalous
anecdote preceded by epigrams on her age, which has affected
her beauty but not her amorous temperament. More
elaborate and detailed, but marred by a coarseness that cannot even, it seems, plead accuracy, the portrait of Anne
Hyde witnesses only to Marvell's hatred of a wretched
woman guilty of being Clarendon's daughter and the Duke
of York's wife. Though the poet consistently denounces, in
the broadest terms, the lewdness of his butts of either sex,
yet he does not create a voluptuous atmosphere in order to
expose its deleterious influence. He deals only in personal
remarks. His scattered censures on the manners of the
Restoration being so obviously partial deserve credit only
so far as they are confirmed by Evelyn's probity or Pepys's
boundless candour. And, artistically speaking, the apt satire
of that frivolous sensuality could be the achievement only

of such men as shared in it, being both accomplices and judges, e.g. Etheredge and Hamilton: they naturally find the tone that does not rouse the suspicion of the average man in the presence of the preacher. That suspicion Marvell raises at once. If he provides us with information concerning the age, he does it indirectly, by showing how angry its corruption could make a soul by inclination merry and even jovial, still respectful of the plain moral code.

Yet circumstance, rather than his own genius, assigned to our poet a satiric province over which he ruled without question: Parliament. From his seat in the House of Commons or in the rooms to which Members retired, 'Spent with *fatigue*, to breath a while Toback', he minutely noted the specific qualities of the *homo parliamentarius*, and also the nature of this collective being, strangely distinct at times from its component individuals, a legislative assembly. In his letters to the Hull Corporation here and there a detail is made picturesque for us by the lapse of centuries. For instance, when daylight fails 'the question [is] put for candles', which are or are not 'brought in' by a division. Or else the House rises earlier than usual, 'the day being extraordinarily cold to which the breaking of one of the House-windows contributed'. In a private letter (24 July 1675) Marvell shows us a tumult: 'upon Dispute of telling right upon Division, both Parties grew so hot, that all Order was lost; Men came running confusedly up to the Table, grievously affronted one by another; every Man's Hand on his Hilt.' Those are memories of a dead past. But in 'The last Instructions', where the poet tries to give a vivid picture of the debates on finance and the war, what strikes the reader, possibly more the foreign than the English one, is an unexpected modernity. Manners, good or bad, that are of recent date elsewhere, already obtained at Westminster. The warping of the mind by habit, which leads to insincere speech and oblique manoeuvring, is perceived in this satire though not explicitly denounced. And at the same time this assembly, in spite of the trickery of its several members, is like any other crowd where Chance decides, and dice, so says the satirist, must choose the winning side. About the same time Pepys writes in his diary: 'The House of Commons a beast not to be understood.'

In 'The last Instructions' the procession of the members of the Court Party is dated by some details: the insolvent debtor who sees in the privileges of the House a means of escaping his creditors belongs to history; gone also are the King's panders. But when we come to the sitting itself we find ourselves in a familiar country. In this metaphorical battle the heat is the greater because the danger is small. The two Coventry brothers, chosen joint-generals,

> accept the Charge with merry glee,
> To fight a Battel, from all Gun-shot free.
>   Pleas'd with their Numbers, yet in Valour wise,
> They feign a parly, better to surprize:

Already some sitting hours lent themselves to snap divisions:

> Thick was the Morning, and the *House* was thin,
> The *Speaker* early, when they all fell in.
> Propitious Heavens, had you not them crost,
> *Excise* had got the day, and all been lost.
> For th' other side all in loose Quarters lay,
> Without Intelligence, Command, or Pay:
> A scatter'd Body, which the Foe ne'r try'd,
> But oftner did among themselves divide.

(Here Marvell seems to regret the lack of organization and discipline of the Country Party: possibly he objected to those limitations of individual members' freedom only when found on the other side.)

The Speaker, chosen by the House, which he should serve but betrays to the Court, is Sir Edward Turnor, the same who in 1662 gave a ruling against Marvell in his quarrel with Clifford. Now he is to pay for his offence, and for once we shall quote in full:

> Dear *Painter*, draw this *Speaker* to the foot:
> Where Pencil cannot, there my Pen shall do't;
> That may his Body, this his Mind explain.
> Paint him in Golden Gown, with Mace's Brain:
> Bright Hair, fair Face, obscure and dull of Head;
> Like Knife with Iv'ry haft, and edge of Lead.
> At Pray'rs, his Eyes turn up the Pious white,
> But all the while his *Private-Bill*'s in sight.

In Chair, he smoaking sits like Master-Cook,
And a *Poll-Bill* does like his Apron look.
Well was he skill'd to season any question,
And make a sawce fit for Whitehall's digestion:
Whence ev'ry day, the Palat more to tickle,
Court-mushrumps ready are sent in in pickle.
When *Grievance* urg'd, he swells like squatted Toad,
Frisks like a Frog to croak a *Taxes* load.
His patient Piss, he could hold longer then
An Urinal, and sit like any Hen.
At Table, jolly as a Country-Host,
And soaks his Sack with *Norfolk*[1] like a Toast.
At night, than *Canticleer* more brisk and hot,
And Serjeants Wife serves him for *Partelott*.

For five years the poet has been awaiting the day of revenge.
This delay has done him the service of clarifying his resentment: instead of a bitter and muddy beverage we have a
hearty and smiling liquor. Marvell's humour here is akin to
that of Chaucer, whom the names of Chanticleer and Partlet
recall inevitably. With the same seductiveness he has the
same awkwardness; here is no more perspective, chiaro-
scuro, order than in the portraits of the Man of Law, the
Franklin, the Cook, from each of which that of Turnor
seems to have borrowed some traits. Whether Chaucer made
individuals sit to him or not, the pilgrims of his Prologue
stand to us as representative of social classes or trades.
Marvell undoubtedly rallies an individual; but today Turnor
has sunk into oblivion, and yet the salt of this piece of
satire has not gone stale because in this hypocritical epicure
and lecher we still recognize, handled burlesquely, some
recurrent features of presidents of legislative assemblies.

In nearly every one of the satires attributed to Marvell
there are found onslaughts on parliamentary corruption and
servility. Too often they oscillate between slanderous per-
sonalities and declamatory generalities. Yet one passage in
'A Dialogue between the Two Horses', without naming any
Member, avoids pure rhetoric thanks to the precision of the
details. In 'a Curst hous of Commons' the renegades of
the Country Party come in for special reprobation: some
of the late 'bold talking members' have been included in

[1] The Serjeant-at-Arms.

the recently made 'rabble of Rascally Lords'; others 'rail at
the Court,—And get good preferment . . . for it'. Bribed
Members:

> give away Millions at every Summons.—
> Yet some of those givers such beggerly Villains
> As not to be trusted for twice fifty shillings.—
> No wonder that Beggers should still be for giving
> Who out of what's given do get a good living.—
> Four Knights and a Knave, who were Publicans made,
> For selling their Conscience were Liberally paid.—
> Yet baser the souls of those low priced Sinners,
> Who vote with the Court for drink and for Dinners.

Marvell's contempt puts lowest in the scale of corruption
the hungry parasites whose intelligence does not exceed
their honesty. Against these he wrote his (if it be his) 'Ballad
call'd the Chequer Inn', a lively parody of Sir John Suckling's 'Ballad of a Wedding'.

And yet, in this House of Commons, so roughly handled
by him, the satirist acknowledges the presence, at least in
1667, of a number of worthy men. Besides the political
friends he mentions by name he praises two groups of
Members for their resistance to Excise. The former is recruited from the urban middle class:

> a seas'nable recruit
> Of Citizens and Merchants held dispute:
> And, charging all their Pikes, a sullen Band
> Of *Presbyterian Switzers*, made a stand.

Most likely we must see here an extended form of hendiadys:
the Citizens and the Presbyterians are the same men. Of
these Marvell writes somewhat condescendingly, with the
man of the world's smile, which might surprise us since his
own electors at Hull were probably as Presbyterian at heart
as they were bourgeois in their way of life. And yet Marvell's fuller sympathy apparently goes to another social class,
one to which he never belonged; according to him the
Opposition owes its victory to the squires (in the sense the
word was then acquiring):

> A *Gross* of *English Gentry*, nobly born,
> Of clear *Estates*, and to no Faction sworn;

Dear Lovers of their King, and Death to meet,
For Countrys Cause, that Glorious think and sweet:
To speak not forward, but in Action brave;
In giving Gen'rous, but in Counsel Grave;
Candidly credulous for once, nay twice;
But sure the *Devil* cannot cheat them thrice.

Of course this praise is largely tactical, as is the solicitude shown in 'The Statue at Charing Cross' for 'the poor Cavaleer' whose 'pensions are stopt' (a strange subject of concern for the former secretary to the Lord Protector). Yes; and yet there rings in those lines on the most English of all English classes a national pride that seems sincere. Without making of Marvell a Monsieur Jourdain north of the Channel, one may note that this bourgeois with Nonconformist leanings, a town dweller most of his life, and something of a bohemian, reserves his greatest admiration for the gentleman-born, rooted in the soil, a fervent Royalist and (though the poet here ignores it) a fanatical Anglican. The remark assumes its full significance if one remembers that the literature of the age, being the reflection of the prejudices of the Courtiers, derides the Squire almost as pitilessly as the Citizen.

There is another sort of men on whom these satires complement the information given by the other contemporary documents, but in a very different spirit: out of prudence rather than sincere respect the banterers of the age abstain from taking the clergy for their butts, at least the higher clergy, prelates and benefit-holders. Marvell, bolder under the cloak of anonymity, shoots a shaft at priests, especially bishops, in almost every satire. In 'The last Instructions' the Archbishop of Canterbury himself is sketched wittily, and for once without savagery. After the disaster at Chatham the Court laments:

Grave *Primate Shelden* (much in Preaching there)
Blames the last Session, and this more does fear.
With *Boynton* or with *Middleton* 'twere sweet;
But with a *Parliament* abhors to meet,
And thinks 'twill ne're be well within this Nation,
Till it be govern'd by a *Convocation*.

Boynton and Middleton are 'languishing' heroines of the
Mémoires de Grammont. Much graver charges are preferred
against Sheldon, and in coarse language, by 'The Loyall
Scot'; but since this part of the poem may not be Marvell's
we mention it only because it attacks, besides the man at its
head, the Anglican ecclesiastical estate as a body. The poem
ridicules *inter alia* its claim to independence of the temporal
power and to a *jus divinum*; a claim inherited by the Church
of England from the Church of Rome:

> The Mitred Hubbub against Pluto Moot
> That Cloven Head must Govern Cloven foot.

(i.e. the Bishops want to rule the Devil himself when they
have reached their last home.) As Marvell showed in *The
Rehearsal Transpros'd* he was ready to defend the temporal
against the spiritual. In his last satires, however, he chiefly
attacks the royal despotism; and, if he implicates the clergy,
it is because they preach to their flocks the doctrine of passive obedience to the sovereign, wicked, impious, and
tyrannical as he may prove. Though it derives from Luther
and was established in England, as regards its substance if
not its wording, by Henry VIII and Elizabeth I, this doctrine is no less odious to Marvell than the preceding one.
In order to discredit it the more surely, the author of
'Britannia and Rawleigh' (if not Marvell, at least in agreement with him on this point) ascribes it to 'a Dame bedeckt
with spotted pride', viz. France. Killing two birds with one
stone, the satirist also makes Hobbes responsible for this
servility, and finally blames the success of the philosophy
of *Leviathan* on the Church of England, a glaring distortion
of the facts. Yet this speech (put in the mouth of a wicked
allegorical character and therefore interpreted by the reader
'the clean contrary way') is the nearest thing to an orderly
and methodical argument that can be found in any of the
satires ascribed to Marvell. 'Britannia and Rawleigh' stands
as his chief, though most precarious, title to a superior position in the satiric hierarchy: outflying political manners
satire soars here to the level of political ideas.

Though the Anglican clergy generally supported the
Stuarts' pretensions to absolute power, Charles II, egged

on by the Duke of York, had come to rely more on his army, however small, as a means of keeping Parliament in awe. At any rate Marvell and his political associates ascribed this intention to him. Some satires strike at the very notion of a standing army. 'The last Instructions' ends with the words, addressed to the King: 'rule without a *Guard*'. Earlier in the same piece Marvell derides the Court's fondness for regular soldiers (as opposed to the Militia). The passage is witty and biting, but one suspects the poet of adapting his opinion to the circumstances: he had never advised Cromwell against maintaining far larger and more formidable forces. True, the military anarchy that followed close upon Oliver's death may have opened his eyes; a letter of 17 November 1660 to his constituents shows him as anxious as any Cavalier to see the Republican Army at last disbanded. He never swerved from this position, but only, one fears, because he did not live long enough. Had he survived to see the War of the League of Augsburg he would have thought William III's Army ever too small, and, during the War of the Succession in Spain, that of Marlborough. Thus at any rate his political heirs, the Whigs, were to behave. To use unpleasant modernisms, Marvell's anti-militarism is accidental, while his anti-clericalism is essential.

On the whole the satires provide little material for a study of Marvell's thought: the texts are too few, some of them too brief, and a doubt still hangs over the authorship. They chiefly avail to prove that on certain points, especially the dynastic problem or even the monarchical form of government, the prose pamphlets do not reveal their author's inmost thoughts but only such dulcified opinions as would not frighten the electors. On all other points we had better consult the more detailed pamphlets, not quite so negative, and of unquestioned authorship.

Thus, if we confine ourselves to the verse satires we find that the discussion of ideas occupies less space than the description of manners; the description of manners yields to the painting of individuals; individuals hardly appear except in motion, in the course of a narrative the matter of which is provided by external events. The poet's predilection

for the 'rimed chronicle' answers to this order of preferences. Of this the most characteristic example is found in
'The last Instructions to a Painter'; having already set forth
the occasion, aim, and contents of the poem, we shall now
explain the staging implied in the title. To do this we must
go back a few years and leave England for the moment.

The Italian Giovanni Francesco Businello described,
c. 1656, a naval victory of the Venetians over the Turks in
a poem addressed to the painter Pietro Liberi, whom he
invited to reproduce it on canvas. Two years later one
Thomas Higgons turned this Venetian *Naval Triumph* into
English verse. Waller, who had written an introductory
poem in praise of this piece of decorated neo-Classicism,
thought the device worthy of imitation: he made use of it
in his 'Instructions To A Painter, For the Drawing of the
Posture and Progress of His Majesties Forces at Sea, Under
the command of His Highness Royal. Together with the
Battel and Victory obtained over the Dutch, June 3, 1665.'
Unluckily for the panegyrist of all English Governments in
turn, set-backs soon took the place of successes and the
next year the theme was transferred from dithyramb to
satire. In 1666 and 1667 four poems, each entitled 'Advice
to a Painter', numbered from second to fifth, derided
Waller's (number one) and attacked the conduct of the war
and of affairs in general. The fact that they were ascribed in
print to the (still living) Sir John Denham suffices to prove
they were not his. The pseudo-Denham, as we may conveniently call their author, writes carelessly and his shape-
less, incorrect, vulgar pieces amuse the modern reader only
by occasional sallies devoid of any literary pretension.

'The last Instructions to a Painter', probably written after
the 'Third Advice', was cast in the same mould. No more
than his immediate predecessor or Waller does Marvell
limit himself to a purely plastic poetry. There is a radical
incompatibility between the 'rimed chronicle' in which he
pleasantly gossips away and the picture in which he pretends
to fix one indivisible moment of English history. Not even
Achilles' shield represented so many diverse scenes, and in
so animated a way. Yet the poet at times remembers that his
narrative is intended to be reproduced on canvas, and then

he sketches individual portraits, or brings a group of characters to a standstill and invites the painter to seize their
attitude, their unfinished gesture:

> Draw next a Pair of Tables op'ning, then
> The *House of Commons* clatt'ring like the Men.
> Describe the *Court* and *Country*, both set right,
> On opposite points, the black against the white.

as in a game of backgammon. But the poet soon wearies of
his graphic enterprise, however rudimentary:

> Here *Painter* rest a little, and survey
> With what small Arts the publick game they play.
> For so too *Rubens*, with affairs of State,
> His lab'ring Pencil oft would recreate.

There follows the analysis of the vile motives that have led
'the close Cabal' to ask for the re-imposition of the Excise
(first imposed by the Long Parliament).

Marvell then merely received from the pseudo-Denham
a device imported from Italy and already popular in England
when used for praise and even more for censure; and he
handles this device rather clumsily, as it seems to the modern
mind. Yet contemporaries liked it, since many poetasters
went on writing such poems to the end of the century and
Marvell himself probably wrote 'Further Advice to a
Painter'. But after this mediocre piece he dismissed his
painter, and then he might have shown his capacity as a
narrative satirist unhampered. The opening of 'An Historical
Poem' probably surpasses anything of that kind before
Absalom and Achitophel; hence our lingering hope or wistful
wish that it might be Marvell's. On the other hand, 'Nostradamus's Prophecy', if definitely proved not to be his, could
be given up without regret, save for one quibble aimed at
Nell Gwyn and other actresses who 'act the parts of Queens
—Within the Curtains' (of the royal bed). This leer apart
and also an allusion to the two kings of Brentford (one more
borrowing from Buckingham's farce) the piece is strained
and sombre. Of course it foretells calamities that have already
happened; the use of the future instead of the preterite and
the liberties taken with chronology make all the difference

with the 'rimed chronicles'. And the device of satirical prog-
nostication is not of Marvell's invention: in England alone
it dates back to the Middle Ages. More original, it seems, is
the theme of 'The Kings Vowes':

> When the Plate was at pawne, and the fobb att low Ebb,
> And the Spider might weave in our Stomack its web;
>> Our Pockets as empty as braine;
>>> Then Charles without acre
>>> Made these Vowes to his Maker—
>> If ere I see England againe,

Then come the articles of this *in petto* declaration; their
number and order vary in manuscript or printed versions,
and they could be added to indefinitely. Did Marvell write
them all? No. Did he write some of them? Again we hope
he did, since several do not lack point, e.g.:

> I will have a fine Tunick and a Sash and a Vest,
> Tho' not rule like the Turk, yet I will be so drest,
> And who knowes but the Mode may soon bring in the rest?

And many stanzas, especially those concerning the public
revenue, are just in the same vein of good-humoured satire,
using the same technique of self-exposure.

The *pièces de circonstance*, such as 'Clarindon's House-Warming', 'The Statue in Stocks-Market', and 'The Statue at Charing Cross', by the very fact that they start from a single incident, often minute, always precisely situated in time and place,
allow the poet's fancy more scope than the 'rimed chronicles'.
The part played by craftsmanship increases in inverse ratio
to the political importance of the incidents related. Thus it
is that in this group we find the best ordonnance, or rather
the least crying sins of composition. The poet tells us what
he knows, eking out certainties with shrewd suppositions.
We should say that nothing interposes between him and us,
did he not occasionally feign to address a person whom he
pesters with embarrassing questions without allowing him
time to answer.

Next to these soliloquies aimed at political Aunt Sallies
we can place the real dialogues, the one between 'Britannia
and Rawleigh', the other 'between the Two Horses'. The

former is too doubtfully Marvell's, too stilted also and humourless, to detain us. But the latter has both a better case as regards authorship and greater liveliness. Yet the two quadrupeds agree too well in Marvell's satire to achieve the individuality with which La Fontaine would have endowed each of them. They hardly enter into a discussion of their respective riders' merits and demerits. It looks as if Charles I's mount tried to plead for this monarch, or at least argue that his cruelty is 'more tolerable' than his son's lust. It seems also that this horse, though made of brass, proves more moderate and even timid, and his fellow, though made of marble, more passionate and bolder in speech (at least when their 'riders are absent; who is't that can hear?'—an element of comedy that quickens the dialogue). But the opposition between the two equine characters does not come out clearly enough, since the various manuscripts and editions vary a good deal in the ascription of the speeches to either. Marvell, if it be he, has once more given only a hint of what he could have done by taking more pains.

To complete this survey of the structural devices we recall that 'The Loyall Scot', like 'Tom May's Death', is a dialogue of the Shades and thus may be directly or indirectly derived from Lucian. Anyhow, Marvell cannot claim here more originality than for his other satirical frameworks. The only one that we can call his, at least provisionally, is the dialogue between the statues of animals, a curious hybrid of the Æsopic fable and the Roman pasquinade. But more damaging than this docility in following the beaten track is the careless workmanship: between the originator, whose unlicked whelps deserve the critic's large indulgence, and the classic, in the wider sense of the word, who brings a slowly elaborated pattern to perfection and relegates his predecessors to oblivion, Marvell plays an historically useful but thankless part. One quality of his, however, we must again acknowledge: variety. It remains striking whatever exclusions from his satirical canon we feel compelled to make.

However necessary it may be to classify the satires according to the devices that determine their structure, prosody provides a still more important criterion. Not that Marvell

reveals himself as a real innovator or a consummate craftsman in verse-making, here any more than in his lyrical
poetry. But the tone of each satire (what in fine matters
most) depends less on the political circumstances, or even
on the author's opinion of persons or events, than on the
rhythm in which it is set: this tone is more cheerful if he
uses a popular metre, more strained if he uses the so-called
heroic couplet.

The latter metrical unit had been chosen by Marvell, we
know, to celebrate the glories of the Protectorate and lament
Oliver's death. We find it again in several satires practically
unchanged, i.e. with very little enjambment. In what has
been called 'the battle of the couplets' Marvell, even in the
freer genre of satire, stands on the side of the closed one. The
only exception is his earliest satire, 'Fleckno', written when
Donne's influence still worked on him unchecked: at least
one couplet in five runs into the next, and some passages
would well illustrate the (rhymed) verse-paragraph:

> He gathring fury still made sign to draw;
> But himself there clos'd in a Scabbard saw
> As narrow as his Sword's; and I, that was
> Delightful, said there can no Body pass
> Except by penetration hither, where
> Two make a crowd, nor can three Persons here
> Consist but in one substance. Then, to fit
> Our peace, the Priest said I too had some wit:

But already by 1649 the closing of the couplet hardly suffers
any exceptions. This conversion, at once sudden and lasting,
is no doubt accounted for by Waller's and Denham's influence, which Marvell felt when he returned from the Con-
tinent. Waller's first volume of verse came out while Marvell
was away from England (in 1645) and Denham's *Cooper's
Hill* (1642) had probably escaped his notice before he left
England. The neo-Classical school tended to limit the use
of the enjambment, and even of the run-on line within the
couplet. In this respect again, Marvell, 'Fleckno' still excepted, equals Dryden's restraint. In 'The last Instructions'
a liberal estimation of run-on lines hardly reaches sixty, i.e.
one in seventeen; in *Absalom and Achitophel* (Part I) the

ratio is one in sixteen, the same as in Waller's 'Instructions to A Painter'. True to say, in 'The last Instructions' a dozen of those enjambments (in the wider French meaning) assume a brusquerie wholly exceptional in Waller and Dryden. But this deliberate abruptness underlines Marvell's notion of the enjambment: he sees in it a device, chiefly satirical, that must always be used wittingly, for a definite effect. Here is, for instance, the Duchess of York preparing poisoned drink, a nocturnal scene:

> Witness ye stars of Night, and thou the pale
> Moon, that o'rcome with the sick steam did'st fail;

The paleness of the moon becomes weird because of the place of the epithet, and the stress on the first syllable of the second line brings out the violence done to the normal rhythm. Here the same Duchess ponders over the unfaithfulness of her husband,

> And nightly hears the hated Guards away
> Galloping with the *Duke* to other Prey.

One catches the pace of the horses in the initial trochee of the second line, which prolongs the first line without any pause. Those two instances border on the tragic, but more commonly the enjambment produces a comic effect:

> Paint *Castlemaine* in Colours that will hold,
> Her, not her Picture, for she now grows old.

Not the canvas but the skin; yet the punctuation, if it be Marvell's, implies a pause at the end of the first line; the second line is then made to look like an afterthought, intended to prevent a misunderstanding. But the next instance allows of no doubt; to her royal lover Castlemaine prefers a footman:

> His brazen Calves, his brawny Thighs, (the Face
> She slights) his Feet shapt for a smoother race.

Such is the animal appetite of the female that the man's countenance stands for nothing. Here now is a political ally of the poet:

> First enter'd forward *Temple*, Conqueror
> Of *Irish*-Cattel and *Sollicitor*.

The device emphasizes the waggishness of the (sincere) praise. But again, though grammar requires no pause, the reciter may well keep the last word of the first line hanging in the air long enough to enhance the surprise at the beginning of the second. Now Clarendon tries to find scapegoats; first he sends against Ruyter's men-of-war . . . the mounted militia!

> Then from the usual *Common-place* he blames
> These; and in Standing-Armies praise declaims.

The unfairness of the charge becomes ludicrous thanks to the place of 'these' (the poor maligned militia-men) and to the stress this normally enclitic pronoun carries here.

These quotations show that Marvell does not boggle at rather pronounced metrical effects. Yet we cannot deny them artistic value provided we take the word artistic to cover farce and caricature: they are not negligences of style. The same cannot be said of certain irregularities found in his satires, especially as regards rhyme. Not over-particular in his lyrical poems, he is even less so in his satires, as might be expected. However, if the identical rhyme appears more frequently, it is always with an obvious comical intention. The members of Parliament are summoned to Westminster in the heart of summer because of the Dutch in the Medway,

> And all with Sun and Choler come adust;
> And threaten *Hyde* to raise a greater Dust.

The heretical consonant *d* emphasizes the quibble. A little further on in the same satire the poet forestalls the objection to his rhyme by blaming the quasi-pun on Clarendon:

> Trembling with joy and fear, *Hyde* them Prorogues,
> And had almost mistook and call'd them Rogues.

Lastly feminine endings, practically absent from the poems in honour of the Lord Protector, are somewhat more numerous here, though not exceeding one per cent. of the total. Again Marvell seems to have considered these hypermetrical syllables as purely burlesque. Here once more is Clarendon:

> See how he Reigns in his new Palace *culminant*,
> And sits in State Divine like *Jove* the *fulminant*!

One Duncombe, Commissioner of the Ordnance, has
failed to provide powder for the English artillery at Chatham
—out of thrift no doubt; he has thus proved worthy to be
made a Commissioner of the Treasury:

> But sure his late good Husbandry in Peeter,
> Show'd him to manage the *Exchequer* meeter:

The same Duncombe had been introduced to us linked in
one couplet with another member of the Court Party:

> Bold *Duncombe* next, of the Projectors chief:
> And old *Fitz-Harding* of the Eaters Beef.

Here, if ever, we catch Marvell imitating Samuel Butler.
We recall Hudibras's horse:

> The Beast was sturdy large and tall
> With Mouth of Meal and Eyes of Wall:

Though not habitually so bold Marvell sometimes does a
piece of tightrope walking; he announces it so that no one
can mistake his purpose. Of two dispatches sent by the
English Government

> The first instructs our (Verse the Name abhors)
> *Plenipotentiary Ambassadors*
> To prove . . .

That is one rocket, but here is a whole display of fireworks;
a scapegoat has been found for all the reverses of the Dutch
war, a minor official at the Admiralty, providentially named
Pett:

> Whose Counsel first did this mad War beget?
> Who all Commands sold thro' the Navy? *Pett.*
> Who would not follow when the *Dutch* were bet?
> Who treated out the time at *Bergen*? *Pett.*

And this goes on with the same zest for twelve lines more.

But all these pranks and licences in the use of the heroic
couplet do not prevent us from perceiving a contrast when
we pass from this metre, which still retains a learned flavour
by virtue of its foreign origin, to the really popular rhythms
in which some of Marvell's happiest satires are written. To
describe the metre of 'Clarindon's House-Warming' as
anapaestic may create a false impression of regularity: 27
only out of 112 lines consist of 4 anapaests, e.g.:

o o / o o / o o / o o
But observ|ing that Mort|als run of|ten behind,

In the others almost any foot may be substituted. And after all these concessions we find ourselves faced with a line that refuses to be scanned in any classical terminology:

As all Chedder Dairys club to the incorporate Cheese

Better acknowledge here the presence of the Old, or at least the Middle, English accentual verse. As far as we know, no real artist had ever used it for satire. Marvell certainly did not bring this easy-going medium to perfection, but he turned it to reasonable profit and showed the promise it held. He thus fought the ankylosis that threatened the poetry of his age, his own included, owing to its excessive submission to syllabic rules.

Unlike the decasyllabic line the accentual verse is chiefly found in stanzas. The only exception is 'A Dialogue between the Two Horses', written in couplets as self-contained as those of 'The last Instructions'. In 'The Statue in Stocks-Market' quatrains are built by the simple process of linking two couplets, as in much popular poetry of the seventeenth century. The cross-rhymed quatrain of 'Clarindon's House-Warming' and 'The Statue at Charing Cross' stands higher artistically. The more doubtful satires show still more craftsmanship in this respect.

Naturally the rhyme here suffers more violence than in the heroic couplets. But the only noteworthy difference is the far greater frequency of feminine rhymes, and here Marvell rivals Butler: buy at/fiat; Amphion/free on; tell ye/belly; then, sirs/Answers; oblige yee/effigie; provide 'um/bestride 'um; find him/behind him; gall us/Sardanapalus; drink 'um/sink 'um. Special mention should be made of a couplet whose rhyme combines wrenching of stress with breaking:

When the Asse so bouldly rebuked the Prophet,
Thou knowest what danger was like to come of it;

This rhyme is as faulty as can be, but it produces its burlesque effect all the better and reveals almost as great ingenuity as the famous couplet in *Hudibras* rhyming 'Philosopher' with 'Ross over'. And while Butler's superior craftsmanship must

be acknowledged, we may wonder whether the droll eccen-
tricity of the rhyme agrees as well with the internal regularity
of his octosyllable as with the free rhythm of Marvell's
accentual verse.

As a matter of personal taste, and without any wish to
generalize, we confess to a preference for Marvell's irregular
satires, which we place above his regular ones. Let us take
two pieces written in the same year and prompted by the
same events, and quote the opening of each. Here are the
heroic couplets:

> After two sittings, now our *Lady State*,
> To end her Picture, does the third time wait.
> But er'e thou fal'st to work, first *Painter* see
> It be'nt too slight grown, or too hard for thee.
> Canst thou paint without Colours? Then 'tis right:
> For so we too without a Fleet can fight.
> Or canst thou dawb a Sign-post, and that ill?
> 'Twill suit our great debauch and little skill.

And now for the stanzas of accentual verse:

> When *Clarindon* had discern'd beforehand,
>   (As the Cause can eas'ly foretel the Effect)
> At once three Deluges threatning our Land;
>   'Twas the season he thought to turn Architect.
>
> Us *Mars*, and *Apollo*, and *Vulcan* consume;
>   While he the Betrayer of *England* and *Flander*,
> Like the King-fisher chuseth to build in the Broom,
>   And nestles in flames like the Salamander.

From the start the second metre seems more hearty than the
first, and the impression persists to the end of the piece.
The Lord Chancellor is handled even more roughly in
'Clarindon's House-Warming' than in 'The last Instructions', but the popular rhythm carries along insults and
obscenities in its fast stream, while the more learned couplet
isolates, sets forth, and stresses each offence against taste.
A comparison between 'Britannia and Rawleigh' or 'Nostradamus's Prophecy' on the one hand and 'A Dialogue
between the Two Horses' on the other, leaving out the
problems of authorship, would show even more convincingly
the influence of the metre on the tone of the satire. In date,
subject, and dramatic form the conversation between the

allegorical figure of the mother country and one of the national heroes closely resembles the 'Dialogue' between Charles I's and Charles II's mounts; but the somewhat vulgar verse of the latter piece contrasts all the more sharply with the rather declamatory rhetoric of the former. And 'Nostradamus's Prophecy', bitter, sombre, monotonous in spite of its brevity, also contrasts with the equally prophetic conclusion of the 'Dialogue' in which the poet passes with ease from the most Rabelaisian tone to an eloquence almost worthy of one of Corneille's characters, and then concludes on a familiar note with a plea in favour of the London coffee-houses, which a Royal Proclamation is trying to suppress. True, this mixture does not wholly avoid incoherence, but one is grateful to the author for having brought so much good humour to the expression of his deepest and most fervent political feelings. Sincerity obtains here as much as in 'Nostradamus's Prophecy', but far more pleasingly.

And yet to this difference in tone there corresponds no difference in the style. Satires in heroic couplets and satires in accentual verse use much the same vocabulary and images: the latter, often far-fetched and intellectual, are the main possession that the lyric poet and the satiric poet hold in common; the former inclining to coarseness and always full of colour, leads on to the prose pamphlets. So that we need not here devote special space to the style of the satires: suffice it to note its intermediate nature and refer the reader to our Chapters III and VII. We advise him, if he wants to form his own opinion on one sample, to choose 'The Statue in Stocks-Market', on account of its shortness, of the almost complete absence of obscure allusions requiring a long historical commentary, and lastly of its sprightliness, not excluding violence but making it tolerable for the civilized reader of today.

Amongst the verse-writers of the Restoration, whose poetry, Milton apart, culminates in political satire, we cannot claim a high rank for Marvell. Between Butler and Dryden his position must obviously be a modest one. And he does not sustainedly surpass minor and mostly anonymous satirists, whence the difficulty we meet in solving problems of authorship. But the same is true of others, even Rochester. This scapegrace (before Grace found him) Marvell duly denounced in his letters for scandalous escapades and, on one occasion, cowardly behaviour, and yet recognized as 'the only man in England that had the true veine of satyr'. This judgement must have been delivered (to Aubrey) very near the end of Marvell's life, when he had ceased writing English verse, for Rochester, however precocious, wrote nothing noteworthy before 1675, the very year in which he praised the wit of *The Rehearsal Transpros'd*. Marvell's self-effacement may be ascribed partly to political caution, but we may subscribe to it so far as to say that 'The History of Insipids' (1676?)—full as it is of Marvellian echoes—transcends Marvell's best satires: the Earl's attacks on King and Court, less headlong, probably because of less deep conviction, but more malicious than the Commoner's, achieve a rarer artistic quality. The latter uses a bludgeon, the former a stiletto.

Rochester was to write his best political satire, the eight-line 'Commons Petition to the King', after Marvell's death, at the time of the so-called Popish Plot. This major political event was to bring into evidence another famous satirist, John Oldham, whom we need not compare with Marvell save to point out how similar are their politics and how different their works. The *Four Satires against the Jesuits* may well be styled original in that they discard the 'rimed chronicle' and anecdotic poetry, to deal in abstract and general denunciation. The anticlerical invective of 'The Loyall Scot' and the device of the villain's confession in 'Britannia and Rawleigh' may have provided patterns for the diatribes against Loyola and his disciples. But Oldham gives these oratorical flights a breadth hitherto unexampled; he intensifies both the qualities and the faults of his predecessors, with all the intemperance of a young man who has just been taking lessons in rhetoric from Juvenal.

Whether or not Marvell deserves to be called the prime English political satirist for a brief period (1667–75) his chief title to a place in the history of the genre rather resides in his paving the way for Dryden. *Absalom and Achitophel* is a 'rimed chronicle' like 'The last Instructions'; the biblical disguise in the one, the convention of the picture to be painted in the other, should not conceal from us the identity of structure. To be sure, the historical circumstances served Dryden better than Marvell; the tragedy that unfolded between 1678 and 1681 provided much richer material than the superficial conflicts of 1667. To be sure also, the progression in Dryden's poem, though more sustained than in Marvell's, could hardly satisfy a French critic of the classical school. It resembles a mighty river whose flow is now and then choked. With these reservations, the evident superiority of the younger writer makes it unnecessary, even cruel to dwell on it. We see it best in the portraits, less numerous but more developed, so that their importance increases and the narrative shrinks proportionally. Read the portraits of Buckingham and Shaftesbury after that of Turnor, in which Marvell has excelled himself: you will find on one side the science of composition, perspective, relievo, light and shade playing against each other, a masterly touch; on the other side stiff draughtsmanship, plain colours, a naïve gaucherie in execution that solicits from us, indeed not unsuccessfully, the amused indulgence of the decadent for the primitive. Lastly, if coarseness and violence have not wholly disappeared from Dryden's poem, feigned moderation shows itself capable of inflicting the cruellest wounds. Marvell had sometimes perceived that essential truth intuitively; he cannot be said to have conformed to it in his satires, especially his more ambitious regular ones.

The immeasurable advance from our poet to Dryden can only be accounted for by the superiority of genius assisted by industry over talent injured by carelessness. Yet one also notes here the difference between two ages of a genre, adolescence and full growth. The gain appears at once, but had it not to be paid for? Without resuming the exploded charge of insincerity against Dryden we may well wonder whether his greater care for the form of his satires does not betoken a less ardent political faith; and even, limiting ourselves to the province of art, whether Marvell's satiric verse with all its faults does not evince a spontaneous verve that indeed is not absent from, but frolics less frequently and vividly in, his great successor's.

VII

THE CONTROVERSIALIST IN PROSE

POLEMICS have no beginning: every combatant always answers an aggressor. If we looked for the origin of the quarrels in which Marvell took part we should go at least as far back as the Martin Marprelate controversy.[1] For practical reasons we shall choose as our starting-point *A Discourse of Ecclesiastical Politie*, which Samuel Parker published at the beginning of 1670.

Younger than Marvell by twenty years, his antagonist to be also came, as we have noted, from a Puritan milieu. Sent to Oxford by a republican father, Samuel gained by prayer and fasting the reputation of being 'one of the preciousest young men in the University'. But when he saw that Charles II had come back to stay he turned against his former friends. Having taken orders in 1664 he rose rapidly in the Church, thanks to his ready pen. His third book, the above-mentioned *Discourse*, voiced the anxiety and resentment of the High Churchmen at the King's disposition to slacken persecution against the Nonconformists after the fall of Clarendon. If the Civil Power, Parker argues, proves remiss, this is due to ignorance of its rights. Though he disagrees with Hobbes on many points, he borrows from the materialistic philosopher a distinction between belief, which commands can never reach, and external action, including speech, which can and must be compelled to conform, since peace in the State requires uniformity. Not the least breath of religious feeling disturbs Parker's logic, but by the standards of the age his book contains little railing; it appeals to reason, as then understood. Hence its success with a restricted but influential section of opinion.

The Dissenters, in the person of John Owen, an Independent minister, answered it meekly and thus brought down

[1] John S. Coolidge, 'Martin Marprelate, Marvell, and *Decorum Personae* as a Satirical Theme', in *P.M.L.A.*, 1959, pp. 526–32, stresses an interesting resemblance between the two prose satirists as regards method.

upon themselves, in 1671, *A Defence and Continuation of the Ecclesiastical Politie*, twice as long as its predecessor, and much more abusive. This silenced Owen by recalling the part he had played during the Civil War, and particularly his friendship with Cromwell. So that, Richard Baxter says, Owen's 'unfitness for this work was a general injury to the Nonconformists'.

But Parker did not rest content with this victory, and in a long preface to a hitherto unpublished tractate, the late *Bishop Bramhall's Vindication of himself and the Episcopal Church From the Presbyterian Charge of Popery* (1672) he could not resist the temptation to trample on Owen again. This time his tone became consistently burlesque, so as to please the less sober part of the reading public, especially the young courtiers. This brought Marvell in. Parker thus made a controversialist of the Member for Hull, now turned fifty. A layman had better not interfere in purely scholastic disputes; but he could give clerics a lesson in raillery. And the political situation favoured the enterprise. The latest development was the King's *Declaration of Indulgence*. This had placed Parker in a difficult position: how could the champion of the unlimited Civil Power protest against the royal decision? The divine right of kings and the divine right of the episcopate clashed. Parker had boldly chosen to affront Charles II (of course mentioning only his Machiavellian ministers) and thus shown that his loyalty to the Crown was conditional.

Marvell knew how to improve his opportunity. *The Rehearsal*, that composite farce, had been acted a few months before with great success. The central character, Mr. Bayes, a grandiloquent playwright, furnished Marvell with a nickname for the ecclesiastical blusterer who had lately been made Archdeacon of Canterbury. Marvell was not thinking of posterity when he took up this device; he sacrificed permanence to popularity and immediate effectiveness. But he did it with such gusto that, in spite of his attempts at blaming his own levity on his antagonist, we feel sure that he was following his own bent.

Neither can he persuade us that Parker stands responsible for the lack of method in *The Rehearsal Transpros'd*, for its desultoriness and wayward course; the very nature of that

class of writings then called 'animadversions' made such
faults inevitable, and the 'Preface' to *Bishop Bramhall's Vindication* certainly does not avoid them, but *The Rehearsal
Transpros'd* sins still more grievously in this respect. Not
only does Marvell take page by page the book he answers,
here carping at a word, there at an historical or geographical
error, there again denouncing a fundamental proposition,
but he introduces into this chaos one more perturbing
element: his poetic fancy. Yet since confusion worse confounded thus becomes less disheartening we can well forgive him. And nobody nowadays cares whether he refuted
Parker's theses properly: they no longer deserve refutation.
If a man of today wants to enjoy *The Rehearsal Transpros'd*
the best way will be to try and forget the Parker of history
and see only the puppet who undergoes a sound thrashing.
Thus the show has hardly any higher moral significance
than Punchinello, then in all its novelty for the gaping
Londoners, but it is as diverting. Every time the cudgel falls
on the representative of an unpopular authority mirth bursts
out anew, and the curtain falls only when showman and
spectators are tired with hitting and laughing.

We cannot, therefore, epitomize Marvell's pamphlet. At
best we can give some idea of its uncertain progress. The
first third derides the preamble of Parker's 'Preface' and his
praise of Bramhall, not without some gibes at the late Archbishop of Armagh (who had when still alive been roughly
handled by Milton). At the same time Marvell indirectly and
cautiously takes up the defence of Calvin and Geneva,
sketches a burlesque biography of Parker, then banters him
on his aversion for 'Mr B[axter]' and 'J[ohn] O[wen]'. When
he thinks he has sufficiently whetted the appetite of his
audience he comes to the heart of the matter: Owen needs
no further defence because not he but 'the King was the
person concern'd from the beginning'. We imagine that
Marvell will now deal with the connexion between Parker's
Preface and the *Declaration of Indulgence* of 1672. But he turns
back to that of Breda in 1660, whence he quickly returns to
Clarendon's fall in 1667, which he recalls with pleasure, and
reaches the first toyings of the Cabal with toleration. He then
shows Parker trying to bring the King round to harsh

measures; the *Discourse of Ecclesiastical Politie* is summed up in six 'aphorisms or hypotheses', which Marvell refutes one by one; to put it in his own words, he gives 'some short rehearsal of Mr. Bayes his six Playes'. He then passes on to the *Defence of the Ecclesiastical Politie* and shows easily that it contradicts the doctrine it pretends to adhere to, at any rate as regards the royal prerogative. The cause of toleration had made some headway, especially in Scotland.

Henceforward the King fell into disgrace with Mr. Bayes, and any one that had eyes might discern that our Author did not afford his Majesty that countenance and favour which he had formerly enjoy'd. So that a book too of J.O.'s happening mischievously to come out at the same season, upon pretence of answering that, he resolved to make his Majesty feel the effects of his displeasure.

His analysis of the *Defence* completed, Marvell at last arrives at the *Declaration of Indulgence*, and again attacks the 'Preface' to *Bishop Bramhall's Vindication*, in which he sees the Anglican persecutors' retort to the King. But hardly have we caught a glimpse of the central idea of *The Rehearsal Transpros'd* when we return to 'J.O.' for some verbal cavil; then Marvell announces: 'till I meet with something more serious, I will take a walk in the garden and gather some of Mr. Bayes his flowers'. And when he tackles the most serious questions, such as the nature of schism or the responsibility for the Civil War, he always does so by way of digression, starting from propositions he culls at random from Parker's 'Preface'. After one more burlesque interlude the tone of the pamphlet rises again to denounce the Hobbesian theory of the sovereign state: 'The truth is . . . Bayes had at first built-up such a stupendous magistrate as never was of God's making. He had put all princes upon the rack to stretch them to his dimension. And as a straight line continued grows a circle, he had given them so infinite a power, that it was extended unto impotency.' But from this height of original thinking we plunge into the old squabbles about the Anglican ceremonies rejected by the Puritans. Parker having asserted that the sovereign could as well settle such matters as define the meaning of words, Marvell makes easy fun of this absurdity.

He then touches on the ultimate consequences of the resort to 'pillories, whipping-posts, gallies, rods, and axes (which are *ratio ultima cleri*, a clergyman's last argument, ay and his first too)'. Among sundry historical examples Marvell quotes a long account in Latin of the persecutions that those Saxons who had been converted to Christianity by Roman missionaries inflicted in the seventh century on their fellow-countrymen converted by Irish missionaries; the reason for Marvell's choice: the historian, Archbishop of Canterbury under Queen Elizabeth, was named Parker. But suddenly the pamphleteer remembers the full title of his antagonist's last work: 'A Preface shewing what grounds there are of fears and jealousies of Popery.' He thereupon accuses Parker of astutely evading a recent law against alarmist rumours of this sort. The future author of *An Account of the Growth of Popery* states his belief 'that Popery could never return into England again' (and yet Marvell, we know, had by this time made a shrewd guess of what had been agreed upon at Dover two years before). However, he condescends to examine Parker's three hypotheses on the part the Non-conformists might play in such a national apostasy. The most important hypothesis being that of a new civil war, Marvell undertakes to prove that the responsibility of the preceding one lies not with the Puritans but with Charles I's ecclesiastical advisers. This is the nicest point his pamphlet has to deal with. His tact enables him to avoid alienating the Royal Martyr's son, but not without making some concessions to the touchiness of the monarchists that must have caused his conscience some pangs. Once he is clear of this strait all is plain sailing to the end. Marvell exposes the disloyal conduct of the bishops since the Restoration: 'It hath been observed, that whensoever his Majesty hath had the most urgent occasions for Supply, [some] of them have made it their business to trinkle with the members of Parliament for obstructing it, unless the king would buy it with a new law against the fanaticks.' (By which name Marvell, like his antagonists, means the Dissenters.) The argument could not fail to move Charles II. And the Court itself finds in Marvell a defender against the charge of atheism. Nay, the mere supposition that 'crafty and sacrilegious statesmen' might mislead the King almost amounts, according to Marvell, to high treason. After insinuating that Parker himself and the Anglican bishops might well bring back Popery in order to bring in the Inquisition Marvell stops short in his review. But in lieu of a conclusion he adds a sort of postscript where, under colour of explaining why he had joined in the fight, he renews his gravest charges against Parker, intending no doubt thus to give them greater weight.

Alluding to the title of Marvell's pamphlet we might call it the performance of a comedy that consists wholly of episodes. And the general impression produced on the spectator is rather destructive than constructive. It aims at discrediting a champion of intolerance, at removing an obstacle on the road to religious freedom. Although Parker's works sometimes contradict one another the Archdeacon's thought proves less elusive than the Member of Parliament's. Should we ascribe this elusiveness to Marvell's incapacity or to his cleverness? Anyhow, the few pages in which he seems to brush Parker aside and give his own views on the problem of liberty, its foundation, conditions, and bounds, should be read with the same caution with which he wrote them. Too many of his biographers have taken at their face value statements lofty indeed but vague enough when scrutinized closely. They have not allowed for tactics because they have not put these statements side by side with Marvell's other utterances and his actions. In order to avoid falling into the same error we had better wait till we have examined the rest of his pamphlets before we try to define the trends that, for lack of a system, determined his public attitude to the problems proposed to him by the life of his country.

Success came at once. The grave Richard Baxter, after telling of Parker's 'Preface', calls *The Rehearsal Transpros'd* 'an answer so exceeding Jocular as thereby procured abundance of readers, and Pardon to the Author'. For, as Baxter himself had recently experienced, the Licensers of the Press, Roger L'Estrange especially, were resolved to silence all possible answerers to Parker. Marvell knew it so well that he had had his pamphlet printed without a licence, and with a burlesque imprint. It seems, however, that trouble began, not with the Licensers but with the Stationers' Company, whose privileges this clandestine publication infringed, and only when a second impression was in progress. Before L'Estrange could intervene he was summoned by the Earl of Anglesey, Lord Privy Seal, in favour with the dissolute King but at heart still a Presbyterian and even then a visitor of Milton's. Anglesey forbade L'Estrange, in the King's name, to suppress the book and even asked him to license it. This L'Estrange did, though unwillingly; he later complained that alterations marked by him on the licensed copy had not been made, and in fact the second impression differs from the first, apart from the correction of a few misprints and trifling typographical changes, mostly in the title-page, which gives the bookseller's name (Ponder), but not the author's.[1]

These dangers past, *The Rehearsal Transpros'd* could well defy the six printed answers launched against it by the intolerant Anglicans. Their only interest today resides in their involuntary acknowledgement of Marvell's success, and in the biographical details (however suspect) they provide on him. They are, in order of publication: *Rosemary and Bayes*, fairly moderate; *A Common-place-book out of the Rehearsal Transpros'd*, very abusive; *The transproser rehearsed* supposedly by Richard Leigh, a minor poet in a vein not wholly unlike Marvell's earlier one, who would prove here a coarse and reckless slanderer; *S'too him Bayes*, remarkable only for the number of its Shakespearian quotations; *A Reproof to the Rehearsal Transpros'd*, Parker's own work; and *Gregory, Father-Greybeard, with his vizard off*, by Edmund Hickeringill, full of buffoonery, bold at times in its attacks against the bibliolatry of the Nonconformists, but answering Marvell only by puns on his name. We may add an anonymous manuscript satire in verse, entitled 'A Love Letter to the Author of the Rehearsall Transposed [*sic*]', which asserts that Marvell has lately been castrated (Leigh calls him a gelding—and Milton a stallion). In fact Parker alone attempts

---

[1] Yet Mrs. Duncan-Jones has made a list (which I hope she will publish) of corrections, suppressions, and additions, not many in number considering the size of the pamphlet but revealing. Marvell in fact cut the anecdote to which L'Estrange objected most, that of 'your Roman Emperor' who was stabbed by 'his Captain of the Life Guard'—clearly an invitation to regicide!

anything like a refutation of the arguments in *The Rehearsal Transpros'd*. But he now trusts less to his logic than to the King's inability to stem the tide of persecution. Parker turns the tables on Marvell who has taxed him with opposing the King's will, and charges the Member for Hull with rebellion against the will of the Commons, who have compelled the King to withdraw his *Declaration of Indulgence*. Therefore, *The Rehearsall Transpros'd: The Second Part*, Marvell's rejoinder to Parker's retort, published in the winter of 1673–4, has to steer cautiously between the renunciation of the hopes in the King voiced in the first part and the antagonizing of the Cavalier Parliament. Having negotiated this difficulty with great skill, Marvell finds it an easy task to finish off Parker. But since his own name appears on the title-page of this *Second Part* the advocate for the Dissenters has to show much more respect than he really feels for the ecclesiastical authorities, including Gilbert Sheldon, the then Archbishop of Canterbury, Parker's patron. On Parker himself he pours more scandal than in the first part; for instance he makes him responsible for the sins committed by his curate at Ickham (Parker was of course a pluralist). The story resembles that of the Scoto-French Morus and Dutch Pontia in Milton's *Defensio Secunda*, praised by Marvell in 1654, and *Pro se Defensio*, the book Marvell had made known at Saumur in 1656; but this English clerical idyll ends more grimly since the curate and his maidservant (if Marvell is to be trusted) procure an abortion to hide their misconduct in a garret of the vicarage. So that Marvell can play the tune of moral indignation more vehemently still, but only after having written of the fornication in a Chaucerian vein.

The same law of acceleration that makes the later pamphlets in a controversy more abusive than the earlier ones affects the disorder of the composition. The first part of *The Rehearsal Transpros'd* would seem to hold a fairly straightforward course if compared to the second. Again and again when you think Marvell has done, he simply tacks about to let fly one more broadside.

Parker, indeed, had been hit below the water-line; he did not fire back any more and the Anglican squadron dispersed. Only two brief anonymous 'Letters' accused Marvell of having slandered the clergy, but even they acknowledged his victory over Parker.[1] Later testimonies confirm this. Gilbert Burnet wrote in 1687:

His [Parker's] extravagant way of writing gave occasion to the wittiest books that have appeared in this age, for Mr. Marvell undertook him and treated him in ridicule in the severest but pleasantest manner possible, and by this one character one may judge how pleasant the books were; for the last king, that was not a great reader of books, read them over and over again.

In the final form of the *History of my Own Time* Marvell's name disappears and the author of *The Rehearsal Transpros'd* is called 'the liveliest droll of the age'; he is said to have had 'all the wits (or as the French say, all the laughers) on his side'. Still more jubilant than the latitudinarian Burnet is a Scottish minister who has taken refuge in Holland, the Reverend Robert MacWard; he piously puns on the 'Mervail . . . raised up' by the Lord 'to fight' Parker 'at his own weapon, who did so cudgel and quell that boasting bravo, as . . . he hath laid his speech'.

More unexpected but no less significant is the praise given to *The Rehearsal Transpros'd* by the Earl of Rochester in 'Tunbridge Wells' (30 June 1675): he wonders that 'pert Bayes' ('Parker', explains a footnote) should still look 'so big and jolly—Tho' Marvell has enough expos'd his folly'. But the most impressive witness, because he hated the Dissenters, is Anthony à Wood, who confesses grudgingly that

---

[1] For the first of these two letters see *André Marvell*, Bibliographie, No. 52, after which should be inserted *Sober Reflections, or a solid confutation of Mr. Andrew Marvel's Works in a letter ab Ignoto ad Ignotum*. Poz un Ruin Ruin y Meduo, London H.H. 1674. This pamphlet of ten pages was discovered by Professor Caroline Robbins; she has located copies at Longleat and in the Union Theological Collection and the McAlpin Collection. It was entered in the Stationers' Register on 17 April 1674.

Under No. 52 of the Bibliographie add: this pamphlet (*An Apology and Advice For some of the Clergy . . .*) is ascribed to the author of *Scepsis Scientifica* by his biographers, e.g. Ferris Greenslet, *Joseph Glanvill*, 1900, p. 81, and Jackson I. Cope, *Joseph Glanvill Anglican Apologist*, 1956, pp. 34–35. They may be right in this but they also make the most unlikely conjecture that Glanvill was the 'J.G.' who threatened to cut Marvell's throat—see the title-page of *The Rehearsall Transpros'd: The Second Part* (information provided by Mrs. Duncan-Jones). Professor Robbins informs me that Thomas Long's *Mr. Hale's Treatise of Schism Examin'd and Censur'd*, London, 1678, contains throughout references to Marvell's 'villainous pamphlet', viz. *The Rehearsal Transpros'd*, and praises Parker. (On Long, 1621–1707, see *D.N.B.*)

'the odds and victory lay on Marvell's side'. Lastly Parker's autobiography, written after his conqueror's death and published posthumously, would of itself prove the severity of the punishment inflicted upon the Anglican divine by one he calls 'spurcus quidam . . . vagus, pannosus et famelicus poetaster'; he who had first appealed to laughter and popular cheers against the sober Nonconformists now charged his witty adversary with having turned all serious things into ridicule but admitted his success: 'populus, ingenti risu excitato, morionem simul contempsit et plausit.' The last word outweighs all the rest.[1]

So great a success dispelled Marvell's professed reluctance to be drawn 'out into publick to be a Writer'. Hence his next pamphlet, *Mr. Smirke; Or, The Divine in Mode* (1676, probably in June). Here again he advocates toleration for the Dissenters; again he defends one divine against another, but this time both the assailant and the assaulted are Anglicans and, paradoxically, the latter has long been a prelate, while the former will don the mitre only seven years later.

Herbert Croft, Bishop of Hereford, had in the Spring of 1675 written and privately printed an appeal to the Lords and Commons, which he did not mean, if we believe his apologist, to make known generally. But a 'covetous bookseller', having procured a copy, published an edition, which brought the author into trouble, though he had not subscribed his name, styling himself 'an humble moderator'. This suspiciously Presbyterian appellation had not, of course, placated the Anglicans and there came out three retorts, one of them the work of so lukewarm an episcopalian as Gilbert Burnet. Such a reception may surprise us since Croft had strongly condemned rebellion on religious grounds and frankly told the Nonconformists: 'your spirit savours some what of the Pharisee', pointing out that no reconciliation could take place unless they yielded something to the Church. He had vindicated the 'Fathers' of that Church in

---

[1] Dennis Davison, 'A Marvell Allusion in the Diary of the Rev. John Ward', in *N.Q.*, January 1955, p. 22, adds one more proof of the popularity of *The Rehearsal Transpros'd*. Ward was vicar of Stratford-upon-Avon from 1662 to his death in 1681.

Henry VIII's and Elizabeth's times from the Puritan charge
of retaining certain popish ceremonies: 'expediency' had
made it advisable to 'wean' the people as gently as possible
from the mass, still their 'delight'. But since it has now
become their 'hate', the same sense of expediency recom-
mends the abolition of the ceremonies, which move Croft
presents to the English, not as a repudiation of their fore-
fathers but as a matter of consistency. The same rule applies
to the hierarchy. All through Croft's appeal, entitled *The
Naked Truth. Or, the true state of the Primitive Church*, moderation and simplicity of style reign, relieved by occasional
touches of humour, and it is sometimes eloquent in the
expression of evangelical charity.

Leaving aside the other answerers to Croft, we shall, like
Marvell, concentrate on Francis Turner, at that time Master
of St. John's College, Cambridge, who published in May
1676 (without his name) *Animadversions Upon a Late Pamphlet Entitled The Naked Truth*; . . . Nor need we say much
even of Turner, who was later to prove a man of character
and principle but appears in this controversy as a paler
copy of Parker, less coarse in invective and also less vigorous
in argument. His attempt at using parody against Croft
evinces no originality and little aptitude. He amuses us most
when he is speaking in earnest, e.g. when, taking as a precedent the compulsory attendance of the Jews in Rome to
a Christian sermon, he explains how far the Dissenters
should be 'punisht': 'I speak nothing more against them or
their greatest Speakers, than that they may be brought to
our Churches and give us a fair hearing.' Of course he considers himself as the pink of tolerance, but he will not budge
one inch from the Elizabethan Establishment, making his
motto of the centurion's decision, in Livy, to stay where
chance had made him halt his soldiers: 'Hic manebimus
optime.'

Against this stick-in-the-mud conservative Marvell
manœuvred very nimbly. Using again the trick that had
recruited mundane readers for *The Rehearsal Transpros'd* he
first fitted Turner with a nickname borrowed from a play,
this time Etherege's *Man of Mode*. He chose a very minor
character, almost a mute, but one who provided a good

actor with opportunities for farcical business. It seems that Mr. Smirke, chaplain to Lady Biggot, was of formal appearance, as neat and starched as his bands, and empty-headed, especially devoid of motherwit. But, by a sort of contamination, Marvell gave Turner some of the features of the chief ridiculous character in the comedy, Sir Fopling Flutter, whose name serves as its sub-title: indeed, both pompous divine and would-be wit consist largely of clothes. Hence Marvell's own double title.

This part of the pamphlet has no more method and no more bears summing-up than *The Rehearsal Transpros'd*. But there is tacked on to *Mr. Smirke* a very different piece of writing: *A Short Historical Essay, concerning General Councils, Creeds, and Impositions, in Matters of Religion*. Turner no longer stands in the way of methodical exposition, and Marvell seriously sets out to undermine the foundations of Anglican intolerance. He opens with due gravity: 'The Christian Religion, as first instituted by our Blessed Saviour, was the greatest security to Magistrates by the obedience which it taught; and was fitted to enjoy no less security under them by a practice conformable to that doctrine.' After a brief review of the first three centuries of Christianity Marvell comes to the point he really has at heart; though he states it explicitly only near the end of the *Essay*: 'How came it that Christianity, which approv'd itself under all persecutions to the heathen emperours and merited their favour so far, till at last it regularly succeeded to the monarchy, would, under those of their own profession, be more distressed?' Looking for an answer to this question Marvell sketches the history of the Church from the abdication of Diocletian to the death of Theodosius the Great, dwelling longest on the Council of Nice. Here composition begins to waver: Marvell suddenly gives up his narrative (in the middle of one of his interminable paragraphs) and returns to the pagan emperors' general toleration of Christianity. Not before he has reached Constantine the Great a second time and denounced his son Valens's indignity does he remember the object of his inquiry. Then at last he formulates the answer implicit in his narrative; his statement makes up for its belatedness by its bluntness, nay its brutality: 'The true and

single cause was the bishops. And they were the cause
against reason' since they would give the Christian princes
more power in the Church than the heathen had. The
bishops 'of all others ought to have preach'd to the Magistrate the terrible denunciations in Scripture against usurp-
ing upon and persecuting Christians'. It only remains now
for the pamphleteer to show how these denunciations apply
to the Anglican clergy. To do this he resorts to an argument
a majori ad minus: the disputes of the fourth and fifth centuries dealt with creeds, those of today deal only with ceremonies; therefore, the modern persecutions far outdo the
ancient ones in absurdity and cruelty. In the last pages
Marvell again writes 'confusedly', as he himself admits; and
one could well say that chronology had provided him, at
little cost, with such coherence as this writing of his evinces.
Yet the *Essay*, like Marvell's next pamphlet, *An Account of
the Growth of Popery*, discussed in Chapter V *supra*, belongs
to a style of composition altogether different from *The
Rehearsal Transpros'd* or *Mr. Smirke* and thus deserves comparative praise for unity, method, and clearness of purpose.

Though its immediate success did not nearly equal that
of his attack on Parker, yet Marvell's handling of Turner
fluttered the ecclesiastical dove-cotes; but this onslaught
upon his brethren delighted the Bishop of Hereford, who
wrote to his lay champion a letter in which the unction of
The Naked Truth gives place to the naïve vanity of an author
sensitive to his enemies' censure and no more charitable to
them than they had been to him. Croft thanked Marvell
profusely and begged for continued protection. Marvell's
answer, very respectful on the surface, may well contain
some irony: in a letter to Sir Edward Harley written a fort-
night before (1 July 1676) he alluded to *The Naked Truth* as
'the poore mans book', but he took great care not to confess
his own authorship of *Mr. Smirke*, or rather of the *Essay
on Councils*, which seems to have given far more offence.
The Bishop of London wanted the Privy Council to take
steps; the Lord Chancellor refused to listen to the Earl of
Anglesey, still Lord Privy Seal, who pleaded for Marvell's
bookseller, again Nathaniel Ponder, imprisoned for having
printed the book without licence. Nor was the resentment

confined to the Anglicans; we see dimly, through Marvell's letter to Harley, that some of the Presbyterians also disapproved of his treatment of the Council of Nice. We may well feel surprised at this touchiness since Marvell might have quoted high Protestant authority, including the XXIst of the XXXIX Articles, for his critical freedom. We shall, however, defer any attempt at accounting for the scandal caused by the *Essay* until the conclusion of this chapter, for we have to relate the last of the controversies in which he took part before we try to define his religious belief.

Not only the authorities but the public knew as early as May that *Mr. Smirke* was Marvell's: identity of manner even more than of purpose showed it to have been written by the same hand as *The Rehearsal Transpros'd*. And this criterion holds good of another pamphlet for which the external evidence of his authorship amounts to very little. In *Remarks Upon a Late Disingenuous Discourse, Writ by one T.D. Under the pretence De Causa Dei . . .*, there is no new departure as regards style and dialectics, save that, instead of giving his adversary (Thomas Danson) a nickname out of a play, Marvell feigns to understand his initials as meaning 'The Discourse', which he ridicules all along as 'It', a stupid and malevolent animal. That his opponent should not be this time a persecuting Anglican but a persecuted Dissenter, at odds with another Dissenter, John Howe, does not cause Marvell to alter his way of jesting. Unfortunately for him the subject hardly lent itself to the same treatment as Parker's and Turner's insistence on uniformity in ceremonies; it was austerely theological: God's prescience of human actions, especially sinful ones, and its 'reconcilableness . . . with the Wisdom and Sincerity of his Counsels, Exhortations, and whatsoever Means He uses to prevent them'. Thus had the question been put to John Howe by the Honourable Robert Boyle (Lady Ranelagh and Lord Orrery's brother), remembered today as a pioneer of chemistry but no less concerned, as a devout Christian, with religious problems. Both men felt the influence of the growing rationalist movement. They also discarded the language of the medieval schools; alas! along with it they discarded metaphysics. The only thing

one can praise in Howe's *Letter* to Boyle is the simplicity
and clarity of his style. His arguments today sound pitiful,
as when he justifies God by invoking the practice of kings
who choose favourites without any special merit to distinguish them. Howe has lost all sense of mystery and thus
leads up to Toland.

On the contrary, Danson, an uncompromising Calvinist,
holds on both to the letter of the Bible and to the scholastic
way of reasoning. We admire his faith and intrepidity, even
if it makes us smile irreverently at times, and start indignantly
at others. And yet his assertion that 'God takes pleasure in
the perishing of unbelievers as well as in the saving of unbelievers' differs not much in spirit from Pascal's 'La justice
[de Dieu] envers les réprouvés est moins énorme et doit
moins choquer que la miséricorde envers les élus'.

Marvell, by this time too timid a Christian to accept
Danson's grim logic, was not enough of a sceptical dilettante
to admire its sublimity from a distance. Persuaded that
human reason can explain, if not the nature of God, at any
rate the manifestations of His will, he protests against a doctrine that seems to him an insult to the Creator. Following
Howe, he rejects the charge of Arminianism against the thesis
he supports, but for all practical purposes he 'evacuates', as
they said then, if not 'the Cross of Christ', at least the Calvinistic interpretation of the dogma of predestination. He
rejects even more hotly the charge of papistry preferred by
Danson against Howe, pointing out, rightly enough, that
the Church of Rome was still divided on this problem. It
remains true that he, like Milton, departs from what was
still the main Protestant tradition to incline towards what
was already the prevailing Roman Catholic interpretation.
We need not take sides here in a theological dispute. But we
must note sorrowfully that Marvell does not do justice to
one of the hardest problems a Christian has to face, if not to
solve. Not to mention the lack of method in the composition
(hardly superior to that of *The Rehearsal Transpros'd* or of
Mr. Smirke), the bantering style and the frivolous, sometimes coarse comparisons shock us far more in this pamphlet
than in those where discipline only, not dogma, was at stake.
We should hope for something better from a writer who

had been a sacred poet, who had experienced mystical ecstasies. But we should not conclude that Marvell takes God's glory and the honour of the Protestant Churches less to heart than Boyle or Howe, or even Danson, 'totus Dei domus zelo calens'. If he tries to move the groundlings to laughter it is in order to discredit an opinion he thinks impious, and liable to make gentle-hearted Christians turn towards the Jesuits. The tumbler of the medieval legend offered to Our Lady his gambols and somersaults in default of anything more dignified. Possibly Marvell plays the jester because of his consciousness that he cannot match his adversary, not only in scholastic argument, which he, like Howe, contemns, but in the field of metaphysics, for which he no longer has a head. With his contemporaries he has come down from those heights and is setting off for the low-lying flats of prosperous empiricism, where Locke will soon establish his bourgeois domination.

Marvell's last pamphlet passed almost unnoticed; very few copies survive, and the only mention of it is found in a life of Howe, published in 1724, by Edmund Calamy, the heir of a name famous in Presbyterian annals. Calamy calls the *Remarks* 'very witty and entertaining'; indeed their wit and fun deserved no more expert praise than that bestowed on them by the grandson of the second fifth of Smectymnuus.

So far we have had to pay rather more attention to those contemporaries of Marvell whom he defends or attacks than to himself, since he takes no initiative and seldom goes beyond negative criticism. But we now come to the qualities that have caused his own writings to outlive those he refuted. Swift's praise, which at first sounds surprising to the modern reader, shows that by the beginning of the eighteenth century the separation had taken place. 'Answerers to Books' are, as a rule, 'like Annuals' and 'fall and die . . . in Autumn', yet: 'There is indeed an Exception, when any great Genius thinks it worth his while to expose a foolish Piece; so we still read *Marvel's* Answer to *Parker* with Pleasure, tho' the Book it answers be sunk long ago.'[1]

---

[1] *A Tale of a Tub*, An Apology for the, &c. (p. 10 in Guthkelch and Smith's edition, 1958). Ronald Paulson, *Theme and Structure in Swift's 'Tale*

But the literary superiority of *The Rehearsal Transpros'd* never lay in its novelty. On the contrary the vogue of the burlesque was already over in France; it persisted in England, as witnessed by the success of *Hudibras*. Marvell, who admired Samuel Butler's wit, had in fact anticipated him; witness these lines in 'Upon Appleton House', describing the resistance offered by the nuns to General Fairfax's ancestor when he entered their house by force:

> Some to the Breach against their Foes
> Their *Wooden Saints* in vain oppose.
> Another bolder stands at push
> With their old *Holy-Water Brush*.
> While the disjointed *Abbess* threads
> The gingling Chain-shot of her *Beads*.
> But their lowd'st Cannon were their Lungs;
> And sharpest Weapons were their Tongues.

Here now is a picture, from the first part of *The Rehearsal Transpros'd*, of the alarum among the Anglican clergy at the *Declaration of Indulgence*. Marvell addresses Parker:

... some of your superiors of your robe did, upon the publishing that Declaration, give the word, and deliver orders through their ecclesiastical camp, to beat up the pulpit drums against Popery. ... So that, though for so many years those your superiors had forgot there was any such thing in the nation as a Popish recusant; though 'polemical and controversial divinity' had for so long been hung up in the halls, like the rusty obsolete armour of our ancestors, for monuments of antiquity, and for derision rather than service; all on a sudden ... happy was he that could climb

---

of a Tub', 1960, has many interesting references to Marvell, and to Parker, as forerunners of Swift, especially pp. 39–45 and 238–45. See also Hugh Macdonald, 'Banter in English Controversial Prose After the Restoration' in *Essays and Studies by Members of the English Association 1946*, pp. 21–39, for useful information on this new style of raillery, in which John Eachard, also esteemed (but not without qualification) by Swift, just preceded Marvell, with *Some Observations upon the Answer to an Enquiry into the Grounds, &c.*, 1671. Mrs. Duncan-Jones informs me that in a pamphlet attributed (wrongly, it seems) to John Eachard, *A free and impartial inquiry into the Causes of that very great Esteem and Honour the Nonconforming Preachers are generally in with their Followers* ... (Imprimatur, April 7, 1673) Marvell is alluded to unmistakably (though not named) as a 'Jester', a 'Jack-Pudding', and a 'Monkey', and that he in return makes a scoffing allusion to the author as a 'Mascarade-Divine'; see *The Rehearsall Transpros'd: The Second Part*, 1673, p. 323.

first to get down one of the old cuirasses or an habergeon that had been worn in the days of Queen Elizabeth ... Some clapp'd it on all rusty as it was, others fell of oyling or furbishing their armour; some piss'd in their barrels, others spit in their pans to scowr them. Here you might see one put on his helmet the wrong way; there one buckle on a back instead of a breast. Some by mistake catched up a Socinian-Arminian argument, and some a Popeish to fight a Papist. Here a dwarf lost in the accoutrements of a giant: there a Don Quixot in an equipage of different pieces and of several parishes. Never was such incongruity and Nonconformity in their furniture. One ran to borrow a sword of Calvin; this man for a musket from Beza; that for a bandeleers even from Keckerman. But when they came to seek match, and bullet, and powder, there was none to be had. The fanaticks had bought it all up, and made them pay for it most unconscionably and through the nose. And no less sport was it to see their leaders. Few could tell how to give the word of command nor understood to drill a company: they were as unexpert as their soldiers were aukward; and the whole was as pleasant a spectacle as the exercising of the trained bands in ——shire.

Reminiscences of Butler combine here with an allusion to Cervantes, though Marvell has lately taken Parker to task for 'growing too early acquainted with Don Quixot, and reading the Bible too late'. Similarly, when Marvell quotes in the second part an anecdote belonging to the Rabelaisian legend, he is careful to add that Parker has long been acquainted with *Gargantua* and calls Hickeringhill 'his [Parker's] second Rabelais', as if, like a good English Puritan, he would shift the opprobrium attached to the French writer's name over to his own adversaries. These had, not ineptly, denounced 'his garagantuan humour', by which they meant such a combination of metaphor and hyperbole as this: Parker, having been made chaplain to a nobleman, 'was transported now with the sanctity of his office, even to ecstasy ... he was seen in his prayers to be lifted up sometimes in the air, and once particularly so high that he crack'd his scull against the chappel ceiling ... that crack of his scull, as in broken looking-glasses, multiplied him in self-conceit and imagination'.

But Marvell can also use the more refined form of parody that ennobles petty thoughts or events by means of lofty expression. Boileau was then providing both the theory of this species of the genre and its best specimen in *Le Lutrin*.

Marvell shows more originality in his parody of the King's Speech, which we should quote in full had we space enough.[1] At that time nobody but a Member of Parliament could write such a piece of satire, and who better than he? Although the external evidence is late and not very solid, the style of the mock-speech, even more than its political drift, vouches for Marvell's authorship. We quote instead from *An Account of the Growth of Popery*, in which pamphlet he is at his soberest, a similar but briefer skit. It is apropos of a French Embassy to England that arrived while King and Commons were wrangling over their respective powers, though pretendedly agreed on the necessity of waging war against France:

There landed immediately after the recess, the Duke of Crequy, the archbishop of Rheims, Monsieur Barillon and a train of three or four hundred persons of all qualities, so that the Lords Spiritual and Temporal of France, with so many of their Commons, meeting the king at Newmarket, it looked like another Parliament and that the English had been adjourned, in order to their better reception. But what address they made to his Majesty, or what Acts they passed, hath not yet been published; but those that have been in discourse were:

'An Act for continuing his Majestie's subjects in the service of France.

'An Act of abolition of all claims and demands of the subjects of France, on account of all prizes made of the English at sea since the year 1674 till that day, and for the future.

'An Act for marrying the Children of the Royal Family to Popish Princes.

'An Act for a further supply of French money.'

But because it appears not that all these, and many others of more secret nature, passed the Royal assent, it sufficeth thus far to have mentioned them. Only it is most certain, that although the English Parliament was kept aloof from the business of war, peace and alliance, as improper for their intermeddling and presumptuous; yet with these three estates of France all these things were negociated and transacted in the greatest confidence. And so they

[1] It is conveniently reprinted in *Andrew Marvell Selected Poetry and Prose*, edited by Dennis Davison, 1952.

were adjourned from Newmarket to London, and there continued
till the return of the English Parliament, when they were dismissed
home with all the signs and demonstrations of mutual satisfaction.

The sting of this passage lies in the use of parliamentary
technicalities and in the opposition between the imaginary
bills and those actually passed by the English Lords and
Commons but not assented to by Charles.

Occasionally the humour does not depend on fanciful
exaggeration, but on straight description of reality, for instance of the Pensionary Parliament. Here political argument
acquires a literary value through a succession of thumbnail
sketches. How could a Member who is also one of the King's
servants move cuts in the expenditure of the department
from which he draws his salary? There is the abstract idea,
which Marvell animates for us. Here we seem to see and
hear one of these interested ministerialists in action: 'What
officer of the navy, but takes himself under obligation to
magnify the expence, extol the management, conceal the
neglect, increase the debts and press the necessity, rigging
and unrigging it to the House in the same moment, and
representing it all at once in a good and a bad condition?'
The name of Samuel Pepys, Member of Parliament for Castle
Rising since 1673, rises inevitably (though perhaps wrongly)
to our mind, but we need not think the worse of him for it
nor accept Marvell's views (in fact long obsolete in his own
country) on the separation of the legislative and executive
powers, to appreciate the quickness of the disputant. When
he stands on his other favourite ground, ecclesiastical satire,
Marvell can also give descriptions that if not impartial are
graphic. In *Mr. Smirke* Francis Turner, or any one of the
sort of authors he belongs to, after having written a pamphlet in favour of religious intolerance, has it sent all over
England, beginning with the Universities 'by an express':

The country cathedralls learn it latest, and arrive [*sic*] by slower
degrees to their understanding, by the carrier. It grows a business
of chapter, and they admire it in a body as a profound book of
theology. Those of 'em that can confide in one another, discourse
it over in private, and then 'tis odds, but, before the laity get
notice of it, they first hear it preach'd over by him whose turn it

is next Sunday in the minster; the rest conceal the fraud for the reputation of the diocess. After the book is grown common the plagiary wonders how, but that proportionable wits jump together, the Exposer [Marvell's other nick-name for Turner] could hit so right upon his notions. But if the dean foresee that 'tis a very vendible book, he you may imagine forestalls the market, and sends up for a whole dicker of 'em to retaile at his best advantage.

Though Marvell has not spent much time in or even near cathedral closes we might say he here anticipates Trollope. In his own age his manner no longer reminds us of Scarron but of Furetière, not of the *Roman Comique* but of the *Roman Bourgeois* (1665).

On rare occasions Marvell rises above common burlesque thanks to his fancy and, while bantering, recovers the language of poetry. In the midst of a farcical scene—Parker and his mistress playing parlour games the first evening of their affair—he who had sung of Damon and Juliana, of Ametas and Thestylis, exclaims:

Is it not strange that in the most benign minutes of a man's life, when the stars smile, the birds sing, the winds whisper, the fountains warble, the trees blossom, and universal nature seems to invite itself to the bridal, when the lion pulls-in his claws and the aspick layes-by its poyson, and all the most noxious creatures grow most amorously innocent; that even then Mr. Bayes alone should not be able to refrain his malignity?

The pleasant picture serves to spring a surprise on us:

As you love yourself, madam, let him not come near you. He has been fed all his life with vipers instead of lampreys, and scorpions for cray-fish; and if at any time he eat chickens, they had been cramb'd with spiders, till he hath so envenomed his whole substance that 'tis much safer to bed with a mountebank before he has taken his antidote.

The quasi-euphuistic hyperbole ends on a piece of coarseness, which dispels the poetic illusion.

More often dirt appears without any poetic alloy. The satires had prepared us for this, but Marvell there conformed to the law of the genre; besides, he painted a corrupt society; lastly, we see him there more as a patriot than a Puritan.

But he now deals with religious matters and the pamphlets have earned him in his own age and with posterity the reputation of a Puritan. He is fully responsible, then, for all the indecency we find here. We must sample it, first as a part of his own temperament and next as representative of what a Puritan, true or merely reputed so, could allow himself to vent, provided of course he refused the same freedom to the children of Baal and Dagon.

If man is a laughing animal it is mainly the animal in man that laughs and causes laughter. The two great physical functions, the digestive and the reproductive, provide the better part of these traditional gibes. Hunger in others is entertaining: 'you were so hungry at that time', Marvell says to Parker, 'that you would have adored an onion, so it had cryed: "Come, eat me" '. But still more entertaining are the necessity of voiding the residue of digestion, and the noises that come out at both ends of the alimentary canal. We shall quote only one instance of this kind of scoff, again addressed to Parker, selecting it because it has been deemed by a good judge to herald Swift: 'But why do I reproach you with these things, which I am persuaded, nay certain, that you take for an honour? I oblige you by the very repetition, and you clap and crow at the wit and malice of your expressions. So some men take a second entertainment in the savoryness of their own belches.'

To those internal servitudes of the flesh Marvell adds other miseries that are external but very close to the skin; lice become his allies against Parker: 'He puts me in mind of the incorrigible scold, that though she was duck'd over head and ears under water, yet stretched up her hands with her two thumbnails in the nit-cracking posture, or with two fingers "devaricated", to call the man still in that language lousy rascal and cuckold.' With this last word we pass on to another province of jesting. The difference here between Marvell's pamphlets and his satires lies chiefly in the substitution of innuendo for plain-spokenness, of a suggestive periphrasis for a coarse word. To Parker, who, taking up a conjecture of Descartes, has placed the seat of the soul in the pineal gland, he remarks, quite gratuitously: ' 'twas civily done, however, that you placed it not in some other glandule'.

Here Marvell anticipates Sterne's pruriency, more corrupt than the bawdry of any Cavalier, and more incompatible with honest Puritanism. Fortunately it is still exceptional in our author.

Anyhow, nobody in the Nonconformist camp seems to have felt ill at ease on account of these various offences against decency; hence the unqualified success of *The Rehearsal Transpros'd*, while the *Essay on Councils*, far less coarse, caused some qualms among the very people it undertook to defend. Since, as we have seen, its matter could hardly disturb even the most conservative Presbyterian, the likeliest explanation is to be found in the light irreverent wit. Under Charles II the meaning of the word was becoming narrower, and approval of the thing less general: to many it seemed that only virtue and piety could serve as butts to the man of wit. Marvell himself occasionally adopts this view. The preface to Danson's pamphlet, he asserts, 'hath all the marks upon it of malice except the wit wherewith that malice is usually accompanied'. To himself he proves more lenient: 'though I carry always some ill nature about me, yet it is, I hope, no more then is in this world necessary for a preservative.' But he at least pretends not to set much store by wit: 'Whether I have any at all, I know not; neither, further than it is not fit for me to reject any good quality wherewith God may have indued me, do I much care; but would be glad to part with it very easily for anything intellectual, that is solid and useful.' The divergence of 'wit' and 'intellect', terms almost synonymous at the beginning of the century, shows how frivolous the former is becoming towards its close. At times, indeed, Marvell distinguishes between true wit (his own) and false wit (his opponents'). After a particularly unwarranted jest at Danson he shakes off the immodesty of it in a sanctimonious manner: 'What sport were here prepar'd for that which is by our moderns called wit, but is no more than the luxuriant sterility of land not broken up or manured!' Yet he could also speak well of wit allied with sense, as when he compares them with the feathers and the head of an arrow respectively: 'I shall treat him [sc. Parker] betwixt jest and earnest. That which is solid and sharp, being imp'd by something more light and airy, may carry further and pierce deeper.'

If we now study Marvell's wit in itself, apart from any moral consideration, another difficulty arises: we shall have to extract the salt from those unfrequented lagoons, his prolix pamphlets; it will not be easy. Let us try, however.

Not seldom this wit takes the form of the French *pointe*, somewhat modernized. Parker 'would never have come into the Church but to take sanctuary'. The quibble on 'Church' and 'sanctuary', both used simultaneously in their concrete and their abstract meanings, saves the sentence from being mere abuse. The House of Commons, after a fifteen months' prorogation, is (according to Marvell) legally dissolved; but what do its Members care provided they can shelter there? This Marvell hints by the mere insertion of one word: 'this House or barn of Commons'.

With hardly less concision and in an even quieter way Marvell shows the crazy condition of the Reformation in the England of the Stuarts by a sly parenthesis: 'Bills . . . of the highest consequence that ever were offered in Parliament since Protestancy came in (and went out of fashion). . .' Elsewhere he dispenses with any warning and simply substitutes a biting word for the expected one; in the above-mentioned review of the *ex officio* ministerialists in the House of Commons, here are a handful of interested officials: 'Or who would have denied money to continue the war with Holland, when he were a commissioner of prizes, of sick and wounded, of transporting the English, or of starving the Dutch prisoners?' Marvell's heart revolts at the treatment inflicted by peculating fellow-countrymen on helpless enemies, but his face remains impassive. Once or twice he resorts to another concealing device, the deliberate anachronism, that very literary weapon wielded just before him by Boileau, next by Rochester and Oldham, and later by Dryden and Pope: why three centuries of persecution against the Christians in the Roman Empire? 'For the Gentile priests could not but observe a great decay in their parishes.'

More commonly learning, waggish but also self-satisfied, spreads out complacently. Marvell laughs at the pedantry of Francis Turner, but Turner might have retorted the charge. What excuses Marvell's pedantry is the variety and novelty of his quotations and allusions. Even in classical antiquity

he unearths anecdotes as yet unstaled. And modern times
contribute their quota: Guelfs and Ghibellines, 'Muleasses,
king of Tunis', the Samoyedes, 'Dancehment Kan', the
'Phtirophagi' of Tartary, the kingdom of Macassar, the
Popish converts of Chiapa. Such erudition recalls Montaigne
(whose *Essays* Marvell had read) in the chapter 'Of cannibals'
and many others; also Burton's *Anatomy of Melancholy* and
Sir Thomas Browne's *Pseudodoxia Epidemica*. It belongs to
the Renaissance, with its superposing on a fundamental
classical culture a vast and capricious reading, in which the
exotic has its share.

That ecclesiastical history should, however, predominate
in these pamphlets, need not surprise us. Such knowledge
was widely diffused then, and we should not praise Marvell's
scholarship for having read, pen in hand, Socrates Scholas-
ticus, Sozomene, and others still more deeply buried in
oblivion nowadays. What belongs to him personally is the
turn he gives to his quotations, the informal English into
which he translates the Greek or Latin originals, and above
all the spirit of his commentaries. We wish we could transcribe the whole relation of the Council of Nice; here at
least is Marvell's refutation of the supreme orthodox argument in favour of this assembly:

But the Holy Ghost was present where there were three hundred
and eighteen bishops, and directed them, or three hundred! Then,
if I had been of their Council, they should have sate at it all their
lives, lest they should never see Him again after they were once
risen. But it concerned them to settle their *quorum* at first by His
dictates; otherwise no bishop could have been absent, or gone
forth upon any occasion but He let him out again; and it behoov'd
to be very punctual in the adjournments!

If this opening bears the stamp of the Member of Parliament
versed in all the chicanery about standing orders, what
follows reveals the *philosophe* by anticipation:

'Tis a ridiculous conception, and as gross as to make Him of the
same substance with the Council. Nor needs there any stronger
argument of His absence, then their pretense to be actuated by
Him, and in doing such work. The Holy Spirit! If so many of
them, when they got together, acted like rational men, 'twas
enough in all reason, and as much as could be expected.

This passage would hardly look out of place in some chapters of the *Essai sur les mœurs*, the *Examen important de Mylord Bolingbroke*, or the article on Councils of the *Dictionnaire philosophique* from which we now quote:

Tous les conciles sont infaillibles, sans doute; car ils sont composés d'hommes. Il est impossible que jamais les passions, les intrigues, l'esprit de dispute, la haine, la jalousie, le préjugé, l'ignorance, règnent dans ces assemblées.

The difference is one of degree, not of kind. Marvell, like Voltaire, sets up reason as the judge of traditions and authorities; if it condemns them, reason uses ridicule to discredit them.

Yet Marvell can lift up the veil of humour and speak his mind without disguise. Here is his final judgement on this same Council of Nice:

I must crave liberty to say, that from one end to the other, though the best of the kind, it seems to me to have been a pityful humane business, attended with all the ill circumstances of other worldly affairs, conducted by a spirit of ambition and contention, the first and so the greatest Œcumenical blow that by Christians was given to Christianity.

But today wider interest will be felt in the following passage since believers and unbelievers alike have to face this problem: are human laws binding *in foro conscientiae*? Parker says yes; Marvell unhesitatingly says no and maintains that a citizen puts himself right with the State by paying the fines and serving the prison terms. The occasion of the argument is the Act against Conventicles. Marvell does his best to show the utilitarian, relative, and temporary nature of this law and human laws in general:

Indeed, how is it possible to imagine, and to what purpose, that ever any magistrate should make laws but for a general advantage? and who again but would be glad to abrogate them when he finds them pernicious to his government? and therefore it is very usual to make at first probationary laws, and for some term of years only; that both the law-giver and the subject may see at leisure how proper they are and suitable for the effect for which they were intended. And indeed all laws however are but probationers of Time; and though meant for perpetuity, yet when

unprofitable, do as they were made by common consent, so expire
by universal neglect, and without repeal grow obsolete.

From this height of eloquence, worthy of Hooker or Bacon,
Marvell at once comes down to his usual familiar style, but
his line of argument remains interesting since it shows, if
not the statesman that circumstances did not allow him to
become, at least the experienced politician, fully able to
bring back theorists to reality; he asserts that civil penalties
do more to keep people within the law than theological or
metaphysical considerations on the basis of legality—a very
liberal view in spite of appearances. To Parker, who complains that laws not binding consciences are not true laws,
Marvell answers with blunt commonsense: 'if they be not
laws, they are at least halters.' But his tone soon rises again:
'. . . as it is unlawful to palliate with God, and enervate His
laws into an humane only and politick consideration; so it is
on the other side, unlawful and unnecessary to give to
common and civil constitutions a divine sanction; and it is
so far from an owning of God's jurisdiction, that it is an
invasion upon it.' We wish the paragraph ended on this
noble and powerful distinction between spiritual and temporal, but it runs on for sixteen more pages of digression
following digression. This prolixity more than anything
else may well discourage the modern reader.

For Marvell's prose raises no barrier. He affects neither
the overwhelming periodicity of Cicero nor the enigmatic
concision of Seneca. He rarely exhausts our attention, like
Milton or, less artfully, Cromwell, with interminable sentences; only occasionally does he strike out *sententiae*, but
some are worthy of Bacon or Hobbes; indeed, apropos of
the former he says: 'a wise man is as it were eternal upon
earth' (this, however, in a subordinate clause).

Usually he writes like a man of the world or a man of
business; even in his more ornate moments the prose of this
poet is not poetic prose. It even lacks resonance. Marvell
wrote for the eye only. And yet he prized the rhythm of
Elizabethan prose, e.g. that of the Liturgy, since he took
the Revisers of 1662 to task for having added 'schism' to
'false doctrine and heresie' in the Litany; they had done it

'though it were to spoil the musick and cadence of the period'. But his own printed prose flows evenly, like Cowley's, which precedes his and may have served him for a model.

Yet the mark of the Renaissance is still found in Marvell's vocabulary and imagery. It yields a far more abundant crop to the lexicographer than his verse. Instead of the gentleman's English of the lyrical poems we have in the pamphlets pedantry and vulgarity, the language of Billingsgate and that of Hyde Park, the technical terms of the army and navy, of Parliament and the Law Courts. When English fails him he does not boggle at French, any more than his contemporaries, or Italian and Spanish, any more than his predecessors. He quotes Latin, Greek, Hebrew, and even Malay.

Nor is his taste in images less catholic, as the quotations already made in this chapter have sufficiently proved. Two groups, however, deserve a special mention. In the first there shines a last gleam of the metaphysical furnace. By their gruesome weirdness these images remind us of Donne: the Duchess of Orléans's death at once reconciled England and France 'as if upon dissecting the princess there had some State philtre been found in her bowels'; the way Danson interprets a defunct divine causes Marvell to exclaim: 'This is the same as to cut off a dead man's hand to subscribe with it to a forgery.' In the second group of images a certain naturalness, or inevitability, announces the coming of the Augustans: to Parker who affirms that the least blow to the Church endangers the stability of the State, Marvell coolly answers: 'There is nothing more natural than for the ivy to be of opinion that the oak cannot stand without its support.' And so we pass on to the moral commonplace that forms the matter of Pope's poetry, expressed in an epigram: the members of the Opposition in the House of Commons profess themselves patriots because ministerial favour has deserted them for others, 'for who would not commend chastity, and rail against whoring, while his rival enjoys their mistress?'

Thus Marvell belongs both to the past and to the future as well by his images as by the build of his sentences. What

is true of the form of his pamphlets may also be surmised of
their matter. But here a difficulty arises: we can tell more
easily what he attacks than what he approves. Let us limit
ourselves to his religious belief. His hostility to the Roman
Church is beyond all doubt, but when it comes to defining
the irreducible opposition between Protestants and Catholics
he mostly tells us in what it does not consist. In the indictment against Popery that stands as a preamble to *An Account*
he deduces all other grievances from the restriction of the
reading of the Bible to the clergy: an argument good enough
for political propaganda, but one that hardly accounts for
his scarcely less fierce abhorrence of the Anglican Prelacy,
innocent of such monopolizing. What then does he charge
the Laudians with? Not their Arminianism, or only when it
suits his present purpose. Their immoderate taste for ceremonies he dislikes, but probably would not demur to them
any more than his father had done, were it not that he sees
the manifestation of a domineering spirit contrary to the
Gospel in the way these ceremonies are enforced. This spirit
was, to him, embodied in the bishops. Did he distinguish
between episcopacy and prelacy? Yes in 1660, though even
a reformed episcopate, shorn of its feudal honours and
powers, probably appeared to him a *pis aller*. At the end of
his life he seems to have worked towards the total abolition
of the order. Going one step further he questioned the
legitimacy of a clergy as a separate body: all the faithful
belong to the 'clerum Domini' and may be called 'clerici'.
The Presbyterian ministers, had they prevailed at the
Restoration, would probably have disgusted him as quickly
as they had Milton at the opening of the Civil War. In the
loose sense of the word he is an Erastian: he looks to the
Civil Power to curb the ingrained intolerance of all eccle-
siastics; hence his oscillation between King and Parliament
according to their readiness to acquit themselves of this
duty.

But his own tolerance has definite bounds; it excludes the
Roman Catholics, like Milton's or Locke's; it includes the
Jews in a grudging manner. The reason is that it rests on a
theological basis: all Christians have the right to interpret
the Bible each in his own way, because it is their duty to do

so, prescribed to them by the Bible itself. Thus Protestants only are free and deserve freedom. Hence, among the persecuted, Marvell's sympathy, at any rate after 1660, restricts itself to the Dissenters. But does it make him a Dissenter? Some of his biographers affirm it, others deny it with equal confidence. We shall nonsuit both parties: for a layman of his generation, a bachelor especially, the Act of Uniformity entailed no necessity of choice, provided no certain test of orthodoxy. In print Marvell sometimes refers to the Church of England, as 'our church' (so does Milton in 1673), but as 'your church' when addressing a high Anglican. The main difference between Marvell and Milton lies in their views of the retention or abolition of the Establishment. The latter speaks as a doctrinaire; the former sticks to Cromwell's religious policy, as liberal as it was illogical: he advocates toleration and works for Comprehension.

Besides, the Established Church, uncompromising on ceremonies and discipline, proved easy-going enough where mere dogma was concerned. From Hales, an Anglican of note, Marvell had received a doctrine that was actually or supposedly tainted with Socinianism, a heresy about which *The Rehearsal Transpros'd* contains equivocal and contradictory remarks. No doubt Marvell remains a Christian in his own eyes, but is he still, to use Voltaire's word, a 'Christolâtre'? Does he not hold out his hand to the Deists?

Of course the open statements of this doctrine were made only after his death: Charles Blount's *Anima Mundi*, published in 1679, was to cause an outcry. But Marvell in his lifetime had been accused of religious indifference and disrespect to the Christian revelation. *A Letter from Amsterdam* (April 1678) says of 'Andrew' that 'for his religion you may place him . . . between *Moses*, the *Messiah*, and *Mahomet*, with this motto in his mouth, *Quò me vertam nescio*'. And in fact *An Account of the Growth of Popery* had just proclaimed the moral and political failure of Christianity: not 'any advantage [has] accrued unto mankind from that most perfect and practical model of society. . .'

What he thought of its purely spiritual aspect he has not told. But in 1687 his favourite nephew, William Popple, was to publish *A rational Catechism* where one might see a

posthumous extension of Marvell's thought. Revelation is
not denied but its necessity is degraded to mere utility: mankind could have done without it 'but that the Vulgar sort
of People . . . are not capable of . . . deep Meditation', and
even the wiser ones 'too frequently, do either slip or break
the fine-spun thread of their own consequences'. Popple
calls the Gospel 'a plain rule of living well' and affirms it
contains no 'hidden mysteries'.

Did Marvell think so meanly? At least one passage in *The
Rehearsal Transpros'd* seems to show that, at least so late as
1672, all sense of the supernatural had not died out in him.
Parker had written: '. . . all Religion must of necessity be
resolv'd into Enthusiasm or Morality. The former is mere
Imposture, and, therefore, all that is true must be reduced
to the latter; . . .' Marvell retorted: 'he overturns the whole
fabrick of Christianity and power of religion. For my part,
if GRACE be resolved into morality, I think a man may as
well make God too to be only a notional and moral existence.' Such a protest could come only from a believer,
unless Marvell just wanted to score off Parker. The riddle
remains unsolved. Perhaps we shall come nearest the truth
if we compare Marvell's deistic sallies to projections from
the general alignment of a building. In other words, he did
not realize the importance of the positions he surrendered
to infidelity, because his mind had more flexibility than
energy or depth.

If so, his thought, less original than representative, marks
the passage of England from the Puritan to the Rationalistic
phase of her history. Still a Protestant while already a free-
thinker, he has, like Hales, 'bidden adieu to Calvin', but
probably not to Saint Paul, and certainly not to Jesus.[1]

[1] Caroline Robbins, 'Marvell's Religion: Was he a New Methodist?' in
Journal of the History of Ideas, 1962, pp. 268–72, makes an interesting attempt
at applying to Marvell a term used, rather ephemerally, by one strict Calvinist
to label a semi-Arminian heresy. She concludes that Marvell retained to the
end his faith in a just yet benevolent God.

VIII

AFTER DEATH

Two days after his death Marvell was buried 'in St Giles church in the Feilds in the South isle by the pulpit'. The ceremony does not seem to have attracted many friends or acquaintances. Aubrey himself, who knew Marvell and was to become his first biographer, evidently did not attend it, since in order to ascertain where the poet's remains lay he had to make inquiries later from the sexton.

If London allowed the defender of public freedom to pass away amid general indifference Hull showed more gratitude; at once and for long Marvell's fame received the local stamp, with all the piety but something of the narrowness this implies. On 24 September the Corporation voted a fairly considerable sum for a monument 'In consideration of the kindnesse the Town and Borough had for Andrew Marvell, Esq. . . . and for his great meritts with the Corporation'. The church of St. Giles was rebuilt in the eighteenth century, so that the disappearance of that 'gravestone' should not surprise us. But a tradition, highly suspect, has it that 'the epitaph . . . erected' above 'was torn down by the zealots of the King's party', possibly during the reaction against the Whigs in 1682. Another tradition, somewhat better established but apparently irreconcilable with the former, asserts that the Rector of St. Giles vetoed the putting up in his church of that monument. These legends, if such we must call them, bear witness to the belief among Marvell's friends that by the end of his life he had become one of the Government's most formidable enemies.

Whether or not placed on or above his tomb, the text of the epitaph, probably composed by William Popple, presents some interest for it avoids the hyperbolical and mendacious style usual in this kind of composition. All the qualities it claims for our poet, 'Wit and Learning, with a singular Penetration and Strength of Judgm^{nt} . . . an unalterable

Steadyn^{ss} in ye Ways of Virtue, . . . Wisdom, Dexterity,
Integrity and Courage' he did possess (though perhaps some
might question the 'unalterable Steadyn^{ss}'). What strikes us
today is not excess of praise but the brevity of the allusion
to Marvell's 'inimitable Writings', while the epitaph insists
lovingly on his conduct as Member of Parliament; the word
it emphasizes is 'Patriot'. For a century and more biographers
were to strike the same note.

Equally characteristic is an anonymous piece, written it
seems before the end of 1678, 'On his Excellent Friend, Mr.
Andrew Marvell', in whom is glorified the foe of 'the grim
Monster, Arbitrary Power'; while many yielded, '*Marvell*,
this Islands watchful Centinel—Stood in the gap, and bravely
kept his Post'. The late Member for Hull's political opponents say the same, though of course in a different tone. In
his 'Epistle to the Whigs' (March 1681/2) Dryden ascribes
the first invention of the seditious doctrines he denounces
to their 'dead Authour's Pamphlet call'd, the *Growth of
Popery*'.[1] And in the preface to *Religio Laici* (November
1682) he calls 'Martin Mar-prelate (the *Marvel* of those times)
. . . the first Presbyterian Scribbler, who sanctify'd Libels
and Scurrility to the use of the Good Old Cause'. This
assimilation had already been made by Parker, and Marvell,
more or less candidly, had rejected it in the *Second Part* of
The Rehearsall Transpros'd. But its use by the leading writer
of the age proves what section of his works, inseparable
from his political and religious activity, lived on in men's
minds after his death.

Dryden indeed had no personal reason to spare his former
colleague in the Latin Secretaryship under Oliver (an

---

[1] E. S. de Beer, 'Dryden: The Kind Keeper', in *N.Q.*, 24 August 1940,
pp. 128–9, suggests that Marvell was the 'poet of scandalous memory'
alluded to in the Dedication of the play (printed in 1680). But the epithet
may well have been aimed at Flecknoe and just mean 'wretched', as de Beer
himself shows. In the same year but on the other side the anonymous
pamphlet entitled *Tell Truth's Answer to Tell-Troth's Letter to Shaftesbury*
defends Marvell's memory: 'any whiffling Cur will venture to beard a dead
Lion . . . little Andrew (as you contemptibly call him) had Wit and Policy
enough to silence the greatest Droll . . .' (Information provided by Professor
Robbins.) In *His Majesties Declaration Defended* . . . 1681, now believed to be
Dryden's (see Macdonald's Bibliography, no. 129), Marvell probably is the
'deceas'd Judas' of the Whigs (p. 3) and he is referred to by name as the
friend of the Petitioners-to-be.

unpleasant memory), for Marvell had made unprovoked attacks on him. Yet the same generosity that prompted the Royalist poet to noble utterances on Milton might have shown itself in the praise of Marvell's literary talent, even when the matter of his pamphlets was condemned. Now the word 'Scribbler' speaks of political prejudice, not critical serenity. And Dryden ignored, then and later, Marvell's lyrical poetry, by then obtainable in print. The volume modestly entitled *Miscellaneous Poems* contained all those pieces that could pass the censorship of 1681. The publisher had indeed thought of including in his collection the pieces in honour of Cromwell, possibly relying on the Whig fervour of the Parliament that met in October 1680 (the brief preface 'To the Reader' is dated the 15th of that month); but a dissolution soon followed, and the publisher's heart failed him: in the printing he stopped halfway through 'A Poem upon the Death of O.C.', and this piece, like 'An Horatian Ode' and 'The First Anniversary' disappeared from the copies put on sale. In spite of this precaution the volume was favourably received only by 'persons of [the author's] persuasion' in political and ecclesiastical matters; and within this group the majority seem to have 'cried up as excellent', on trust, out of gratitude for services rendered in another field, a kind of poetry that did not well agree with their own austerity: many of those who bought the *Miscellaneous Poems* only cared for the portrait in the frontispiece. Far from politics' interfering in 1681 with Marvell's success as a poet, he seems to have been indebted to them for whatever noise his finest work then made. Reason for the silence that soon fell on it must be sought in the changes of taste during the thirty years that separated composition (at least the greater part of it) from publication. Other belated metaphysicals, such as Henry Vaughan and Thomas Traherne, fared no better even though they were excellent Royalists and pious Anglicans. Dryden himself had passed from extravagant imitation of Donne to a respectful but decisive condemnation of his manner. His indifference to Marvell's lyrical poetry is that of the adult for the playthings of his childhood.

Among the political works the prose pamphlets were more widely read than the verse satires until the Glorious

Revolution. A second edition, late in 1678, and a French translation of the *Growth of Popery* in 1680, a continuation of the same in English by a Whig in 1682, two editions of the *Essay* on Councils, in 1680 and 1687, witness to their popularity. Besides the reprinting of the *Growth of Popery* among the *State Tracts* used to justify the dethronement of James II, the year 1689 saw the first three of those *Collections*, now called for short *State Poems*, in which appear (sometimes toned down politically) all those verse satires that may be Marvell's, and others wrongly attributed to him. Among the heroes of the recent past he ranks first, as shown by the title-pages of two of those volumes where 'A—— M——l, Esq.' alone precedes the rest, lumped together as 'other Eminent Wits'. At this time, we may say, Marvell's political influence affects the course of history most vigorously and successfully; it deserves to be numbered among the causes that, in the last years of the seventeenth century and the first of the eighteenth brought the English people to that organization of politics and religion so many features of which still survive. This is why one of the agents of that transformation, Defoe, admires Marvell; possibly takes his cue, in his own *True-Born Englishman*, from some lines of 'A Dialogue between the Two Horses'; and quotes, to the end of his life, this same satire, agreeable, in spite of some flights of fancy, to his own prosaic and bourgeois temperament.

In the first decade of the eighteenth century the *Essay* on Councils reappeared twice, and the third edition shows that its admirers stood on the extreme borders of Christianity, where religion can hardly be distinguished from Deism. Therefore we are not surprised to see Marvell as the addressee of an imaginary letter from John Toland, who certainly admired him and whose own name was enough to scandalize pious souls. But soon the boldness of the *Essay* became trite and it joined Marvell's other pamphlets in oblivion. The almost excessive praise given by Swift in 1710 to the 'answer to Parker' marks the term, not the starting-point of a reputation. The best of the style and wit of *The Rehearsal Transpros'd* and *Mr. Smirke* has passed into *The Battle of the Books* and *A Tale of a Tub*;[1] the rest looks prolix and heavy beside

[1] Irvin Ehrenpreis, 'Four of Swift's Sources', in *M.L.N.*, 1955, p. 95, adds

more recent, and truly classic, prose works. About the same time current politics drifted away from the problems to which Marvell had devoted his polemical talent. The Whigs, now safely in power under George I, continued to honour him as is shown by the dedication of Thomas Cooke's edition to the Duke of Devonshire, one of the leaders of the ruling oligarchy. This contains both the lyrical poems and the satires, and its preface compares Marvell to Aristides; but pleas for the freedom of the Press, protests against parliamentary corruption, even attacks on the bishops appealed little to Sir Robert Walpole, who gagged the independent playwrights, notably Fielding, declared that every Member of Parliament had his price, and placed in every episcopal see a pliant Whig, full of indulgence for the Dissenters and severe only to the over-zealous Anglicans.

Accordingly it was now the Tories' turn to seize the weapons discarded by their opponents. Rather than 'the Tories', we should say 'the Opposition', an incongruous combination where Bolingbroke and Pulteney had little in common beyond the will to overthrow the Administration. The chief Press organ of that coalition, *The Craftsman*, published two essays on Marvell in 1735: the former reprovingly assimilates the 'modern Whigs' to the 'old Tories' and fights them with arguments out of *The Rehearsal Transpros'd*; the latter is a pastiche of the *Essay* on Councils really aimed at Walpole's prelates though nominally at those of Charles II. But if an infidel like Bolingbroke or his disciple Wyndham could delight in such *jeux d'esprit*, Tories of the old rock continued to execrate Marvell: Roger North, far from a malicious man, calls *The Growth of Popery* 'the worst . . . of the Libels of that Time'; he stigmatizes Marvell's 'infamous Practices', charges him with having written a 'base Pamphlet' against the Christian religion (the *Essay* no doubt) and sums up his censure in the word 'free-thinker'.

Though in Anglican orders, William Mason, Thomas Gray's friend, did not resent rather too personal views on dogma or banter aimed at the clergy. A true-blue Whig but also the scion of a family that held high municipal offices at

one more possible borrowing or reminiscence from *The Rehearsall Transpros'd* (Part II): wit is also compared to whipped cream in *The Battle of the Books*.

Hull when our poet sat for it in Parliament, Mason could not but choose him for the hero of his 'Ode to Independency'. He shows us the deified personification's 'fav'rite Swain' wandering in his youth along the 'lone beach' of Humber where he 'artless wove his Doric lay'. The goddess tells the poet that the situation now is too serious for him to continue writing amatory verse, and Marvell goes to war against 'Freedom's foes'. His triumph over Parker stands as his main title to fame. And naturally his 'awful poverty' occupies the place of honour in this panegyric.

Poorly as they read today, Mason's lines served Marvell's reputation in their time. Published in 1756 they preluded to a recrudescence of the Whig admiration for the incorruptible Member of Parliament and the avenging satirist. But Marvell owed it less to the author of *Caractacus* than to George III and his attempt at reviving the Prerogative. Possibly out of a misgiving that parliamentary government was going to be called in question, the 'republican' collector Thomas Hollis, in the very year of the new sovereign's accession, bought a portrait of Marvell, had it engraved, and distributed it among the patriots. Less disinterested but more pugnacious, Charles Churchill called the Stuarts' great enemy to the rescue of the liberties of England from the Earl of Bute (himself a Stuart). The Albion of 1763 is even more wretched than that of the Restoration: then, at least the 'honest rimes' of 'the hardy poet' made rascals tremble and blush. No Whig could mistake the unnamed scourge of the Court Party. Elsewhere Churchill[1] devotes seven of his most eloquent couplets to his predecessor's virtue, which will 'place his Hull above the Roman name'; he thus voices Marvell's eighteenth-century fame more efficiently than Mason had done in his prolix ode.

In the year of Churchill's premature death (1764) Robert Nettleton, Marvell's grand-nephew, placed in the restored church of St. Giles a new epitaph, which insisted even more than the first on the 'patriot'. Nettleton also gave the newly opened British Museum his great-uncle's most authentic

---

[1] No more than the preceding editors of Churchill does Douglas Grant, Oxford, 1956, collect these lines; for their ascription to the satirist, Edward Thompson (iii, 487) thus remains the only authority.

portrait. After his death Nettleton's papers and those of
another grandnephew of the poet's, as well as a collection
of documents made by Hollis, came into the hands of a
native of Hull, Captain Edward Thompson, a sailor and
occasionally a poet, but above all an enthusiastic Whig, who
resolved to erect to the glory of Hull's M.P. a monument
more lasting than brass. In 1772 Cooke's edition had been
reprinted. But Thompson aimed higher: he would publish
Marvell's works in verse and prose. He was the first to
include the poems on Cromwell but marred this achievement by claiming for his hero psalms written by Addison
and Watts and a ballad by Mallet. This vagary of the spirited
but uncritical editor[1] started a tedious controversy that
dragged through the nineteenth and even into the twentieth
century, giving Marvell's genuine poetry the worst sort of
advertisement.

This first complete edition, which came out in 1776 and
consisted of three magnificent volumes costing a guinea
each, provided the occasion for a so-called democratic
demonstration of the Whigs, excluded from power by
George III's policy. A noisy and not over-scrupulous
Opposition did not hesitate to call up memories of the Civil
War, including its climax on 30 January 1648/9, or even to
glorify, rather against logic, the tyrant Cromwell. The list
of the 146 subscribers thus presents an interest more political than literary: at its head we read the name of the
notorious Duke of Cumberland, but the first of these subscribers in the estimation of posterity is 'Edmund Burke,
Esquire', the Burke of the *Reflections on the Causes of the
Present Discontents* and of the speeches in favour of the
American Whigs.[2]

What had become, amidst all this dust of the Forum, of those
delicate poems of Marvell's in praise of the countryside?

---

[1] His reputation has been somewhat improved by Hugh Macdonald's
discovery of one of his 'manuscript books', *v. supra*, p. 163, n. 1.

[2] Caroline Robbins, *The Eighteenth-century Commonwealthman*, 1959, gives
abundant proof of the continuity of the 'Republican' tradition from the
Restoration to the loss of the American colonies: Marvell's influence counts
for much in this survival. See also the same historian's letter to *T.L.S.* of
19 December 1958, p. 737, for the use of 'Andrew Marvell' as a *nom de plume*
in 1773 by a Philadelphian in a protest against municipal tyranny.

What of his love poetry? Early in the century Addison, without naming him, had shown acquaintance with Marvell's 'To his Coy Mistress',[1] and in 1727 *Tonson's Miscellany* had, surprisingly enough, included nine of his lyrical pieces. But explicit critical praise in print limits itself to a physician's lecture on *Human Physiognomy* (1747) where 'Eyes and Tears' is quoted for its 'pathetic and engaging manner', for the 'expressive ... language ... wherein [the author] has shewn, that Tears are a Blessing peculiar only to human Nature'. This is not much, and yet much more than Edward Thompson could say; if he thinks it his duty to mention Marvell's love poetry he barely sees in it the proof that the poet 'whose gallantries are unknown' was 'unfortunate in the choice of his fair friend', and passes on to more important subjects. The subscribers, self-satisfied after having evinced their public spirit and enriched their libraries with fine calf-bindings, do not seem to have perused the poetical contents much. In spite of their proud independence in politics they bowed to the Dictator of Letters. Now Samuel Johnson did not even pay Marvell the compliment of naming him in his 'Life of Cowley' among the 'metaphysical poets' on whom he passed a death sentence.[2] We might ascribe this contemptuous silence to Tory and Anglican prejudice. But neither did the rival collections of Anderson, Bell, or Chalmers, those necropolises of the pseudo-classical school, provide a niche for our too imaginative poet. He was, too, ignored by such a catholic anthologist as Thomas Headley in 1787, and by George Ellis in the first edition of his *Specimens of English Poetry* (1790).

[1] See my 'Marvell and Addison: A Note to No. 89 of *The Spectator*', in *R.E.S.*, 1934, pp. 447–50.

[2] Yet Mrs. Duncan-Jones points out to me that Johnson's *Dictionary* includes several quotations from Marvell's verse: 'The last Instructions' (under EXCISE)—'Ametas and Thestylis' (under NOR)—'On Blood's Stealing the Crown' (under SURCINGLE). I could rank the first of these three quotations with the Tory kidnappings of Marvell (*v. supra*, what is said of *The Craftsman*) but this explanation does not hold for the third quotation (inaccurate and made from memory) since Marvell and Johnson differed radically on ecclesiastical vestments and the Church generally. The second quotation, entirely non-political, seems to reveal some appreciation of Marvell's lighter love poetry, but not necessarily acquaintance with the 1681 volume or even Cooke's edition of 1726, since 'Ametas and Thestylis' had been included in *Tonson's Miscellany*, 1727 (see *André Marvell*, Bibliography, No. 104 *bis*).

One must leave the eighteenth century behind to find in the second edition of the same anthology (1801) 'Daphnis and Chloe' (expurgated) and 'Young Love' (abridged). Marvell's reputation thus began, however timidly, to free itself from politics. This deserves the more notice since Ellis, one of the authors of *The Rolliad* and a collaborator in the *Anti-Jacobin*, seemed better prepared to enjoy the manner of Marvell's satires than that of his love poetry. Yet he showed himself so eclectic that his admission of Marvell into the *Specimens* has no revolutionary significance. But in 1806 William Lisle Bowles presented our poet as the direct opposite of Pope,[1] defied the pseudo-classics by preferring the former to the latter, and exalted in the author of 'Upon Appleton House' the qualification that the nineteenth century was to prize above all others in a poet, love of nature.

It is curious that Pope's chief champion, after Byron, against Bowles, the same Thomas Campbell whose poems bear the indelible mark of the eighteenth-century tradition, should have granted Marvell a very honourable place in his *Specimens of the British Poets* (1819); more curious still that the martial author of 'Hohenlinden' and 'The Battle of the Baltic' should have selected, not 'An Horatian Ode' but Bermudas', 'Young Love', and above all that protest against bloodshed, 'The Nymph complaining for the death of her Faun'. Yet, in his preliminary notice, most of which deals with the Member for Hull, Campbell can say no more of Marvell's poetry than that 'it comes from the heart, warm, pure, affectionate'.

A judgement of greater importance had been pronounced the year before by William Hazlitt: 'Some of [Marvell's] verses are harsh, as the words of Mercury; others as musical as in Apollo's lute.' True, Hazlitt's haughty taste treated the satires with excessive scorn and 'An Horatian Ode' was known to him only indirectly; he had heard it 'praised by one whose praise is never high but of the highest things'. Does the definition fit Charles Lamb, more interested in

---

[1] Pope himself does not seem ever to have named Marvell or even alluded to him; but he had certainly read his satires; see Benjamin Boyce, 'An Annotated Volume from Pope's Library', in *N.Q.*, February 1958, pp. 55–57, and W. J. Cameron, 'Pope's Annotations on "State Affairs" Poems', ibid., July 1958, pp. 291–3.

originality than concerned with literary precedence? Anyhow Lamb knew Marvell as early as 1800, and we are told
by Leigh Hunt that they had both tried to make Hazlitt
relish the humour of 'The Character of Holland': in vain,
for Hazlitt had not 'animal spirits enough' to enjoy those
burlesque exaggerations. He gravely explained why such
tricks should not raise a laugh, but Lamb and Hunt refuted
him with peals of laughter.

If he could not persuade Hazlitt of the quality of Marvell's
humour[1] Lamb did more for our poet with the well-read public than any other critic before or since. After a first laudatory
mention in 1820, he quoted five stanzas of 'The Garden'
in one of his *Essays of Elia* (September 1821) and, to note
the aspect of Marvell's genius that appears there, hit upon the
happy phrase 'witty delicacy'. Three years later he coined the
epithet 'garden-loving' and considered it so characteristic
and peculiar to Marvell that he omitted the poet's name.

However important the part played by Lamb it must not
disguise the fact that the general change in poetical taste
favoured the growth of Marvell's reputation. Witness two
articles published in the *Retrospective Review* (1824 and 1825)
where 'The Nymph complaining for the death of her Faun'
is called 'the most interesting of all his poems'.

But traditions die hard, especially when they contain some
element of truth. Wordsworth, whom his worship of nature
might have led to Marvell's poetry as to Wither's and
Vaughan's, names our poet but thrice, twice as a satirist[2]

---

[1] Neither, it seems, did he infect his former Blue-Coat fellow schoolboy
with his own enthusiasm for Marvell's poetry. *Coleridge on the Seventeenth
Century*, edited by Roberta Florence Brinkley, 1955, provides only negative
evidence (the references to Donne are many). The first volume (1794–1804)
of *The Notebooks of Samuel Taylor Coleridge*, edited by Kathleen Coburn, 1957,
however, contains quotations, with occasional comment, from *The Rehearsal
Transpros'd*. See Nos. 702–8, and the editor's notes.

[2] Una Venable Tuckerman, 'Wordsworth's Plan for His Imitation of
Juvenal', in *M.L.N.*, 1930, pp. 209–15, shows that by the end of 1795 the
English Girondin considered the Member for Hull as an equivalent to the
homo novus from Arpinum (Satire VIII, ll. 231–53)—also that the sobered
Wordsworth of 1802 copied the 'Horatian Ode' in Notebook W—and that
his library contained Guy Miège's *Relation of Three Embassies*.

There is a mention of Marvell in Wordsworth's letter to Walter Scott of
7 November 1805, again as a satirist and a source of information on Restoration politics; see *The Early Letters of William and Dorothy Wordsworth*, edited
by Ernest de Selincourt, 1935, p. 541.

and once, in a famous political sonnet against the French Revolutionists (1802), along with Algernon Sidney, Harrington, and Vane, as one of those 'great men . . . that called Milton friend'. Other writers indeed speak of Marvell at much more length without saying more of his poetry. Isaac D'Israeli, in his *Quarrels of Authors* (1814) gives a fairly readable narrative of the controversy with Parker, but from the very start a rhetorical sentence relegates Marvell to political history of an anecdotal sort: he 'placed the oblation of his genius on a temporary altar, and the sacrifice sunk with it; he wrote to the times, and with the times his writings have passed away'. It is amazing how many biographers or critics, for over half a century, copied that verdict on Marvell, probably without giving his lyrical poetry a hearing.

And yet D'Israeli provided, almost exclusively, the information used by the most fiery, if not the most judicious, of all Marvell's admirers. When Landor in his *Imaginary Conversations* (imaginary indeed!) sets face to face Milton and Marvell, or Marvell and 'Bishop Parker', or Marvell and Henry Marten (the libertine regicide), he does not seem to have any suspicion of the existence of his hero's non-political poetry; on the other hand, the legend that had grown around the Member for Hull in the course of the eighteenth century reaches its perfect state in Landor. The epithet 'republican', first flung at Marvell by a Tory, had been taken up by the Whigs, who apparently gave it the etymological meaning of 'devoted to the common weal', but Landor credited Marvell with his own political faith, kindled in 1793 at the French conflagration. It is the Oxford undergraduate expelled for his Jacobinism who exclaims: 'I am a republican and will die one.' As he sees Oliver through Napoleon, Landor congratulates Marvell upon his having 'scorned to serve an usurper' and makes the Protector's sometime Latin Secretary say that 'Cromwell was hypocritical and perfidious'.

Thus, parallel with his new poetical reputation, Marvell's former one, political and religious, continues, and even 'vires acquirit eundo'. Waiving minor pieces of evidence[1]

[1] Save this one (pointed out to me lately by Professor Robbins): John Clare contributed to Hone's *Every-day Book*, June 1825, a poem entitled

we shall mention the first *Life of Andrew Marvell* that stands
on its own bottom; it was written by a Yorkshireman named
John Dove and published in 1832 with an epigraph from
Paradise Lost praising the heroic patriot, God's soldier who
'among innumerable false' remained steadfast, 'alone'. True,
Dove quotes Marvell's lyrical poems extensively and taste-
fully, but one can estimate the biographer turned literary
critic by his reproaching Donne's disciple with 'commonplace similes'. The reviewers of the volume strike the same
note; for instance, *The Westminster Review* enrolls Marvell
among the philosophical radicals, argues from his incorruptible poverty against a recent law establishing a property
qualification for candidates to Parliament, and concludes:
'The admiration for Marvell is to be based, not on his
intellectual, but on his moral qualities.'

Not only ephemeral journalism but criticism with more
pretension to permanence continued to be written on Marvell as if Hazlitt and Lamb had not dethroned Johnson.
A man of fairly catholic taste, though a Dissenting minister,
Henry Rogers, who relished the jokes of *The Rehearsal Transpros'd* and even of the *Remarks*, gave *The Edinburgh Review*
in 1844 an essay on Marvell, judicious enough, save for the
conclusion. What a shock to hear that 'the two best' of the
poems ascribed to him by Thompson are not his (meaning
Addison's and Watts's psalms)! For Rogers our poet's sense
of the ridiculous was stronger than his sense of beauty. Such
an opinion looks queer today, but it did not then. Leigh
Hunt published in that very year 1844 a poetical anthology
under the title *Imagination and Fancy*, in which Marvell does
not appear; but he took good care not to omit him two
years later from another anthology devoted to *Wit and
Humour*. In the same decade Marvell was for Macaulay an
'austere republican' who wrote satires in heroic couplets

'Death' (the one beginning 'Why should man's aspiring mind') fathered by
him on Marvell. In a letter to Henry Francis Carey on 7 January 1829 he
confesses the literary fabrication, and adds: 'I had read that Marvel was a
great advocate for liberty. . . .' In a much earlier (1817) letter to Holland he
had written: 'like the Poet Marvell I had not Sixpence to bless me' (see the
index to J. W. and Anne Tibble's edition of Clare's letters). In fact the poem
is very little like Marvell, whom Clare, it seems, knew only through Ellis's
Specimens.

before Pope had brought this medium to perfection. And down to 1860 critics, biographers, pamphleteers, lecturers emulously took up the legendary character, embellishing him with all the additions suggested to them by a facile and vulgar imagination; e.g. to the temptation of the Lord Treasurer's guineas is added that of 'Dalilas', who later become 'voluptuous houries' or 'frail beauties of the court'. The only notable exception in England is Miss Mitford, whose love of nature prepared her to understand Marvell's most characteristic poetry; yet even she cannot forbear to blame the abundance of conceits and wish that 'the stern Roundhead' had 'left' them 'to his old enemies, the Cavaliers'.

To find Lamb's true successor one must cross the Atlantic. As early as 1836 a young writer, destined to write his country's most beautiful verse, in order to express his admiration for Marvell's least classic, most *précieux* poem, 'The Nymph complaining for the death of her Faun', daringly used the words 'truth', 'nature', and 'pathos'. Edgar Poe admits 'the outrageous hyperbole and absurdity' of the conceit on the 'Lilies without, Roses within', but he vindicates it, or rather glorifies it, as the fittest expression of 'the passionate grief, and more passionate admiration of the bereaved child'. This is a poet's criticism indeed, but how much more just in its intemperance than the self-conscious fairness of a Rogers!

Even before Poe, Emerson felt a warm admiration for Marvell's poetry, though he did not express it in print until much later; and the influence of 'Upon Appleton House' appears clearly in 'Woodnotes'.[1] But in England the decisive impulsion, amplifying the effect of that given by Lamb, came from Palgrave in the first edition of *The Golden Treasury* (1861). The brief commentary on the three selected pieces:

---

[1] Robert L. Brant, 'Hawthorne and Marvell', in *American Literature*, November 1958, p. 366, convincingly derives the final line of *The Scarlet Letter* from the last stanza of 'The unfortunate Lover'.

Herman Melville makes a curious use of the phrase 'starry Vere' ('Upon Appleton House', l. 724) in *Billy Budd*, chapter i (vol. xiii, pp. 26–27 in the Standard Edition of Melville's *Works*). His acquaintance with Marvell's poetry would, however, have been more remarkable in an earlier work (*Billy Budd* was completed in 1891). I owe the reference to Mrs. Duncan-Jones.

'An Horatian Ode', 'The Garden', and 'Bermudas', asserted
that 'In imaginative intensity Marvell and Shelley are closely
related.' One may wonder why the anthologist failed to support his assertion by including the piece in which this quality
appears at its strongest; the answer lies in Victorian prudery,
which would have been more incomprehensible to Marvell
than his mistress's coyness. But Palgrave must have suffered
when he sacrificed to a debased version of puritanism the
poem that his friend Tennyson would read to him, 'dwelling
. . . on the magnificent hyperbole, the powerful union of
pathos and humour'. Edward Fitzgerald, who also loved
Marvell, reveals to us that the sudden vision of eternity—
'But at my back I alwaies hear . . .'—haunted Tennyson as
early as *c*. 1840 and that it struck him as 'sublime'.[1] And in
his old age Queen Victoria's poet laureate would tell his
family 'that he had made Carlyle laugh for half-an-hour at
the following line from "The Character of Holland": "They
with mad labour, fish'd the land to shore" '. Yet the dyspep-
tic prophet failed to mention the poet of the Protectorate in
his *Cromwell*. For this neglect Marvell was avenged by James
Russell Lowell, for whom his funeral elegy, 'in part noble
and everywhere humanly tender, is worth more than all
Carlyle's biography as a witness to the gentler qualities of
the hero, and of the deep affection that stalwart nature could
inspire in hearts of truly masculine temper'.

With *The Golden Treasury* in every respectable household
it became almost impossible to write, as a biographer of the
Member for Hull had still been able to do in 1853: 'Perhaps
few of the persons who have heard of the name of Marvell
at all, have heard his name mentioned as a poet.' But there
remained the task of uniting into one stream the different
currents of his reputation and showing the essential identity
of the poet, the Puritan, and the patriot. This has not yet
been fully accomplished, but an article in *The Cornhill Magazine* (by John Ormsby) at least managed, in 1869, to present
in a 'Gallery' of portraits the various personages who are
known to posterity under the one name of Andrew Marvell,

---

[1] J. Philip Goldberg points out 'Two Tennysonian Allusions to a Poem
by Andrew Marvell', viz. 'The Nymph complaining for the death of her
Faun'. The allusions are found in *The Princess* (1847) and *Maud* (1855).

all the time avoiding prejudice and exclusiveness and combining sense with sensibility.

Hardly had this synthesis been attempted when Grosart's edition of Marvell's complete works, for all its glaring faults, brought much fresh material to the critics. The editor, inebriated with Carlylean enthusiasm, could not give a sober biography or even portrait of Marvell, but he at least took care to neglect no aspect of his hero.

After Grosart the oscillations of Marvellian criticism became less wide. A judicious poise might have been reached as early as 1885 by Edmund Gosse in *From Shakespeare to Pope* if his anxiety to justify the advent of neo-Classicism had not occasioned excessively severe judgment of 'a good deal' in Marvell's poetry, which he called 'infantile'. 'A little' might have been not wholly unfair. On the biographical side the life contributed by C. H. Firth to the *Dictionary of National Biography* in 1893 is a masterly sketch that later research has done little more than fill in.

In the decadent nineties a new attitude appeared, at once (to borrow the poet's astrological phrasing) in conjunction with and in opposition to the eighteenth-century assessment of Marvell: accepting the postulate that he had deliberately sacrificed his lyrical gifts to his civic duties, some critics, instead of praising, denounced this renunciation. A. C. Benson led the way when in 1892, quoting Dante and Browning most inappropriately, he accused the Member for Hull of having made 'the great denial' and 'left us . . . Just for a handful of silver' and 'a ribbon'; going still further in imaginative boldness he wrote: 'It is perhaps to Milton's example and probably to his advice, that we owe the loss of a great English poet.' This *fin de siècle* dilettantism lived on well into the twentieth century and may not have disappeared entirely even today. It serves at any rate to make us appreciate better, in contrast with it, the touching and healthy nature of the somewhat naïve, even clumsy worship of Marvell's memory in the town he represented in Parliament for twenty years. This worship was manifested most solemnly on the occasion of the tercentenary of the poet's birth. Speeches, toasts, and sermons (for a very broadminded bishop, the Right Reverend H. Hensley Henson,

did the author of the *Essay* on Councils the honour of re-
admitting him into Anglican orthodoxy) chiefly extolled an
energetic life not directed by self-interest.

In London the celebration was mostly literary. Among
several articles of varied importance towers Mr. T. S. Eliot's
in the *Times Literary Supplement*. Profound even to obscurity,
crowded with unexpected parallels that sometimes dazzle
while they aim at enlightening the reader, the poet of *The
Waste Land* subtly analyses the wit of which Marvell is the
representative *par excellence*, 'a tough reasonableness beneath
the slight lyric grace'; or again, 'this alliance of levity and
seriousness (by which the seriousness is intensified)'. Mr.
Eliot justly praises Marvell's 'bright, hard precision', far
more 'suggestive' than the 'mistiness' and 'vagueness'
of many a nineteenth-century poet—William Morris for
instance; and infers from the contrast that 'the suggestive-
ness is the aura around a bright clear centre', so 'that you
cannot have the aura alone'. There is some truth too in the
statement that Marvell's 'precise taste . . . finds for him the
proper degree of seriousness for every subject which he
treats'. But while we may grant that some of Marvell's pieces
achieve a 'classic' balance, shall we go so far as to say with
the American-born critic, who served his poetic apprenticeship in Paris: 'This wit which pervades the poetry of Marvell
is more Latin, more refined than anything that succeeded it'
in English literature? A Frenchman hardly dare make this
judgment his.

The other event of the twenties was the admirable edition
of the *Poems and Letters of Andrew Marvell* by H. M. Margoliouth (1927). For the first time the research worker could
start from a firm basis and avoid tedious wanderings in the
Wood of Error. And indeed some useful work has since been
done towards the further annotation of the poems as well as
in the field of biography. But literary criticism of a more
ambitious kind has been peculiarly active: Marvell's lyrical
pieces, being mostly short, lent themselves perfectly to the
explication de texte, then newly taken up by the British and
the Americans with the neophyte's fervour. Much ingenuity
has been spent on discovering ambiguities, some plausible,
others not; in Marvell possibly more than in any one of

his fellow metaphysicals (Donne alone excepted). On the strength of his rare successes he has been raised to a rank his warmest admirers of the generation now passing away had never dreamt of for him. Let us hope no reaction will follow the exaggerations of some indiscreet fans. Meanwhile we must try to sum up our own estimate of the man in as well as outside his work.

Several portraits have reached us as being Marvell's, but they resemble one another so little that one hesitates to accept them all as authentic. What have these in common?— the dreamy young man, gazing queerly, of the miniature that belongs to the Duke of Buccleuch—the man with a high and broad forehead painted by Hanneman in 1658—and the one whose brow is more than half concealed by a flowing head of curly hair (or a periwig) in the picture presented by Nettleton to the English nation. While the first might possibly be authentic and the second almost certainly is not, the third, which has the best title and agrees in all but its serenity with the haggard Hollis portrait (dated 1661), now at Hull, and the engraving in the frontispiece of the 1681 edition of the poems, also agrees best with Aubrey's physical description of Marvell: 'He was of a middling stature, pretty strong sett, roundish faced, cherry cheek't, hazell eie, browne haire.' This is the Member for Hull in the Cavalier Parliament, and we may try to explain away iconographic problems by relating each portrait to a different age of the sitter. Shall we do the same when we have to assign to one author 'The Nymph complaining for the death of her Faun' and 'The last Instructions to a Painter' or *The Rehearsal Transpros'd*? And can we draw one moral portrait of the man? assemble so many diverse features? Was the true Marvell an improvident idler or a thrifty burgess chiefly concerned with Parliamentary control of royal extravagance? the friend of Milton or of City merchants and bankers? Shall we see him as an apostate from the Apollonian cult, or as a wit who changes his manner only so far as his successive subjects demand? the last child of the Renaissance or the forerunner of Dryden and Swift?

And yet the man Marvell, creates the same impression of health and poise morally as he does physically. Issued from

peasant stock, the vitality of the race shows in him no symp-
tom of exhaustion; but, being the son of a clergyman and
a learned clergyman at that, he has nothing either of the
literary upstart in whom a sudden ascent causes a sort of
dizziness. His education is the best normal education of the
time, Grand Tour included. The twofold imprint, Christian
and pagan that it left on him—what cultured European has
not borne it, willy-nilly, since the Renaissance? The dis-
crepancy shows less in him than in Spenser, and hardly more
than in Milton. As to the inconsistencies in his conduct,
public events chiefly account for them, and he shares them
with many of his contemporaries. Almost alone in that age
Milton strikes right ahead, with increasing boldness; his
course is a straight line where Marvell's is a zigzag line that
sometimes splits in two.

So far there is nothing more mysterious than what
ordinary human nature offers. All his life through Marvell,
like every complete man, was by turns tender and vindictive,
enthusiastic and cynical, earnest and droll. He did not speak
in the same key as tutor to Mary Fairfax or William Dutton
and as companion to Lovelace: should this surprise us?
He was a good son on the whole, a good brother and uncle,
if not a good husband, a staunch friend, a dogged foe. His
full-blooded temperament, even without the stimulus of
Canary wine, predisposed him to sudden fits of anger and
quarrels; life taught him prudence and even dissembling.
He could be active enough, but he preferred leisure. His
ambition was moderate and no dreams of immortality either
as an author or as a statesman seem to have haunted him.
He had plain tastes and yet the necessity of making a living
seems to have played a far more important part in his career
than the desire to live after death. He just managed to avoid
poverty, which ill agrees with independence and self-respect,
yet he did not yield to the temptation of riches. Neither a
Bohemian nor a bourgeois, he had something of both.[1]

---

[1] Marvell's bourgeois side has been made more evident of late by the
fuller revelation of his ties with moneyed men in the City (*v. supra*, pp. 148–9).
It appears also, unexpectedly and indirectly, in a hitherto unpublished private
letter (*v. supra*, p. 125, n. 1) of 25 April 1677, where superiority of brains,
over French great nobles and 'the Archbishop of Rheims first Duc and Pair
of France', is claimed for 'Monsieur Barillon a Counsellor of Parliament'.

Interested in ideas, even bookish, he could get out of his books when required, and in this he stands out among his fellow poets of equal gifts; better than Milton he achieves the combination of the scholar and the man of action. For this superiority he paid the price of remaining an amateur at a time when the man of letters was establishing his status. For him it never was 'un métier que de faire un livre'. He wrote for his own pleasure or at the call of duty; no work of his seems to have had for him an existence independent of circumstances or his own fancy.

Supposing he did cease after 1653 to write the lyrical poetry we prize so highly this (conjectural) drying up of inspiration need not be accounted for by the coarsening influence of political life: 'le poète mort jeune à qui l'homme survit' is met more often than the poet who survives as long as the man. And around him the poetical atmosphere was changing so fast that he may well have felt out of date.

Instead of wondering how Marvell could join in the conflict between parties one should wonder how he could keep so long out of public life. Save in the Church (to which, unlike his father, he had no call) he could turn his education to no better use. Though he ended in the Opposition he had not the temperament of the systematic opponent. Irreverence was not congenital in his composition. After having worshipped Cromwell he looked for another hero to whom he might proffer his allegiance, and when he died he may have thought he had found him in Shaftesbury, or even in Monmouth. If the republican spirit consists essentially in preferring principles to men, no one was ever less of a Republican than Marvell. If he appears at times as a solitary it is against his will and because his political associates have ratted. Soon he joins another group. Neither a courtier nor an irreconcilable though he may have looked like both in turn, pugnacious yet cautious, personally incorruptible yet not averse from manœuvring and pretty far from over-scrupulous, such he reveals himself in his political career.

As regards religion, a sensuous temperament, repressed by a Calvinistic education, finds a vent in poetry without damage to faith. But later the critical faculty eats deep into dogma. Yet his conduct bears to the end the stamp of his education rather than of his temperament or intellect. In that way the Puritan prevails in Marvell. The paternal doctrine determines his actions: without it he might, voluptuous and sceptical, have adopted the Restoration style of life; because of it he comes into conflict with his environment. Besides, love of country reinforces the influence of religion: for Marvell England should be the champion of the Protestant cause, largely because only thus can she play a leading role in Europe.

The intensity and the narrowness of his patriotism (the one quality being almost inseparable from the other) make the most obvious difference between Marvell and his French contemporaries. These praise the *Grand Roy* sincerely enough on the occasion of his conquests; but their heart is not in it, they do not feel responsible for the conduct of public affairs; frontiers do not bound their thought; not the Frenchman but man in general, man after Descartes's definition, is their proper study. It will require the reverses of the War of the Succession in Spain to cause the patriotic feeling to reappear, distinct from monarchic loyalty. But under Charles II an ordeal, negligible in comparison, finding in Marvell a well-prepared soil, produced the same effects as did the first years of the eighteenth century in Fénelon and Vauban. And even in Cromwell's glorious years the greatness of England is already our poet's main concern. The secret of the continuity of his career might be found there if his absence during the Civil War did not remain unaccountable and if his intimate poetry did not reveal his eagerness, amounting almost to egotism, for personal satisfactions sought in religion, woman, and nature.

Even more than the man the writer is hard to take in at one glance. Not but that some features are found all through his works: from 'Fleckno' to the *Remarks* the wit that expresses itself in the choice of images, the perception of hitherto unsuspected analogies, remains the fundamental characteristic. But subjects and tone diverge too widely: we could only repeat here severally the conclusions of the chapters devoted to the lyrical poetry, the satires, the pamphlets, without welding them into one. As to establishing a hierarchy between those three parts of the works, it would nowadays be superfluous.

And yet, in spite of its eventual victory, Marvell's lyrical poetry will always suffer with some for having been long unrecognized. The pure historian of literature, who measures the importance of a book by the number of books it engenders, may easily ignore the folio of 1681. Marvell died without poetical posterity but, for the reader not set on determinist continuity, this extinction of a literary line appeals to a high emotion. 'Never more' sounds in our ears as we read Marvell's octosyllabics and endows them with a resonance they did not possess three centuries ago.

On the contrary the history of literature finds its proper pabulum in the satires and the pamphlets, which it rightly sees as the rough drafts of greater works to come. More aptly still, it considers Marvell as a link between two generations and notes that he plays this part almost alone. He is not wholly a belated metaphysical, like Henry Vaughan; he does not anticipate the future, like Hobbes; across the chasm of 1660 he throws the bridge of his personality.

So does Marvell appear in our time. The history of his reputation in the past should warn us to abstain from venturing into prophecy. Yet those whom his poetry charmed long before its present vogue and caused to wonder how it had not charmed all successive generations, can reaffirm their faith that it will live as long as the English language. And to those who read them, his poems will ever give, along with the enjoyment of their beauty, the sense of the spiritual contradictions from which springs England's poetical and political greatness.

ADDENDA

p. 17, *n.* 1. The fancy title of Ruth Nevo's *The Dial of Virtue*, Princeton, 1963, had screened this important book from my critical attention as regards her treatment of the 'Horatian Ode' and Marvell's poems on Cromwell generally. She interprets the earlier work by the later, a method particularly dangerous when dealing with our poet (whose biography she knows only in a dim way): she reads into the pagan Ode the Messianic enthusiasm of 'The First Anniversary' (p. 102), which she styles 'a republican manifesto' ('republican' is a word she often uses but never defines historically) though written in a monarchical spirit; and she even invokes 'On Blake's Victory', where this spirit runs to idolatry. She has plenty of ideas and a manly, assured, style. But she has little Latin and less French: she writes, twice, '*jus divinus*', and she anglicizes, prematurely, two words in the title of the only French book in her bibliography.

George Williamson, in *Milton and Others*, 1965, devotes an essay entitled 'Bias in Marvell's Horatian Ode' to an attractive vindication of the poet's consistency, all his life through, with respect to Charles I and Cromwell, whom he never ceased to honour jointly. The demonstration, unfortunately, is vitiated by several biographical errors or omissions, and, as regards the Ode itself, by an untenable interpretation of the word 'Arts' in the last stanza: it cannot refer back to Cromwell's conduct as described earlier in the poem; it must, syntactically, be taken in exclusive connexion with 'the Sword erect' used to 'gain . . . Pow'r' and indispensable to 'maintain' it.

p. 23, *n.* 1. L. N. Wall, 'Thomas Randolph and Marvell's "Coy Mistress"', in *Notes and Queries*, 1968, p. 103, calls attention to one more echo from that son of Ben's.—See also *infra*, Bibliographical Appendix, under Leishman.

p. 25, *n.* 1. Woledge had been anticipated by Edward Bliss Reed, 'The Poems of Thomas Fairfax', in *Transactions of the Connecticut Academy of Arts and Sciences*, July 1909, p. 248 (quoted by Leishman, *The Art of Marvell's Poetry*, p. 294, n. 1).

p. 43, *ll.* 32–33. E. E. Duncan-Jones, in a not yet published article, quoted by Leishman, *ut supra*, pp. 134–6, notes that Pliny (Book XV, ch. xv) had also warned man against impious innovations in 'graffing', though his condemnation is not so sweeping as that in Leviticus.

p. 49, *n* 1. And, of course, 'the Mower whets his sithe' in 'L'Allegro', l. 66.

p. 50, *ll.* 28–29. Geoffrey H. Hartman (see *infra*, Bibliographical Appendix) quotes J. C. Scaliger, *Poetices*, Book III, ch. 99, who lists eleven sorts of pastorals, the fourth of these being 'Fœnisecia'. But Hartman confesses: 'I have not been able to find a Classical or Neolatin example' of them.

p. 54, *n.* 1 (*and p.* 90, *Additional note*). The attempt to explicate this poem made on the largest scale so far is Stanley Stewart's *The Enclosed Garden, The Tradition and the Image in Seventeenth Century Poetry*, 1966: 226 pages; only the last 34 deal directly with 'The Garden', but the author's 'purpose' has been all along to demonstrate the importance of the historical 'context' in the study of 'a work of art', choosing this one as most in need of such an approach. So far so good; but even if all the impressive illustrations of the literary fortunes, all over Christendom, from St. Bernard to some of Marvell's contemporaries, of the 'Hortus conclusus' in the 'Song of Songs' are correctly interpreted by the industrious collector, and even if it were granted that echoes of the 'Song' are overheard in 'The Garden', the highly ingenious historian and critic would have failed to prove that Marvell here is thinking of the Christian God, much less that his poem is 'eucharistic' (p. 177). That the poet experiences an ecstasy few critics deny, certainly not I (see *supra*, pp. 54 and 90, in the text) but his originality, at that date, is that he communes not with an allegory but with real, vegetable nature, alone present in the poem.

p. 54, *ll.* 23–25. Yet he must be credited with a special knowledge of some horticultural devices; see 'Andrew Marvell and the Grafter's Art', by Nicholas A. Salerno, to appear in *Études Anglaises*, no. ii, 1968.

p. 56, *l.* 23. Drayton, in his *Polyolbion* (1613) xiii, 147 sqq., expresses some pity for the hunted deer, but only *in extremis*, after relating the chase with much gusto (noted by Edward Le Comte, 'Marvell's "The Nymph Complaining for the Death of her Fawn"', in *Modern Philology*, 1952, p. 100).

p. 62, *n.* 1. Perhaps I should mention here that the presence, in Stanza viii of 'The Garden', of 'the androgynous Adam', modestly hazarded as a query by Ruth Wallerstein in 1950 (*Studies in Seventeenth Century Poetics*, pp. 333–4), has become an article of faith with several of her critical successors. It promises to be as long-lived as the belief that ll. 615–6 of 'Upon Appleton House' contain an allusion to Christ's crucifixion, a belief formulated by William Empson in 1932 and still going strong.

p. 70, *n.* 1. Karl Joseph Höltgen, in his review of the first edition of the present book (in *Anglia*, 1966, p. 243), has some interesting references to emblem-books that help to visualize Marvell's 'Times winged Charriot' and illustrate the devouring of his children by Chronos, identified with Cronos.

p. 164, *n.* 2. Miss Wedgwood has also written an introduction for Marvell's *Poems*, published by the Folio Society, 1964. In this introduction (which unfortunately contains some minor biographical inaccuracies) she uses the same epithet 'Puritan' to describe Marvell's 'virtues' that she had used in her book for his 'opinions', and considers it as sufficiently precise. Thus fortified by her high authority as an historian of the English seventeenth century I can bear more confidently attacks by some reviewers of the first edition of the present book against my use of the middle adjective in its sub-title.

Ruth Nevo (see *supra*) also covers political literature through the seventeenth century. Her treatment of Marvell's satires of the Restoration presents less originality than that of the poems centring on Cromwell and therefore lies open to fewer objections; the only one I shall raise here is that she practically ignores all of those satires except 'The last Instructions', probably because it offers the least resistance to her theory that Marvell arrived at the 'mixed style'—a phrase she apparently coins out of a sentence of Dryden's 'Discourse Concerning . . . Satire' (1693). Even so she greatly exaggerates the importance of the 'panegyric' and of the corresponding 'high' style; their ratio to the 'philippic' written mostly in the 'low' style is rather less than one to ten in 'The last Instructions.'

p. 222, *last paragraph*. Caroline Robbins, 'Absolute Liberty: the Life and Thought of William Popple, 1638–1708', in *William and Mary Quarterly*, 1967, pp. 190–223, produces hitherto unpublished or unnoticed evidence, showing that Marvell's nephew was more deeply and feelingly religious than would appear from *A rational Catechism*. There is not much about Marvell in this article, but Popple proves interesting in his own right, and likeable, though hardly heroic.

p. 231, *after l.* 8. John Butt, in footnote 1, last paragraph, of p. 19 of Leishman's *Art of Marvell's Poetry*, notices Marvell's 'inclusion in *The Lives of the Poets of Great Britain and Ireland* (vol. iv, 1753), attributed to Theophilus Cibber, but in fact the work of Robert Shiels'. Of the two poems quoted one is 'A Dialogue between the Resolved Soul and Created Pleasure', said to be 'written with a true spirit of poetry, the numbers are various, and harmonious', remarkable praise at that date.

E. E. Duncan-Jones, 'Smart and Marvell', in N._Q._, May 1967, quotes two long lines from 'Jubilate Agno', written during Christopher Smart's confinement in a madhouse, 1761–3, alluding to 'Marvel' in connexion with Hull, possibly with a reference to the woodpecker in 'Upon Appleton House' but probably with a very confused memory of seventeenth-century politics.

_p._ 237, _l._ 1. Louis Bonnerot, _Matthew Arnold poète_, 1947, p. 529, quotes from a letter in which Arnold, on 31 December 1861, calls Sainte-Beuve's attention to Marvell's 'Horatian Ode', lately unearthed by Palgrave, with the result that three years later the French critic used this information against his fellow countryman Taine (who had ignored Marvell altogether): Milton was not the only poet to celebrate Cromwell: 'Il existe une Ode d'Andrew Marvell qui appartient au même mouvement de Renaissance chrétienne[?] et patriotique' (Lundi 6 juin 1864. _Nouveaux Lundis_, vol. viii, 1867, p. 100).

BIBLIOGRAPHICAL APPENDIX

THE following list, which does not pretend to completeness, will show what a spate of publications devoted to Marvell has occurred in recent years, witnessing to the growing interest in the poet. Since this abundance of criticism is of mixed quality, some guidance through it may prove acceptable.

BOOKS

Joan Bennett, *Five Metaphysical Poets*, Cambridge, 1964, adds Marvell to her *Four Metaphysical Poets* of 1934, and deals with him no less lovingly and delicately (reviewed by me in *Études Anglaises*, 1965, pp. 80–81).

Dennis Davison, *Marvell: Poems*, London, 1964, in a series intended for 'the advanced sixth former' and the undergraduate, provides an introduction to the lyrical poet, helpful also for the general reader (reviewed by me, rather carpingly, in the *Modern Language Review*, 1966, pp. 288–9, where he is blamed for the sins of his critical generation).

Frank Kermode, ed., *Andrew Marvell Selected Poetry*. The Signet Classic Poetry Series, New York: The New American Library, London: The New English Library. Pp. xlvii+189, 1967. Though modernized, the text is trustworthy; the annotation, in a highly condensed form, contains a good deal that is original and helpful, along with a few questionable interpretations; the introduction gives, for the main lyrical poems, an eclectic summary of recent research and critical opinion, sifted and judged by a nimble and independent mind.

Lawrence W. Hyman, *Andrew Marvell*, New York, 1964, has at least no illusion as regards the lasting quality of his criticism; his last sentence expresses the hope that he has given 'present-day readers . . . what is significant for this decade' (reviewed by me in *Études Anglaises*, 1966, pp. 183–4).

J. B. Leishman, *The Art of Marvell's Poetry*, 1966, has done good service to the lyrical poet, though his premature death left this book in an imperfect condition. It really deals with Marvell's immediate predecessors and contemporaries as well as with Marvell himself and provides much information about his sources, Latin and English. It is the work of a man of taste and culture (reviewed by me in *Études Anglaises*, 1966, pp. 184–5).

William A. McQueen and Kiffin A. Rockwell, *The Latin Poetry of Andrew Marvell*, Chapel Hill, 1964, will prove helpful not only for its translations, careful if not unimpeachable, but for its annotation, largely original.

Paoli Gulli' Pugliatti, ed., *Andrew Marvell Selected Poems Scelta, Intro-duzione e Commento*, Bari, 1967, testifies to the growing interest in Marvell's lyrical poetry south of the Alps. The extensive bibliography shows the editor's diligence in acquainting herself with all that has been written on Marvell in this century, and her sensitiveness to the poems is manifest. The annotation, however, is unequal, and disappointingly fails to connect the English poet with his Italian predecessors.

Harold E. Toliver, *Marvell's Ironic Vision*, New Haven, 1965, aims high and, if he fails in his attempt at reducing the poems to a philosophical formula, shows powers that may be turned to better use when disciplined (reviewed by me, at some length, in English, in *Anglia*, 1966, pp. 235–41, as an *exemplum* of what is called, antiphrastically, 'close reading').

John M. Wallace, *Destiny his Choice: The Loyalism of Andrew Marvell*, Cambridge University Press, 1968, incorporates the article mentioned *supra*, p. 17, n. 1, and another, 'Andrew Marvell and Cromwell's Kingship: "The First Anniversary" ', in *E.L.H.*, 1963, pp. 209–35, which I had failed to see, somewhat revised. The book as a whole is an attempt to prove Marvell's perfect consistency and candour all through his life and especially in his political career. This it achieves by ignoring, misreading, or dismissing summarily all the evidence showing that Marvell's political thought fluctuated (legitimately) and that he did not speak his whole mind in his prose pamphlets—but of course he was quite honest and reasonably truthful for one involved in the politics of a troubled and dangerous age (see *supra*, p. 242). Professor Wallace's large-scale painting of the historical background to the poems on Cromwell, documented by wide reading of seventeenth-century pamphleteers and recent historians, will prove useful and instructive. His industrious plodding in that field does not prepare the reader for the wild flights of New Criticism in the last chapter, paradoxically devoted to 'Upon Appleton House'.

ARTICLES

Harry Berger, Jr., 'Marvell's "Garden" Still Another Interpretation', in *Modern Language Quarterly*, 1967, pp. 285–304, cheerfully sets himself to show that Marvell's wit 'should be viewed as a form of phenomenological *action*'. Of one of the meanings he discovers he admits that 'this is straining some', but maintains that his own freedom 'accords well with . . . the extravagant farce-character of some of the arguments' used by Marvell in Stanza iii. He has, however, some surprisingly sensible and conservative remarks about the dial in Stanza ix. Yet one might say of the article what its author says of the Soul in its 'Dialogue' with Created Pleasure: 'Its self-satisfaction makes [it] faintly insufferable'.

The same critic has also written an article entitled 'Andrew Marvell The Poem as Green World', in *Forum for Modern Language Studies*, 1967, pp. 302–3, which I have not seen.

Ann Evans Berthoff, 'The Allegorical Metaphor: Marvell's "The Definition of Love"', in *Review of English Studies*, 1966, pp. 16–29, and 'The Voice of Allegory in Marvell's "The unfortunate Lover"', in *Modern Language Quarterly*, 1966, pp. 41–50, applies brilliantly to those two poems a very personal notion of allegory, soon to be given its full scope in a book. In those two articles the New Criticism is seen at its most seductive.

Paola Colaiacomo, 'Alcuni Aspetti della Poesia di Andrew Marvell', in *English Miscellany*, Rome, 1960, pp. 75–111, has so far been ignored, not only by me but (at least in print) by all other Marvellians; and yet she has launched the most vigorous attack of the last ten years against new-fangled views of Marvell's poetry and swept away such Empsonian ambiguities as 'the Fall' symbolized by the poet's 'fall on grass' in Stanza v of 'The Garden'. She rightly stresses (anticipating Leishman's book, noticed *supra*) Marvell's dependence upon Latin, especially Virgilian, and neo-Latin, e.g. Pontanus's and Poliziano's, poetry (references to be added to note 2 of page 25, *supra*). But, in spite of her intense patriotism, she has discovered only a very few echoes from Italian poetry, viz. from Marino's. She mars a good case by wanting to prove too much and ends with a sentence of shocking depreciation.

John S. Coolidge, 'Marvell and Horace', in *Modern Philology*, 1965, pp. 111–20, takes up the parallel between the two poets' political conversions (see *supra*, p. 15, n. 2), arguing more closely. While he somewhat exaggerates the likeness, he ignores the obvious metrical justification for the title of Marvell's poem.

Dennis Davison, 'Notes on Marvell's "The Garden"', in *Notes and Queries*, 1966, pp. 25–26, provides many more parallels with poems probably or certainly known to Marvell (to be added to those referred to in note 1 of page 23, *supra*).

E. E. Duncan-Jones, 'Marvell's Letter to Sir John Trott', in *Notes and Queries*, 1966, pp. 26–27, detects 'a curious political innuendo' (aimed at Clarendon) in what apparently is a letter of condolence for the death of a son (see *supra*, p. 124). Her argument is both convincing and revealing of Marvell's temper.

S. L. Goldberg, 'Andrew Marvell', in *The Melbourne Critical Review*, 1960, pp. 41–56, and 'Marvell: Self and Art', ibid, 1965, pp. 32–44, gallantly attempts 't'immure the *Circle* in the *Quadrature*' by reducing all that really matters (to him) of Marvell's poetry to a single formula: 'the loss of gain'. The 'engaged' poet ends as a forerunner of D. H. Lawrence.

Robin Grove, 'Marvell', in *The Melbourne Critical Review*, 1963, pp. 31–43, begins with a sensible and welcome refutation of the excessive claims made recently for 'Upon Appleton House' (see *supra*, p. 63, n. 1) but proceeds to enhance the merit of 'An Horatian Ode' by overloading it with questionable complexities.

Geoffrey H. Hartman, 'Marvell, St. Paul, and the Body of Hope', in *ELH*, 1964, pp. 175–94, builds upon foundations that are not merely unsafe, like those of some of his predecessors (see *supra*, p. 70, n. 1) but non-existent: there is no 'hope' in 'The Garden', all is enjoyment in the present tense; and in the Mower poems 'hope' belongs to the past, having been succeeded by disappointment.

Joan Hartwig, 'The Principle of Measure in "To his Coy Mistress"', in *College English*, 1964, pp. 572–5, improves upon some of her predecessors (see 'Marvell and the New Critics', in *Review of English Studies*, 1957, pp. 388–9) in using Aristotle to interpret first the phrase 'vegetable love' and then the whole poem. She establishes an 'equation . . . between time and space and motion' that might have interested Marvell but of which he can hardly have been conscious.

Lawrence W. Hyman, 'Marvell's "Coy Mistress" as Fact or Poem', in *Modern Language Quarterly*, 1965, pp. 463–6, gives, under a somewhat tendentious title, a comparative review of Legouis's and Toliver's books, preferring the latter as more up to date though already rather too 'predictable'.

Frank Kermode, 'Marvell Transprosed', in *Encounter*, 1966, pp. 77–84, though mainly a combined review of Toliver's, Leishman's, and Legouis's books, opens with original and illuminating remarks on the appeal of Marvell's poetry to the English reader of today.

Bruce King, 'In Search of Andrew Marvell', in *A Review of English Literature*, October 1967, pp. 31–41, gives a survey of recent books and articles, and thus covers much the same ground as the present Appendix, in which it is a last-minute inclusion, and to which it should serve as a useful counterpoise, if not corrective, for we agree about as often as we disagree. Praise and blame are generously distributed, but one would like to have the critic's own modernistic views set forth directly. While waiting until he himself does 'provide the intense, exacting analysis of poetry we have come to expect', one will regret that mere prose is not dealt with so carefully as it was before 'time and fashion caught up with' the old guard whose supreme ambition was scholarship; readers of the present book may see for themselves (pp. 43–44, *supra*) whether I 'describe Marvell's "Garden" as prophesying eighteenth century English parks' (of course my remark applies to 'The Mower against Gardens') and (pp. 53–54, *supra*) whether I deny the presence in 'The Garden' and 'Upon Appleton House' of 'mystic raptures'; the negative adjective 'no' before this phrase in Bruce King's article is an interpolation.

Isabel G. MacCaffrey, 'Some Notes on Marvell's Poetry, Suggested by a Reading of his Prose', in *Modern Philology*, 1964, pp. 261–9, is supplemented by Kitty Datta, ibid., 1966, pp. 319–21. Both articles are scholarly and useful contributions to a methodical study of Marvell's imagination and style.

William A. McQueen, 'The Missing Stanzas in Marvell's "Hortus"', in *Philological Quarterly*, 1965, pp. 173–9, deserves consideration; it should be read in connexion with pp. 45, n. 1, and 64 *supra*.

Earl Miner, ' "The Poetic Picture, Painted Poetry" of *The Last Instructions to a Painter*', in *Modern Philology*, 1965–6, pp. 288–94, brings out interesting resemblances between Marvell's satire and contemporary pictures, engravings, and cartoons. But he hardly succeeds in persuading a Frenchman that 'The last Instructions' achieves artistic unity and is a carefully composed poem.

Earl Miner, 'The Death of Innocence in Marvell's *Nymph Complaining for the Death of her Faun*', in *Modern Philology*, 1967, pp. 9–16, follows, without being aware of it, in the wake of Ruth Nevo (see *infra*); but Mr. Miner extends the notion of innocence, painfully transmuted into experience, to include the fate of England in the Civil War: the same lesson emanates from the 'pastoral tragedy', which 'suggests a national epic', as from the 'Horatian Ode'. In spite of his carefulness and tactfulness this critic shares the partiality of his generation for hitherto hidden meanings, e.g. at ll. 53–54, where he brings in as lovers the 'Troopers' of l. 1 (whom Marvell had left behind at l. 24), which leads him to ask himself, logically enough: 'have there been passages between the Troopers and the Nymph?' (p. 10a).

Ruth Nevo, 'Marvell's Songs of Innocence and Experience', in *Studies in English Literature 1500–1900*, 1965, pp. 1–21, forces the lyrical poems into a Blakean antithesis but relies mostly upon Ficino to confer upon them a philosophical interest. Using *petitio principii* confidently and undeterred by *non sequitur*, she adds to the stock of 'puns' lately discovered in Marvell, the *non plus ultra* being the identification of his four-footed fawn with 'the lustful offspring of satyrs, half-man, half-beast' (p. 9). Yet she sensibly dismisses some of her predecessors' vagaries.

Jack E. Reese, 'Marvell's "Nymph" in a New Light', and Pierre Legouis, 'Réponse à Jack E. Reese', in *Études Anglaises*, 1965, pp. 398–403, pursue the controversy started by Leo Spitzer (see *supra*, p. 61, n. 1).

Earl J. Schultze, 'The Reach of Wit: Marvell's "The Definition of Love"', in *Papers of the Michigan Academy of Science, Arts, and Letters*, 1965, pp. 563–74, overreaches himself; indeed this performance looks like a *reductio ad absurdum* of the allegorical method; yet the critic sees it all 'clearly', happier than St. Paul, who was content, in this life, to 'see through a glass, darkly'. The poem becomes 'Socratic and Christian', with 'the begetting of Christ by Grace upon virginity' as 'the exuberant . . . counterpart for the vexatious begetting of man's love by despair upon impossibility'. The words 'vexation' and 'exuberance', which form the leitmotiv of the article, I do not profess to understand; but such other words and phrases as 'pleasing', 'sheer fun', 'gracefully', seem to me critically inept praise for Marvell's most sombre and deeply moving poem. Those interested in the cartography of it (see *supra*, p. 75 and n. 1) may be referred to Schulze's entirely original interpretation (p. 568) of 'the distant poles': Marvell (distinct, it seems, from 'the speaker') stands at the terrestrial pole, and the 'extended Soul' (metamorphosed into the 'beloved') at the celestial pole, a politic compromise between the two contrary opinions held so far.

Donal Smith, 'The Political Beliefs of Andrew Marvell', in *University of Toronto Quarterly*, 1966, pp. 55–67, tries to make of the Member for Hull a Trimmer in the school of Halifax. Some of his quotations from this statesman are interesting, but his thesis seems untenable: Smith takes Marvell's public statements at their face value and ignores his private letters (see *supra*, p. 146).

James R. Sutherland, 'A Note on the Satirical Poetry of Andrew Marvell', in *Philological Quarterly*, 1966, pp. 46–53, is 'more concerned with the poems than with the poet'; he deals in a lively manner with 'The last Instructions' and 'A Dialogue between the Two Horses'; the reader may well be puzzled by the inversion of the notes numbered 7 and 8, respectively referring to the one and the other piece.

Frank J. Warnke, 'Play and Metamorphosis in Marvell's Poetry', in *Studies in English Literature 1500–1900*, 1965, pp. 23–30, deserves credit for rediscovering Marvell's playfulness (obvious enough in many, perhaps most, of his poems); but the critic does not make it the more playful by grafting it upon the theories of Johan Huizinga in *Homo Ludens* and applying to it the vocabulary of modern anthropology: he considers Mary Fairfax 'as an agent of the fertility principle' (p. 26), her part being, however, to discipline that 'fertility', and Little T. C. as at once a 'love object' and 'the mind of man itself' (p. 28). But he does not go against his own principles, since, to him, 'Marvell's poetry is ... scarcely ... reducible to meaning in the accepted sense of the word' (p. 29).

Robert Wilcher, 'Details from the Natural Histories in Marvell's Poetry', in *Notes and Queries*, 1968, pp. 101–2, provides useful references from Topsell and Pliny.

J. B. Winterton, 'Some Notes on Marvell's "Bermudas"', in *Notes and Queries*, 1968, p. 102, tortures syntax in order to introduce into ll. 23–24 'the loss of innocence', decidedly a topic in vogue today.

Some other recent publications of which Marvell occupies a more or less important part are mentioned in the Addenda.

INDEX